C

COLLECTED POEMS

1925–1948

Collected Poems
1925-1948

by

LOUIS MACNEICE

Faber and Faber Limited

24 Russell Square

London

First published in this edition in mcmxlix
by Faber and Faber Limited
24 Russell Square London W.C.1
Second impression mcmli
Third impression mcmliv
Fourth impression mcmlxii
Printed in Great Britain by
R. MacLehose and Company Limited
The University Press Glasgow

SC 50-1976

PREFACE

This collection includes the bulk of my published verse. While resisting the temptation to 'collect' only what I most admire I have omitted certain poems which I now dislike or which overlap others that I have kept; two or three, however, have been kept mainly at the request of my friends. There are a few poems here which have not appeared in my previous volumes while in Section II I have reprinted a dozen poems from *Blind Fireworks* which might be called juvenilia. The arrangement of this collection should be clear from the Table of Contents; I thought it best to separate the shorter pieces from the longer while *Autumn Journal* falls naturally and not only on chronological grounds in the middle. Within each group the order of poems is not necessarily chronological. The earliest poem here is *Genesis* (summer, 1925) and the latest, excepting the dedicatory sestina, *The Window* (October, 1948). I have included no translations.

In preparing this book for the press I have also resisted the temptation to make many revisions, since I feel that after three or four years from the date of writing a poet should leave even not-so-well alone. Within that time limit I have to some extent revised; outside it I have merely altered titles where the original titles were makeshift and made a couple of word changes for the sake of factual accuracy; I have also cut three lines from the early poem *Breaking Webs*.

The books in which these poems have previously appeared are the following: *Poems* (1935), *Out of the Picture* (1937), *Letters from Iceland* (1937), *The Earth Compels* (1938), *Autumn Journal* (1939), *Plant and Phantom* (1941), *Springboard* (1944), *Holes in the Sky* (1948)—all published by Faber and Faber—and *Blind Fireworks* (1929) published by Victor Gollancz. Of the poems written since *Holes in the Sky*, *The North Sea* and *Mahabalipuram* have appeared in *The New Statesman and Nation*.

To Hedli

Acting younger than I am and thinking older
I have buried so many stray moments in this volume
That I feel shrunk; as though those April answers
Had withered off their Question and now turning,
As the year turns, I bind up ghost and image
To give them, Hedli, to you, a makeshift present.

For having lived, and too much, in the present,
Askance at the coming gods, estranged from those older
Who had created my fathers in their image,
I stand here now dumbfounded by the volume
Of angry sound which pours from every turning
On those who only so lately knew the answers.

So I lay my ear to the ground and no one answers
Though I know that the Word, like a bulb, is there, is present
And there the subterranean wheels keep turning
To make the world gush green when, we being older,
Others will be in their prime to drench a volume
In the full leaf of insight and bloom of image.

At one time I was content if things would image
Themselves in their own dazzle, if the answers
Came quick and smooth and the great depth and volume
Of the cold sea would wash me the chance present,
Bone or shell or message from some older
Castaway for whom there was no returning.

But now I am not content, the leaves are turning
And the gilt flaking from each private image
And all the poets I know, both younger and older,
Condemned to silence unless they divine the answers
Which our grim past has cached throughout our present
And which are no more than groped for in this volume.

9

Still at this point I tender you this volume
In hopes, my dearest, that your fingers turning
These pages may let fall, among those present,
Some greeting on my waifs and wraiths of image
And half-blind questions that still lack their answers,
Which lack grows no way less as I grow older.

Older and older. Which was the right turning?
Rhythm and image and still at best half answers
And at half volume. But take this; it is a present.

November, 1948.

CONTENTS

CONTENTS

CONTENTS

V

VI

1939–1940

CONTENTS

VII

1941–1944

CONTENTS

VIII

1944–1947

CONTENTS

IX

1940–1948

I

1933—1937

I

AN ECLOGUE FOR CHRISTMAS

A. I meet you in an evil time.
B.   The evil bells
   Put out of our heads, I think, the thought of everything else.
A. The jaded calendar revolves,
   Its nuts need oil, carbon chokes the valves,
   The excess sugar of a diabetic culture
   Rotting the nerve of life and literature;
   Therefore when we bring out the old tinsel and frills
   To announce that Christ is born among the barbarous hills
   I turn to you whom a morose routine
   Saves from the mad vertigo of being what has been.
B. Analogue of me, you are wrong to turn to me,
   My country will not yield you any sanctuary,
   There is no pinpoint in any of the ordnance maps
   To save you when your towns and town-bred thoughts
        collapse,
   It is better to die *in situ* as I shall,
   One place is as bad as another. Go back where your instincts
        call
   And listen to the crying of the town-cats and the taxis again,
   Or wind your gramophone and eavesdrop on great men.
A. Jazz-weary of years of drums and Hawaiian guitar,
   Pivoting on the parquet I seem to have moved far
   From bombs and mud and gas, have stuttered on my feet
   Clinched to the streamlined and butter-smooth trulls of the
        élite,
   The lights irritating and gyrating and rotating in gauze—
   Pomade-dazzle, a slick beauty of gewgaws—
   I who was Harlequin in the childhood of the century,
   Posed by Picasso beside an endless opaque sea,
   Have seen myself sifted and splintered in broken facets,
   Tentative pencillings, endless liabilities, no assets,
   Abstractions scalpelled with a palette-knife
   Without reference to this particular life.
   And so it has gone on; I have not been allowed to be
   Myself in flesh or face, but abstracting and dissecting me
   They have made of me pure form, a symbol or a pastiche,
   Stylised profile, anything but soul and flesh:
   And that is why I turn this jaded music on
   To forswear thought and become an automaton.

[19]

B. There are in the country also of whom I am afraid—
    Men who put beer into a belly that is dead,
    Women in the forties with terrier and setter who whistle and
        swank
    Over down and plough and Roman road and daisied bank,
    Half-conscious that these barriers over which they stride
    Are nothing to the barbed wire that has grown round their
        pride.
A. And two there are, as I drive in the city, who suddenly
        perturb—
    The one sirening me to draw up by the kerb
    The other, as I lean back, my right leg stretched creating
        speed,
    Making me catch and stamp, the brakes shrieking, pull up
        dead:
    She wears silk stockings taunting the winter wind,
    He carries a white stick to mark that he is blind.
B. In the country they are still hunting, in the heavy shires
    Greyness is on the fields and sunset like a line of pyres
    Of barbarous heroes smoulders through the ancient air
    Hazed with factory dust and, orange opposite, the moon's
        glare,
    Goggling yokel-stubborn through the iron trees,
    Jeers at the end of us, our bland ancestral ease;
    We shall go down like palaeolithic man
    Before some new Ice Age or Genghiz Khan.
A. It is time for some new coinage, people have got so old,
    Hacked and handled and shiny from pocketing they have
        made bold
    To think that each is himself through these accidents, being
        blind
    To the fact that they are merely the counters of an unknown
        Mind.
B. A Mind that does not think, if such a thing can be,
    Mechanical Reason, capricious Identity.
    That I could be able to face this domination nor flinch—
A. The tin toys of the hawker move on the pavement inch by
        inch
    Not knowing that they are wound up; it is better to be so
    Than to be, like us, wound up and while running down to
        know—
B. But everywhere the pretence of individuality recurs—

A. Old faces frosted with powder and choked in furs.
B. The jutlipped farmer gazing over the humpbacked wall.
A. The commercial traveller joking in the urinal.
B. I think things draw to an end, the soil is stale.
A. And over-elaboration will nothing now avail,
   The street is up again, gas, electricity or drains,
   Ever-changing conveniences, nothing comfortable remains
   Un-improved, as flagging Rome improved villa and sewer
   (A sound-proof library and a stable temperature).
   Our street is up, red lights sullenly mark
   The long trench of pipes, iron guts in the dark,
   And not till the Goths again come swarming down the hill
   Will cease the clangour of the pneumatic drill.
   But yet there is beauty narcotic and deciduous
   In this vast organism grown out of us:
   On all the traffic-islands stand white globes like moons,
   The city's haze is clouded amber that purrs and croons,
   And tilting by the noble curve bus after tall bus comes
   With an osculation of yellow light, with a glory like
      chrysanthemums.
B. The country gentry cannot change, they will die in their
      shoes
   From angry circumstance and moral self-abuse,
   Dying with a paltry fizzle they will prove their lives to be
   An ever-diluted drug, a spiritual tautology.
   They cannot live once their idols are turned out,
   None of them can endure, for how could they, possibly,
      without
   The flotsam of private property, pekinese and polyanthus,
   The good things which in the end turn to poison and pus,
   Without the bandy chairs and the sugar in the silver tongs
   And the inter-ripple and resonance of years of dinner-gongs?
   Or if they could find no more that cumulative proof
   In the rain dripping off the conservatory roof?
   What will happen when the only sanction the country-
      dweller has—
A. What will happen to us, planked and panelled with jazz?
   Who go the theatre where a black man dances like an eel,
   Where pink thighs flash like the spokes of a wheel, where we
      feel
   That we know in advance all the jogtrot and the cake-walk
      jokes,

[21]

     All the bumfun and the gags of the comedians in boaters and
        toques,
     All the tricks of the virtuosos who invert the usual—
B. What will happen to us when the State takes down the manor
        wall,
     When there is no more private shooting or fishing, when the
        trees are all cut down,
     When faces are all dials and cannot smile or frown—
A. What will happen when the sniggering machine-guns in the
        hands of the young men
     Are trained on every flat and club and beauty parlour and
        Father's den?
     What will happen when our civilisation like a long pent
        balloon—
B. What will happen will happen; the whore and the buffoon
     Will come off best; no dreamers, they cannot lose their dream
     And are at least likely to be reinstated in the new régime.
     But one thing is not likely—
A.   Do not gloat over yourself
     Do not be your own vulture, high on some mountain shelf
     Huddle the pitiless abstractions bald about the neck
     Who will descend when you crumple in the plains a wreck.
     Over the randy of the theatre and cinema I hear songs
     Unlike anything—
B.   The lady of the house poises the silver tongs
     And picks a lump of sugar, 'ne plus ultra' she says
     'I cannot do otherwise, even to prolong my days'—
A. I cannot do otherwise either, tonight I will book my seat—
B. I will walk about the farm-yard which is replete
     As with the smell of dung so with memories—
A. I will gorge myself to satiety with the oddities
     Of every artiste, official or amateur,
     Who has pleased me in my rôle of hero-worshipper
     Who has pleased me in my rôle of individual man—
B. Let us lie once more, say 'What we think, we can'
     The old idealist lie—
A.   And for me before I die
     Let me go the round of the garish glare—
B.   And on the bare and high
     Places of England, the Wiltshire Downs and the Long Mynd
     Let the balls of my feet bounce on the turf, my face burn in
        the wind

My eyelashes stinging in the wind, and the sheep like grey
    stones
Humble my human pretensions—
A.   Let the saxophones and the xylophones
And the cult of every technical excellence, the miles of canvas
    in the galleries
And the canvas of the rich man's yacht snapping and tacking
    on the seas
And the perfection of a grilled steak—
B.   Let all these so ephemeral things
Be somehow permanent like the swallow's tangent wings:
Goodbye to you, this day remember is Christmas, this morn
They say, interpret it your own way, Christ is born.

ECLOGUE BY A FIVE-BARRED GATE

(*Death and two Shepherds*)

D. There is no way here, shepherds, read the wooden sign,
    Your road is a blind road, all this land is mine.
1. But your fields, mister, would do well for our sheep.
2. They could shelter from the sun where the low hills dip.
D. I have sheep of my own, see them over there.
1. There seems no nater in 'em, they look half dead.
2. They be no South Downs, they look so thin and bare.
D. More than half, shepherds, they are more than half dead.
    But where are your own flocks you have been so talking of?
1. Right here at our elbow—
2.   Or they *was* so just now.
D. That's right, shepherd, they was so just now.
    Your sheep are gone, they can't speak for you,
    I must have your credentials, sing me who you are.
1. I am a shepherd of the Theocritean breed,
    Been pasturing my songs, man and boy, this thirty year—
2. And for me too my pedigree acceptances
    Have multiplied beside the approved streams.
D. This won't do, shepherds, life is not like that,
    And when it comes to death I may say he is not like that.
    Have you never thought of Death?
1.   Only off and on,
Thanatos in Greek, the accent proparoxytone—

[23]

2. That's not what he means, he means the thing behind the word
      Same as took Alice White the time her had her third—

D. Cut out for once the dialect and the pedantry,
      I thought a shepherd was a poet—

1.   On his flute—

2.   On his oat—

D. I thought he was a poet and could quote the prices
      Of significant living and decent dying, could lay the rails level
          on the sleepers
      To carry the powerful train of abstruse thought—

1. What an idea!

2.   But certainly poets are sleepers,
      The sleeping beauty behind the many-coloured hedge—

D. All you do is burke the other and terrible beauty, all you do is
          hedge
      And shirk the inevitable issue, all you do
      Is shear your sheep to stop your ears.
      Poetry you think is only the surface vanity,
      The painted nails, the hips narrowed by fashion,
      The hooks and eyes of words; but it is not that only,
      And it is not only the curer sitting by the wayside,
      Phials on his trestle, his palms grown thin as wafers
      With blessing the anonymous heads;
      And poetry is not only the bridging of two-banked rivers.

2. Whoever heard of a river without a further bank?

D. You two never heard of it.
      Tell me now, I have heard the cuckoo, there is tar on your
          shoes,
      I surmise that spring is here—

2.   Spring be here truly,
      On Bank Holiday I wore canvas shoes,
      Could feel the earth—

D.   And that being so, tell me
      Don't you ever feel old?

2.   There's a question now.

1. It is a question we all have to answer,
      And I may say that when I smell the beans or hear the thrush
      I feel a wave intensely bitter-sweet and topped with silver—

D. There you go again, your self-congratulation
      Blunts all edges, insulates with wool,
      No spark of reality possible.
      Can't you peel off for even a moment that conscious face?

All time is not your tear-off jotter, you cannot afford to
    scribble
So many so false answers.
This escapism of yours is blasphemy,
An immortal cannot blaspheme for one way or another
His trivialities will pattern in the end;
But for you your privilege and panic is to be mortal
And with Here and Now for your anvil
You must strike while the iron is hot—
2.   He is an old man,
    That is why he talks so.
D.   Can't you understand me?
    Look, I will set you a prize like any of your favourites,
    Like any Tityrus or tired Damon;
    Sing me, each in turn, what dream you had last night
    And if either's dream rings true, to him I will open my gate.
2. Ho, here's talking.
1.   Let me collect myself.
D. Collect yourself in time for if you win my prize—
2. I'm going to sing first, I had a rare dream.
1. Your dream is nothing—
D.   The more nothing the better.
1. My dream will word well—
2.   But not wear well—
D. No dreams wear at all as dreams.
    Water appears tower only while in well—
    All from the same comes, the same drums sound
    In the pulsation of all the bulging suns,
    And no clock whatever, while winding or running down,
    Makes any difference to time however the long-legged
        weights
    Straggle down the cottage wall or the child grows leggy
        too—
1. I do not like your talking.
2.   It gives giddiness
    Like the thrumming of the telephone wires in an east wind
    With the bellyache and headache and nausea.
D. It is not my nature to talk, so sing your pieces
    And I will try, what is repugnant too, to listen.
1. Last night as the bearded lips of sleep
    Closed with the slightest sigh on me and I sank through the
        blue soft caves

[25]

Picked with light delicate as the chink of coins
Or stream on the pebbles I was caught by hands
And a face was swung in my eyes like a lantern
Swinging on the neck of a snake.
And that face I knew to be God and I woke,
And now I come to look at yours, stranger,
There is something in the lines of it—

D.   Your dream, shepherd,
Is good enough of its kind. Now let us hear yours.

2.   Well, I dreamt it was a hot day, the territorials
Were out on melting asphalt under the howitzers,
The brass music bounced on the houses. Come
I heard cry as it were a water-nymph, come and fulfil me
And I sped floating, my feet plashing in the tops of the wheat
But my eyes were blind,
I found her with my hands lying on the drying hay,
Wet heat in the deeps of the hay as my hand delved,
And I possessed her, gross and good like the hay,
And she went and my eyes regained sight and the sky was full
      of ladders
Angels ascending and descending with a shine like mackerel—
Now I come to tell it it sounds nonsense.

D. Thank you, gentlemen, these two dreams are good,
Better than your daytime madrigals.
If you really wish I will give you both the prize,
But take another look at my land before you choose it.

1.   It looks colder now.

2.   The sheep have not moved.

1.   I have a fancy there is no loving there
Even among sheep.

D.   They do not breed or couple.

1 & 2. And what about us, shall we enjoy it there?

D. *Enjoy what where?*

2.   Why, life in your land.

D. I will open this gate that you may see for yourselves.

1.   You go first.

2.   Well, you come too.

1 & 2. We will go together to these pastures new . . .

D. So; they are gone; life in my land . . .
There is no life as there is no land.
They are gone and I am alone
With a gate the façade of a mirage.

[26]

ECLOGUE FROM ICELAND

Scene: The Arnarvatn Heath. Craven, Ryan and the ghost of Grettir. Voice from Europe.

R.   This is the place, Craven, the end of our way;
        Hobble the horses, we have had a long day.

C.   The night is closing like a fist
        And the long glacier lost in mist.

R.   Few folk come this time of year.
        What are those limping steps I hear?

C.   Look, there he is coming now.
        We shall have some company anyhow.

R.   It must be the mist—he looks so big;
        He is walking lame in the left leg.

G.   Good evening, strangers. So you too
        Are on the run? I welcome you.
        I am Grettir Asmundson,
        Dead many years. My day is done.
        But you whose day is sputtering yet
        I forget. . . . What did I say?
        We forget when we are dead
        The blue and red, the grey and gay.
        Your day spits with a damp wick,
        Will fizzle out if you're not quick.
        Men have been chilled to death who kissed
        Wives of mist, forgetting their own
        Kind who live out of the wind.
        My memory goes, goes——Tell me
        Are there men now whose compass leads
        Them always down forbidden roads?
        Greedy young men who take their pick
        Of what they want but have no luck;
        Who leap the toothed and dour crevasse
        Of death on a sardonic phrase?
        You with crowsfeet round your eyes
        How are things where you come from?

C.   Things are bad. There is no room
        To move at ease, to stretch or breed—

G.   And you with the burglar's underlip
        In your land do things stand well?

R.   In my land nothing stands at all

But some fly high and some lie low.

G.   Too many people. My memory will go,
Lose itself in the hordes of modern people.
Memory is words; we remember what others
Say and record of ourselves—stones with the runes.
Too many people—sandstorm over the words.
Is your land also an island?
There is only hope for people who live upon islands
Where the Lowest Common labels will not stick
And the unpolluted hills will hold your echo.

R.   I come from an island, Ireland, a nation
Built upon violence and morose vendettas.
My diehard countrymen like drayhorses
Drag their ruin behind them.
Shooting straight in the cause of crooked thinking
Their greed is sugared with pretence of public spirit.
From all which I am an exile.

C.   Yes, we are exiles,
Gad the world for comfort.
This Easter I was in Spain before the Civil War
Gobbling the tripper's treats, the local colour,
Storks over Avila, the coffee-coloured waters of Ronda,
The comedy of the bootblacks in the cafés,
The legless beggars in the corridors of the trains
Dominoes on marble tables, the architecture
Moorish mudejar churriguerresque,
The bullfight—the banderillas like Christmas candles,
And the scrawled hammer and sickle:
It was all copy—impenetrable surface.
I did not look for the sneer beneath the surface.
Why should I trouble, an addict to oblivion
Running away from the gods of my own hearth
With no intention of finding gods elsewhere?

R.   And so we came to Iceland—

C.   Our latest joyride.

G.   And what have you found in Iceland?

C.   What have we found? More copy, more surface,
Vignettes as they call them, dead flowers in an album—
The harmoniums in the farms, the fine-bread and pan-
    cakes
The pot of ivy trained across the window,
Children in gumboots, girls in black berets.

[28]

R.   And dead craters and angled crags.

G.   The crags which saw me jockey doom for twenty
Years from one cold hide-out to another;
The last of the saga heroes
Who had not the wisdom of Njal or the beauty of Gunnar
I was the doomed tough, disaster kept me witty;
Being born the surly jack, the ne'er-do-well, the loiterer
Hard blows exalted me.
When the man of will and muscle achieves the curule
      chair
He turns to a bully; better is his lot as outlaw
A wad of dried fish in his belt, a snatch of bilberries
And riding the sullen landscape far from friends
Through the jungle of lava, dales of frozen fancy,
Fording the gletcher, ducking the hard hail,
And across the easy pastures, never stopping
To rest among the celandines and bogcotton.
Under a curse I would see eyes in the night,
Always had to move on; craving company
In the end I lived on an island with two others.
To fetch fire I swam the crinkled fjord,
The crags were alive with ravens whose low croak
Told my ears what filtered in my veins—
The sense of doom. I wore it gracefully,
The fatal clarity that would not budge
But without false pride in martyrdom. For I,
Joker and dressy, held no mystic's pose,
Not wishing to die preferred the daily goods
The horse-fight, women's thighs, a joint of meat.

C.   But this dyspeptic age of ingrown cynics
Wakes in the morning with a coated tongue
And whets itself laboriously to labour
And wears a blasé face in the face of death.
Who risk their lives neither to fill their bellies
Nor to avenge an affront nor grab a prize
But out of bravado or to divert ennui
Driving fast cars and climbing foreign mountains.
Outside the delicatessen shop the hero
With his ribbons and his empty pinned-up sleeve
Cadges for money while with turned-up collars
His comrades blow through brass the Londonderry Air
And silken legs and swinging buttocks advertise

[29]

The sale of little cardboard flags on pins
G.   Us too they sold
The women and the men with many sheep.
Graft and aggression, legal prevarication
Drove out the best of us,
Secured long life to only the sly and the dumb
To those who would not say what they really thought
But got their ends through pretended indifference
And through the sweat and blood of thralls and hacks
Cheating the poor men of their share of drift
The whale on Kaldbak in the starving winter.

R.   And so today at Grimsby men whose lives
Are warped in Arctic trawlers load and unload
The shining tons of fish to keep the lords
Of the market happy with cigars and cars.

C.   What is that music in the air—
Organ-music coming from far?

R.   Honeyed music—it sounds to me
Like the Wurlitzer in the Gaiety.

G.   I do not hear anything at all.

C.   Imagine the purple light on the stage

R.   The melting moment of a stinted age

C.   The pause before the film again
Bursts in a shower of golden rain.

G.   I do not hear anything at all.

C.   We shall be back there soon, to stand in queues
For entertainment and to work at desks,
To browse round counters of dead books, to pore
On picture catalogues and Soho menus,
To preen ourselves on the reinterpretation
Of the words of obsolete interpreters,
Collate delete their faded lives like texts,
Admire Flaubert, Cézanne—the tortured artists—
And leaning forward to knock out our pipes
Into the fire protest that art is good
And gives a meaning and a slant to life.

G.   The dark is falling. Soon the air
Will stare with eyes, the stubborn ghost
Who cursed me when I threw him. Must
The ban go on for ever? I,
A ghost myself, have no claim now to die.
Now I hear the music again—

[30]

Strauss and roses—hear it plain.
The sweet confetti of music falls
From the high Corinthian capitals.

C. Her head upon his shoulder lies. . . .
Blend to the marrow as the music dies.

G. Brought up to the rough-house we took offence quickly
Were sticklers for pride, paid for it as outlaws—

C. Like Cavalcanti whose hot blood lost him Florence

R. Or the Wild Geese of Ireland in Mid-Europe.
Let us thank God for valour in abstraction
For those who go their own way, will not kiss
The arse of law and order nor compound
For physical comfort at the price of pride:
Soldiers of fortune, renegade artists, rebels and sharpers
Whose speech not cramped to Yea and Nay explodes
In crimson oaths like peonies, who brag
Because they prefer to taunt the mask of God,
Bid him unmask and die in the living lightning.
What is that voice maundering, meandering?

VOICE. Blues . . . blues . . . high heels and manicured hands
Always self-conscious of the vanity bag
And puritan painted lips that abnegate desire
And say 'we do not care' . . . 'we do not care'—
I don't care always in the air
Give my hips a shake always on the make
Always on the mend coming around the bend
Always on the dance with an eye to the main
Chance, always taking the floor again—

C. There was Tchekov,
His haemorrhages drove him out of Moscow
The life he loved, not born to it, who thought
That when the windows blurred with smoke and talk
So that no-one could see out, then conversely
The giants of frost and satans of the peasant
Could not look in, impose the evil eye.

R. There was MacKenna
Spent twenty years translating Greek philosophy
Ill and tormented , unwilling to break contract,
A brilliant talker who left
The salon for the solo flight of Mind.

G. There was Onund Treefoot
Came late and lame to Iceland, made his way

[31]

	Even though the land was bad and the neighbours
	jealous.
C.	There was that dancer
	Who danced the War, then falling into coma
	Went with hunched shoulders through the ivory gate.
R.	There was Connolly
	Vilified now by the gangs of Catholic Action.
G.	There was Egil
	Hero and miser who when dying blind
	Would have thrown his money among the crowd to hear
	The whole world scuffle for his hoarded gold.
C.	And there were many
	Whose commonsense or sense of humour or mere
	Desire for self assertion won them through
R.	But not to happiness. Though at intervals
	They paused in sunlight for a moment's fusion
	With friends or nature till the cynical wind
	Blew the trees pale—
VOICE.	Blues, blues, sit back, relax
	Let your self-pity swell with the music and clutch
	Your tiny lavendered fetishes. Who cares
	If floods depopulate China? I don't care
	Always in the air sitting among the stars
	Among the electric signs among the imported wines
	Always on the spree climbing the forbidden tree
	Tossing the peel of the apple over my shoulder
	To see it form the initials of a new intrigue
G.	Runes and runes which no one could decode
R.	Wrong numbers on the 'phone—she never answered.
C.	And from the romantic grill (Spanish baroque)
	Only the eyes looked out which I see now.
G.	You see them now?
C.	But seen before as well.
G.	And many times to come, be sure of that.
R.	I know them too
	These eyes which hang in the northern mist, the brute
	Stare of stupidity and hate, the most
	Primitive and false of oracles.
C.	The eyes
	That glide like snakes behind a thousand masks—
	All human faces fit them, here or here:
	Dictator, bullying schoolboy or common lout,

[32]

Acquisitive women, financiers, invalids,
Are capable all of that compelling stare
Stare which betrays the cosmic purposelessness
The nightmare noise of the scythe upon the hone,
Time sharpening his blade among high rocks alone.

R The face that fate hangs as a figurehead
 Above the truncheon or the nickelled death.

G. I won the fall. Though cursed for it, I won.

C. Which is why we honour you who working from
 The common premisses did not end with many
 In the blind alley where the trek began.

G. Though the open road is hard with frost and dark.

VOICE. Hot towels for the men, mud packs for the women
 Will smooth the puckered minutes of your lives.
 I offer you each a private window, a view
 (The leper window reveals a church of lepers).

R. Do you believe him?

C. I don't know.
 Do you believe him?

G. No.
 You cannot argue with the eyes or voice;
 Argument will frustrate you till you die
 But go your own way, give the voice the lie,
 Outstare the inhuman eyes. That is the way.
 Go back to where you came from and do not keep
 Crossing the road to escape them, do not avoid the
  ambush,
 Take sly detours, but ride the pass direct.

C. But the points of axes shine from the scrub, the odds
 Are dead against us. There are the lures of women
 Who, half alive, invite to a fuller life
 And never loving would be loved by others.

R. Who fortify themselves in pasteboard castles
 And plant their beds with the cast-out toys of children,
 Dead pines with tinsel fruits, nursery beliefs
 And South Sea Island trinkets. Watch their years
 The permutations of lapels and gussets,
 Of stuffs—georgette or velvet or corduroy—
 Of hats and eye-veils, of shoes, lizard or suède,
 Of bracelets, milk or coral, of zip bags
 Of compacts, lipstick, eyeshade and coiffures
 All tributary to the wished ensemble

c   [33]   M.C.P.

The carriage of body that belies the soul.

C.   And there are the men who appear to be men of sense,
Good company and dependable in a crisis,
Who yet are ready to plug you as you drink
Like dogs who bite from fear; for fear of germs
Putting on stamps by licking the second finger,
For fear of opinion overtipping in bars,
For fear of thought studying stupefaction.
It is the world which these have made where dead
Greek words sprout out in tin on sallow walls—
Clinic or polytechnic—a world of slums
Where any day now may see the Gadarene swine
Rush down the gullets of the London tubes
When the enemy, x or y, let loose their gas.

G.   My friends, hounded like me, I tell you still
Go back to where you belong. I could have fled
To the Hebrides or Orkney, been rich and famous,
Preferred to assert my rights in my own country,
Mine which were hers for every country stands
By the sanctity of the individual will.

R.   Yes, he is right,

C.   But we have not his strength

R.   Could only abase ourselves before the wall
Of shouting flesh

C.   Could only offer our humble
Deaths to the unknown god, unknown but worshipped,
Whose voice calls in the sirens of destroyers.

G.   Minute your gesture but it must be made—
Your hazard, your act of defiance and hymn of hate,
Hatred of hatred, assertion of human values,
Which is now your only duty.

C.   Is it our only duty?

G.   Yes, my friends.
What did you say? The night falls now and I
Must beat the dales to chase my remembered acts.
Yes, my friends, it is your only duty.
And, it may be added, it is your only chance.

[34]

ECLOGUE BETWEEN THE MOTHERLESS

A.   What did you do for the holiday?

B.   I went home.
      What did you do?

A.   O, I went home for the holiday.
      Had a good time?

B.   Not bad as far as it went.
      What about you?

A.   O quite a good time on the whole—

(both) Quite a good time on the whole at home for the holiday

A.   As far as it went—In a way it went too far,
      Back to childhood, back to the backwoods mind;
      I could not stand a great deal of it, bars on the brain
      And the blinds drawn in the drawingroom not to fade the
          chair covers

B.   There were no blinds drawn in ours; my father has married
         again—
      A girl of thirty who had never had any lovers
      And wants to have everything bright

A.   That sounds worse than us.
      Our old house is just a grass-grown tumulus,
      My father sits by himself with the bossed decanter,
      The garden is going to rack, the gardener
      Only comes three days, most of our money was in linen

B.   My new stepmother is wealthy, you should see her in
         jodhpurs
      Brisking in to breakfast from a morning canter.
      I don't think he can be happy

A.   How can you tell?
      That generation is so different

B.   I suppose your sister
      Still keeps house for yours?

A.   Yes and she finds it hell.
      Nothing to do in the evenings.

B.   Talking of the evenings
      I can drop the ash on the carpet since my divorce.
      Never you marry, my boy. One marries only
      Because one thinks one is lonely—and so one was
      But wait till the lonely are two and no better

A.   As a matter
      Of fact I've got to tell you

[35]

B.   The first half year
Is heaven come back from the nursery—swansdown
    kisses—
But after that one misses something

A.   My dear,
Don't depress me in advance; I've got to tell you—

B.   My wife was warmth, a picture and a dance,
Her body electric—silk used to crackle and her gloves
Move where she left them. How one loves the surface
But how one lacks the core—Children of course
Might make a difference

A.   Personally I find
I cannot go on any more like I was. Which is why
I took this step in the dark

B.   What step?

A.   I thought
I too might try what you

B.   Don't say that you
And after all this time

A.   Let's start from the start.
When I went home this time there was nothing to do
And so I got haunted. Like a ball of wool
That kittens have got at, all my growing up
All the disposed-of process of my past
Unravelled on the floor—One can't proceed any more
Except on a static past; when the ice-floe breaks
What's the good of walking? Talking of ice
I remembered my mother standing against the sky
And saying 'Go back in the house and change your shoes'
And I kept having dreams and kept going back in the
    house.
A sense of guilt like a scent—The day I was born
I suppose that that same hour was full of her screams

B.   You're run down

A.   Wait till you hear what I've done.
It was not only dreams; even the crockery (odd
It's not all broken by now) and the rustic seat in the
    rockery
With the bark flaked off, all kept reminding me, binding
My feet to the floating past. In the night at the lodge
A dog was barking as when I was little in the night
And I could not budge in the bed clothes. Lying alone

[36]

I felt my legs were paralysed into roots
And the same cracks in what used to be the nursery ceiling
Gave me again the feeling I was young among ikons,
Helpless at the feet of faceless family idols,
Walking the tightrope over the tiger-pit,
Running the gauntlet of inherited fears;
So after all these years I turned in the bed
And grasped the want of a wife and heard in the rain
On the gravel path the steps of all my mistresses
And wondered which was coming or was she dead
And her shoes given to the char which tapped through
     London—
The black streets mirrored with rain and stained with
     lights.
I dreamed she came while a train
Was running behind the trees (with power progressing),
Undressing deftly she slipped cool knees beside me,
The clipped hair on her neck prickled my tongue
And the whole room swung like a ship till I woke with
     the window
Jittering in its frame from the train passing the garden
Carrying its load of souls to a different distance.
And of others, isolated by associations,
I thought—the scent of syringa or always wearing
A hat of fine white straw and never known in winter—
Splinters of memory. When I was little I sorted
Bits of lustre and glass from the heap behind the hen-
     house;
They are all distorted now the beautiful sirens
Mutilated and mute in dream's dissection,
Hanged from pegs in the Bluebeard's closet of the brain,
Never again nonchalantly to open
The doors of disillusion. Whom recording
The night marked time, the dog at the lodge kept barking
And as he barked the big cave opened of hell
Where all their voices were one and stuck at a point
Like a gramophone needle stuck on a notched record.
I thought 'Can I find a love beyond the family
And feed her to the bed my mother died in
Between the tallboys and the vase of honesty
On which I was born and groped my way from the cave
With a half-eaten fruit in my hand, a passport meaning

	Enforced return for periods to that country?

Enforced return for periods to that country?
Or will one's wife also belong to that country
And can one never find the perfect stranger?

B.   My complaint was that she stayed a stranger.
I remember her mostly in the car, stopping by the white
Moons of the petrol pumps, in a camelhair rug
Comfortable, scented and alien.

A.   That's what I want,
Someone immutably alien—
Send me a woman with haunches out of the jungle
And frost patterns for fancies,
The hard light of sun upon water in diamonds dancing
And the brute swagger of the sea; let her love be the drop
From the cliff of my dream, be the axe on the block
Be finesse of the ice on the panes of the heart
Be careless, be callous, be glass frolic of prisms
Be eyes of guns through lashes of barbed wire,
Be the gaoler's smile and all that breaks the past.

B.   Odd ideals you have; all I wanted
Was to get really close but closeness was
Only a glove on the hand, alien and veinless,
And yet her empty gloves could move

A.   My next move
Is what I've got to tell you, I picked on the only
One who would suit and wrote proposing marriage

B.   Who is she?

A.   But she can't have yet received it;
She is in India.

B.   India be damned.
What is her name?

A.   I said I cannot offer
Anything you will want

B.   Why?

A.   and I said
I know in two years' time it will make no difference.
I was hardly able to write it at the claw-foot table
Where my mother kept her diary. There I sat
Concocting a gambler's medicine; the afternoon was cool,
The ducks drew lines of white on the dull slate of the pool
And I sat writing to someone I hardly knew
And someone I shall never know well. Relying on that
I stuck up the envelope, walked down the winding drive,

All that was wanted a figurehead, passed by the lodge
Where the dog is chained and the gates, relying on my
    mood
    To get it posted
B.   Who is the woman?
A.   relying
B.   Who is the woman?
A.   She is dying
B.   Dying of what?
A.   Only a year to live
B.   Forgive me asking
    But
A.   Only a year and ten yards down the road
    I made my goal where it has always stood
    Waiting for the last
B.   You must be out of your mind;
    If it were anyone else I should not mind
A.   Waiting for the last collection before dark
    The pillarbox like an exclamation mark.

VALEDICTION

Their verdure dare not show . . . their verdure dare not show . . .
Cant and randy—the seals' heads bobbing in the tide-flow
Between the islands, sleek and black and irrelevant
They cannot depose logically what they want:
Died by gunshot under borrowed pennons,
Sniped from the wet gorse and taken by the limp fins
And slung like a dead seal in a boghole, beaten up
By peasants with long lips and the whisky-drinker's cough.
Park your car in the city of Dublin, see Sackville Street
Without the sandbags in the old photos, meet
The statues of the patriots, history never dies,
At any rate in Ireland, arson and murder are legacies
Like old rings hollow-eyed without their stones
Dumb talismans.
See Belfast, devout and profane and hard,
Built on reclaimed mud, hammers playing in the shipyard,
Time punched with holes like a steel sheet, time
Hardening the faces, veneering with a grey and speckled rime
The faces under the shawls and caps:

This was my mother-city, these my paps.
Country of callous lava cooled to stone,
Of minute sodden haycocks, of ship-sirens' moan,
Of falling intonations—I would call you to book
I would say to you, Look;
I would say, This is what you have given me
Indifference and sentimentality
A metallic giggle, a fumbling hand,
A heart that leaps to a fife band:
Set these against your water-shafted air
Of amethyst and moonstone, the horses' feet like bells of hair
Shambling beneath the orange cart, the beer-brown spring
Guzzling between the heather, the green gush of Irish spring.
Cursèd be he that curses his mother. I cannot be
Anyone else than what this land engendered me:
In the back of my mind are snips of white, the sails
Of the Lough's fishing-boats, the bellropes lash their tails
When I would peal my thoughts, the bells pull free—
Memory in apostasy.
I would tot up my factors
But who can stand in the way of his soul's steam-tractors?
I can say Ireland is hooey, Ireland is
A gallery of fake tapestries,
But I cannot deny my past to which my self is wed,
The woven figure cannot undo its thread.
On a cardboard lid I saw when I was four
Was the trade-mark of a hound and a round tower,
And that was Irish glamour, and in the cemetery
Sham Celtic crosses claimed our individuality,
And my father talked about the West where years back
He played hurley on the sands with a stick of wrack.
Park your car in Killarney, buy a souvenir
Of green marble or black bog-oak, run up to Clare,
Climb the cliff in the postcard, visit Galway city,
Romanticise on our Spanish blood, leave ten per cent of pity
Under your plate for the emigrant,
Take credit for our sanctity, our heroism and our sterile want
Columba Kevin and briny Brandan the accepted names,
Wolfe Tone and Grattan and Michael Collins the accepted
    names,
Admire the suavity with which the architect
Is rebuilding the burnt mansion, recollect

The palmy days of the Horse Show, swank your fill,
But take the Holyhead boat before you pay the bill;
Before you face the consequence
Of inbred soul and climatic maleficence
And pay for the trick beauty of a prism
In drug-dull fatalism.
I will exorcise my blood
And not to have my baby-clothes my shroud
I will acquire an attitude not yours
And become as one of your holiday visitors,
And however often I may come
Farewell, my country, and in perpetuum;
Whatever desire I catch when your wind scours my face
I will take home and put in a glass case
And merely look on
At each new fantasy of badge and gun.
Frost will not touch the hedge of fuchsias,
The land will remain as it was,
But no abiding content can grow out of these minds
Fuddled with blood, always caught by blinds;
The eels go up the Shannon over the great dam;
You cannot change a response by giving it a new name.
Fountain of green and blue curling in the wind
I must go east and stay, not looking behind,
Not knowing on which day the mist is blanket-thick
Nor when sun quilts the valley and quick
Winging shadows of white clouds pass
Over the long hills like a fiddle's phrase.
If I were a dog of sunlight I would bound
From Phoenix Park to Achill Sound,
Picking up the scent of a hundred fugitives
That have broken the mesh of ordinary lives,
But being ordinary too I must in course discuss
What we mean to Ireland or Ireland to us;
I have to observe milestone and curio
The beaten buried gold of an old king's bravado,
Falsetto antiquities, I have to gesture,
Take part in, or renounce, each imposture;
Therefore I resign, good-bye the chequered and the quiet hills
The gaudily-striped Atlantic, the linen-mills
That swallow the shawled file, the black moor where half
A turf-stack stands like a ruined cenotaph;

Good-bye your hens running in and out of the white house
Your absent-minded goats along the road, your black cows
Your greyhounds and your hunters beautifully bred
Your drums and your dolled-up Virgins and your ignorant dead.

ODE

Tonight is so coarse with chocolate
    The wind blowing from Bournville
That I hanker after the Atlantic
    With a frivolous nostalgia
Like that which film-fans feel
    For their celluloid abstractions
The nifty hero and the deathless blonde
    And find escape by proxy
From the eight-hour day or the wheel
    Of work and bearing children.

If God is boundless as the sea or sky
The eye bounds both of them and Him,
We always have the horizon
Not to swim to but to see:
God is seen with shape and limit
More purple towards the rim,
This segment of His infinite extension
Is all the God of Him for me.

And you too, my love, my limit,
So palpable and your hair shot with red—
I do not want a hundred wives or lives
Any more than I want to be too well-read
Or have money like the sand or ability like the hydra's heads
To flicker the tongues of self-engendering power,
I want a sufficient sample, the exact and framed
Balance of definite masses, the islanded hour.

I would pray for that island; mob mania in the air,
I cannot assume their easy bravery
Drugged with a slogan, chewing the old lie
That parallel lines will meet at infinity;
As I walk on the shore of the regular and rounded sea

I would pray off from my son the love of that infinite
Which is too greedy and too obvious; let his Absolute
Like any four-walled house be put up decently.

Let us turn to homeliness,
Born in the middle of May
Let him accumulate, corroborate while he may
The blessedness of fact
Which lives in the dancing atom and the breathing trees
And everywhere except in the fancy of man
Who daubs his slush on the hawthorn and the may.

Let him have five good senses
The feeling for symmetry
And the sense of the magnet,
His mind deft and unflustered
To change gear easily
And let not the blasphemy
Of dusty words deceive him.

May he hit the golden mean
Which contains the seasonal extreme,
May he riot in the diving sun
And die in the crystal dream,
May his good deeds flung forth
Like boomerangs return
To wear around his neck
As beads of definite worth.

May he pick up daintily
The ambiguous joys,
As a bee in May the blossom of fruit
Cross-fertilise his data and distil
From the drum balalaika fiddle and organ
From sun's gunnery splintering glass
More than the twanging dazzle or the dazzling noise.

To get permanence, to hear the personance
Of all the water-gullies and blackbirds' songs
Drained off or died twenty years back
To make one's flesh of them and so renounce the mask
Of the sham soul, the cask bobbing empty
On leaden waves, the veneer the years crack.

[43]

To ride two horses at once, a foot on each
Tilting outward on space abstract and packed
With the audience of the dead and the unborn,
To pay his debts to each
To beach his boat so that others can use it
To throw his bread on the waters, the best deposit.

That people are lovable is a strange discovery
And there are many conflicting allegiances;
The pedals of a chance bicycle
Make a gold shower turning in the sun,
Trains leave in all directions on wild rails
And for every act determined on and won
There is a possible world denied and lost.

Do not then turn maudlin or weathercock,
We must cut the throat of the hour
That it may not haunt us because our sentiments
Continued its existence to pollute
Its essence; bottled time turns sour upon the sill.

The children play in the park; the ducklings
Rise and scurry on the water, a car
Changes down, the sandwichmen
Move up and down with the never-changing news.
Do not brood too much on the forking paths.

The leaves dark green on top, light green under, seas of green
Had brought him on full flood, the colour laid on in slices
As by a mason's trowel or ice cream in sliders
Bought in dusty streets under the yellow-green beeches,
A little while ago the green was only peppered
But now we gape at a wealthy wave and a tidal tower of green.

Coral azalea and scarlet rhododendron
Syringa and pink horse-chestnut and laburnum
Solid as temples, niched with the song of birds,
Widen the eyes and nostrils, demand homage of words.
And we have to turn from them,
Compose ourselves, fit out an ethic:
Have I anything to hand my son,
Scarab or compass for his journey?

[44]

Only so far, so far as I can find, symbols;
No decalogue, no chemical formula;
Unanalysed scent and noise, the fly on the pane,
The tulips banked on the glass-and-black hearse
A memory of a cock crowing in the dark like a curse
The remembered hypnotism of an aeroplane in June—

Watching the cricket from between
Slabs of green and slabs of blue and slowly ladled clouds
We looked at the sky through straw hats,
The sky was turned into black and white small stars.
Then came, southward as always, the angel
His song like the heat dancing on the gravel
High above the bat-chock and the white umpires
Moving south while the clapping of a run turns chill in echo
And his own drone is whittled to the point of a pin
So that dozing boys fumble the ghost of sound.

But this identical sound the then epitome
Of summer's athletic ease and the smell of cut grass
Will sometime be our augury of war
When these tiny flies like nibs will calmly draw our death
A dipping gradient on the graph of Europe
And over the hairy flatnesses of Russia
This sound when we have died will linger to a wisp
And the endless corn wave tiredly.

Humming and buzzing, the bomber and the fly on the pane
And the telephone wires hung on dead pines,
In Ireland once a string of bright-red haws
Hung, thrown up by children, on those wires:
Not to hang so, O God, between your iron spires!
The town-dweller like a rabbit in a greengrocer's
Who was innocent and integral once
Now, red with slit guts, hangs by the heels
Hangs by the heels gut-open against the fog
Between two spires that are not conscious of him.

Therefore let not my son, halving the truth
Be caught between jagged edges;
And let him not falsify the world
By taking it to pieces;

[45]

The marriage of Cause and Effect, Form and Content
Let him not part asunder.
Wisdom for him in the time of tulips
Monastic repose, martial élan,
Then the opening mouth a dragon or a voluptuary—
These moments let him retain like limbs
His time not crippled by flaws of faith or memory.

In the Birmingham Market Hall at this time
There are horseshoe wreaths of mauve stock
Fixed with wire and nailed with pale pink roses
The tribute to a life that ran on standard wheels—
May his life be more than this matter of wheels and wire.

I remember all the houses where parents
Have reared their children to be parents
(Cut box and privet and the parrot's voice)
To be clerks to total the flow of alien money
To be florists to design these wreaths and wedding bouquets.

I cannot draw up any code
          There are too many qualifications
Too many asterisk asides
          Too many crosses in the margin
But as others, forgetting the others,
          Run after the nostrums
Of science art and religion
          So would I mystic and maudlin
Dream of the both real and ideal
          Breakers of ocean.
I must put away this drug.

Must become the migrating bird following felt routes
The comet's superficially casual orbit kept
Not self-abandoning to sky-blind chutes
To climb miles and kiss the miles of foam
For nothing is more proud than humbly to accept
And without soaring or swerving win by ignoring
The endlessly curving sea and so come to one's home.
And so come to one's peace while the yellow waves are roaring.

HOMAGE TO CLICHÉS

With all this clamour for progress
This hammering out of new phases and gadgets, new trinkets and
     phrases
I prefer the automatic, the reflex, the cliché of velvet.
The foreseen smile, sexual, maternal, or hail-fellow-met,
The cat's fur sparking under your hand
And the indolent delicacy of your hand
These fish coming in to the net
I can see them coming for yards
The way that you answer, the way that you dangle your foot
These fish that are rainbow and fat
One can catch in the hand and caress and return to the pool.
So five minutes spent at a bar
Watching the fish coming in, as you parry and shrug
This is on me or this is on me,
Or an old man momentously sharpens a pencil as though
He were not merely licking his fur like a cat—
The cat's tongue curls to the back of its neck, the fish swivel
     round by the side of their tails, on the abbey the arrows of
     gold
On the pinnacles shift in the wind—
This is on me this time
Watch how your flattery logic seduction or wit
Elicit the expected response
Each tiny hammer of the abbey chime
Beating on the outer shell of the eternal bell
Which hangs like a Rameses, does not deign to move
For Mahomet comes to the mountain and the fish come to the
     bell.
What will you have now? The same again?
A finger can pull these ropes,
A gin and lime or a double Scotch—
Watch the response, the lifting wrist the clink and smile
The fish come in, the hammered notes come out
From a filigree gothic trap.
These are the moments that are anaplerotic, these are the gifts to
     be accepted
Remembering the qualification
That everything is not true to type like these
That the pattern and the patina of these

[47]

Are superseded in the end.
Stoop your head, follow me through this door
Up the belfry stair.
What do you see in this gloom, this womb of stone?
I see eight bells hanging alone.
Eight black panthers, eight silences
On the outer shell of which our fingers via hammers
Rapping with an impertinent precision
Have made believe that this was the final music.
Final as if finality were the trend of fish
That always seek the net
As if finality were the obvious gag
The audience laughing in anticipation
As if finality were the angled smile
Drawn from the dappled stream of casual meetings
(Yet oh thank God for such)
But there is this much left over
There is very much left over:
The Rameses, the panther, the two-ton bell
Will never move his sceptre
Never spring, never swing
No, no, he will never move . . .
What will you have, my dear? The same again?
Two more double Scotch, watch the approved response
This is the preferred mode ;
I have shut the little window that looks up the road
Towards the tombs of the kings
For I have heard that you meet people walking in granite
I have shut up the gates under padlock
For fear of wild beasts
And I have shut my ears to the possible peal of bells,
Every precaution—
What will you have, my dear? The same again?
Count up our fag-ends
This year next year sometime never
Next year is this year, sometime is next time, never is sometime
Never is the Bell, Never is the Panther, Never is Rameses
Oh the cold stone panic of Never—
The ringers are taking off their coats, the panther crouches
The granite sceptre is very slightly inclining
As our shoes tap against the bar and our glasses
Make two new rings of wet upon the counter

[48]

Somewhere behind us stands a man, a counter
A timekeeper with a watch and a pistol
Ready to shoot and with his shot destroy
This whole delightful world of cliché and refrain—
What will you have, my dear? The same again?

LETTER TO GRAHAM AND ANNA

Reykjavik.
August 16th, 1936.

To Graham and Anna: from the Arctic Gate
I send this letter to N.W. 8,
Hoping that Town is not the usual mess,
That Pauli is rid of worms, the new cook a success.
I have got here, you see, without being sick
On a boat of eight hundred tons to Reykjavik.
Came second-class—no air but many men;
Having seen the first-class crowd would do the same again.
Food was good, mutton and bits of fishes,
A smart line-up of Scandinavian dishes—
Beet, cheese, ham, jam, smoked salmon, gaffalbitar,
Sweet cucumber, German sausage, and Ry-Vita.
So I came here to the land the Romans missed,
Left for the Irish saint and the Viking colonist.
But what am I doing here? Qu'allais-je faire
Among these volcanic rocks and this grey air?
Why go north when Cyprus and Madeira
De jure if not de facto are much nearer?
The reason for hereness seems beyond conjecture,
There are no trees or trains or architecture,
Fruits and greens are insufficient for health,
Culture is limited by lack of wealth,
The tourist sights have nothing like Stonehenge,
The literature is all about revenge.
And yet I like it if only because this nation
Enjoys a scarcity of population
And cannot rise to many bores or hacks
Or paupers or poor men paying Super-Tax.
Yet further, if you can stand it, I will set forth
The obscure but powerful ethics of Going North.
Morris did it before, dropping the frills and fuss,

D   [49]   M.C.P.

Harps and arbours, Tristram and Theseus,
For a land of rocks and sagas. And certain unknown
Old Irish hermits, holy skin and bone,
Camped on these crags in order to forget
Their blue-black cows in Kerry pastures wet.
Those Latin-chattering margin-illuminating monks
Fled here from home without kit-bags or trunks
To mortify their flesh—but we must mortify
Our blowsy intellects before we die,
Who feed our brains on backchat and self-pity
And always need a noise, the radio or the city,
Traffic and changing lights, crashing the amber,
Always on the move and so do not remember
The necessity of the silence of the islands,
The glacier floating in the distance out of existence,
The need to grip and grapple the adversary,
Knuckle on stony knuckle, to dot and carry
One and carry one and not give up the hunt
Till we have pinned the Boyg down to a point.
In England one forgets—in each performing troupe
Forgets what one has lost, there is no room to stoop
And look along the ground, one cannot see the ground
For the feet of the crowd, and the lost is never found.
I dropped something, I think, but I am not sure what
And cannot say if it mattered much or not,
So let us get on or we shall be late, for soon
The shops will close and the rush-hour be on.
This is the fret that makes us cat-like stretch
And then contract the fingers, gives the itch
To open the French window into the rain,
Walk out and never be seen at home again.
But where to go? No oracle for us,
Bible or Baedeker, can tell the terminus.
The songs of jazz have told us of a moon country
And we like to dream of a heat which is never sultry,
Melons to eat, champagne to drink, and a lazy
Music hour by hour depetalling the daisy.
Then Medici manuscripts have told of places
Where common sense was wedded to the graces,
Doric temples and olive-trees and such,
But broken marble no longer goes for much.
And there are some who scorn this poésie de départs

[50]

And say 'Escape by staying where you are;
A man is what he thinks he is and can
Find happiness within.' How nice to be born a man.
The tourist in space or time, emotion or sensation,
Meets many guides but none have the proper orientation.
We are not changing ground to escape from facts
But rather to find them. This complex world exacts
Hard work of simplifying; to get its focus
You have to stand outside the crowd and caucus.
This all sounds somewhat priggish. You and I
Know very well the immediate reason why
I am in Iceland. Three months ago or so
Wystan said that he was planning to go
To Iceland to write a book and would I come too;
And I said yes, having nothing better to do.
But all the same we never make any choice
On such a merely mechanical stimulus.
The match is not the cause of fire, so pause
And look for the formal as well as the efficient cause.
Aristotle's pedantic phraseology
Serves better than common sense or hand to mouth psychology.
ἔσχε τὴν φύσιν—'found its nature'; the crude
Embryo rummages every latitude
Looking for itself, its nature, its final pattern,
Till the fairy godmother's wand touches the slattern
And turns her to a princess for a moment
Beyond definition or professorial comment.
We find our nature daily or try to find it,
The old flame gutters, leaves red flames behind it.
An interval of tuning and screwing and then
The symphony restarts, the creature lives again—
Blake's arabesques of fire; the subtle creature
Swings on Ezekiel's wheels, finding its nature.
In short we must keep moving to keep pace
Or else drop into Limbo, the dead place.
I have come north, gaily running away
From the grinding gears, the change from day to day,
The creaks of the familiar room, the smile
Of the cruel clock, the bills upon the file,
The excess of books and cushions, the high heels
That walk the street, the news, the newsboys' yells,
The flag-days and the cripple's flapping sleeve

[51]

The ambushes of sex, the passion to retrieve
Significance from the river of passing people,
The attempt to climb the ever-climbing steeple
And no one knows what is at the top of it,
All is a raffle for caps which may not fit,
But all take tickets, keep moving; still we may
Move off from movement or change it for a day;
Here is a different rhythm, the juggled balls
Hang in the air—the pause before the soufflé falls.
Here we can take a breath, sit back, admire
Stills from the film of life, the frozen fire;
Among these rocks can roll upon the tongue
Morsels of thought, not jostled by the throng,
Or morsels of un-thought, which is still better,
(Thinking these days makes a suburban clatter).
Here we can practise forgetfulness without
A sense of guilt, fear of the tout and lout,
And here—but Wystan has butted in again
To say we must go out in the frightful rain
To see a man about a horse and so
I shall have to stop. For we soon intend to go
Around the Langjökull, a ten day's ride,
Gumboots and stockfish. Probably you'll deride
This sissy onslaught on the open spaces.
I can see the joke myself; however the case is
Not to be altered, but please remember us
So high up here in this vertiginous
Crow's-nest of the earth. Perhaps you'll let us know
If anything happens in the world below?

THE HEBRIDES

On those islands
The west wind drops its messages of indolence,
No one hurries, the Gulf Stream warms the gnarled
Rampart of gneiss, the feet of the peasant years
Pad up and down their sentry-beat not challenging
Any comer for the password—only Death
Comes through unchallenged in his general's cape.
The houses straggle on the umber moors,
The Aladdin lamp mutters in the boarded room

[52]

Where a woman smoors the fire of fragrant peat.
No one repeats the password for it is known,
All is known before it comes to the lips—
Instinctive wisdom. Over the fancy vases
The photos with the wrinkles taken out,
The enlarged portraits of the successful sons
Who married wealth in Toronto or New York,
Console the lonely evenings of the old
Who live embanked by memories of labour
And child-bearing and scriptural commentaries.
On those islands
The boys go poaching their ancestral rights—
The Ossianic salmon who take the yellow
Tilt of the river with a magnet's purpose—
And listen breathless to the tales at the ceilidh
Among the peat-smoke and the smells of dung
That fill the felted room from the cave of the byre.
No window opens of the windows sunk like eyes
In a four-foot wall of stones casually picked
From the knuckly hills on which these houses crawl
Like black and legless beasts who breathe in their sleep
Among the piles of peat and pooks of hay—
A brave oasis in the indifferent moors.
And while the stories circulate like smoke,
The sense of life spreads out from the one-eyed house
In wider circles through the lake of night
In which articulate man has dropped a stone—
In wider circles round the black-faced sheep,
Wider and fainter till they hardly crease
The ebony heritage of the herded dead.
On those islands
The tinkers whom no decent girl will go with,
Preserve the Gaelic tunes unspoiled by contact
With the folk-fancier or the friendly tourist,
And preserve the knowledge of horse-flesh and preserve
The uncompromising empire of the rogue.
On those islands
The tethered cow grazes among the orchises
And figures in blue calico turn by hand
The ground beyond the plough, and the bus, not stopping,
Drops a parcel for the lonely household
Where men remembering stories of eviction

Are glad to have their land though mainly stones—
The honoured bones which still can hoist a body.
On those islands
There is echo of the leaping fish, the identical
Sound that cheered the chiefs at ease from slaughter;
There is echo of baying hounds of a lost breed
And echo of MacCrimmon's pipes lost in the cave;
And seals cry with the voices of the drowned.
When men go out to fish, no one must say 'Good luck'
And the confidences told in a boat at sea
Must be as if printed on the white ribbon of a wave
Withdrawn as soon as printed—so never heard.
On those islands
The black minister paints the tour of hell
While the unregenerate drink from the bottle's neck
In gulps like gauntlets thrown at the devil's head
And spread their traditional songs across the hills
Like fraying tapestries of fights and loves,
The boar-hunt and the rope let down at night—
Lost causes and lingering home-sickness.
On those islands
The fish come singing from the drunken sea,
The herring rush the gunwales and sort themselves
To cram the expectant barrels of their own accord—
Or such is the dream of the fisherman whose wet
Leggings hang on the door as he sleeps returned
From a night when miles of net were drawn up empty.
On those islands
A girl with candid eyes goes out to marry
An independent tenant of seven acres
Who goes each year to the south to work on the roads
In order to raise a rent of forty shillings,
And all the neighbours celebrate their wedding
With drink and pipes and the walls of the barn reflect
The crazy shadows of the whooping dancers.
On those islands
Where many live on the dole or on old-age pensions
And many waste with consumption and some are drowned
And some of the old stumble in the midst of sleep
Into the pot-hole hitherto shunned in dreams
Or falling from the cliff among the shrieks of gulls
Reach the bottom before they have time to wake—

Whoever dies on the islands and however
The whole of the village goes into three day mourning,
The afflicted home is honoured and the shops are shut
For on those islands
Where a few surnames cover a host of people
And the art of being a stranger with your neighbour
Has still to be imported, death is still
No lottery ticket in a public lottery—
The result to be read on the front page of a journal—
But a family matter near to the whole family.
On those islands
Where no train runs on rails and the tyrant time
Has no clock-towers to signal people to doom
With semaphore ultimatums tick by tick,
There is still peace though not for me and not
Perhaps for long—still peace on the bevel hills
For those who still can live as their fathers lived
On those islands.

II

_1925—1929_

THE CREDITOR

The quietude of a soft wind
Will not rescind
My debts to God, but gentle-skinned
His finger probes. I lull myself
In quiet in diet in riot in dreams,
In dopes in drams in drums in dreams
Till God retire and the door shut.
But
Now I am left in the fire-blaze
The peacefulness of the fire-blaze
Will not erase
My debts to God for His mind strays
Over and under and all ways
All days and always.

TRAINS IN THE DISTANCE

Trains came threading quietly through my dozing childhood,
Gentle murmurs nosing through a summer quietude,
Drawing in and out, in and out, their smoky ribbons,
Parting now and then, and launching full-rigged galleons
And scrolls of smoke that hung in a shifting epitaph.
Then distantly the noise declined like a descending graph,
Sliding downhill gently to the bottom of the distance
(For now all things are there that all were here once);
And so we hardly noticed when that metal murmur came.
But it brought us assurance and comfort all the same,
And in the early night they soothed us to sleep,
And the chain of the rolling wheels bound us in deep
Till all was broken by that menace from the sea,
The steel-bosomed siren calling bitterly.

GENESIS

A million whirling spinning-wheels of flowing gossamer,
A million hammers jangling on the anvils of the sky,
The crisp chip of chisels and the murmuring of saws
And the flowing ripple of water from a million taps,

With the champ of griffin-horses with their heads in sacks of hay
And sawdust flitting to and fro in new-born fragrancy.
But not the same for all—flooding over weedy rocks
A green sea singing like a dream, and on the shore
Fair round pebbles with eggy speckles half transparent,
And brown sodden tangles of odorous wrack.

GLASS FALLING

The glass is going down. The sun
Is going down. The forecasts say
It will be warm, with frequent showers.
We ramble down the showery hours
And amble up and down the day.
Mary will wear her black goloshes
And splash the puddles on the town;
And soon on fleets of macintoshes
The rain is coming down, the frown
Is coming down of heaven showing
A wet night coming, the glass is going
Down, the sun is going down.

POUSSIN

In that Poussin the clouds are like golden tea,
And underneath the limbs flow rhythmically,
The cupids' blue feathers beat musically,
And we dally and dip our spoon in the golden tea.
The tea flows down the steps and up again,
An old-world fountain, pouring from sculptured lips,
And the chilly marble drop like sugar slips
And is lost in the dark gold depths, and the refrain
Of tea-leaves floats about and in and out,
And the motion is still as when one walks and the moon
Walks parallel but relations remain the same.
And thus we never reach the dregs of the cup,
Though we drink it up and drink it up and drink it up,
And thus we dally and dip our spoon.

EVENING INDOORS

In this evening room there is no stir, no fuss;
The silken shade of the oil-light is diaphanous,
And so come other noises through the noise of the clock
Transparent as the shade, as a girl's frock.
There is no crease, no fold ruffling the room at all;
The glass fringe of the shade seems a summer waterfall,
Like August insects purring over mown grass
The flames blend and pass, incend and end and pass.
Like the calm blue marriage of the sky and sea,
Or a blue-veiled Madonna beaming vacancy,
See that Madonna snuff out the shaded light
And stroke with soothing hand asleep the night.

ELEPHANT TRUNK

Descending out of the grey
Clouds elephant trunk
Twitches away
Hat;
THAT
Was *not* what I expected,
A
Misdirected
Joke it seemed to me;
"What about a levitation?" I had said,
Preening head for halo,
All alert, combed, sanctified,
I thank Thee, Lord, I am not like other men
WHEN
Descending out of the grey
Clouds elephant trunk. . . .

(and so *ad nauseam.*)

RIVER IN SPATE

The river falls and over the walls the coffins of cold funerals
Slide deep and sleep there in the close tomb of the pool,
And yellow waters lave the grave and pebbles pave its mortuary

[61]

And the river horses vault and plunge with their assault and
    battery,
And helter-skelter the coffins come and the drums beat and the
    waters flow,
And the panther horses lift their hooves and paw and shift and
    draw the bier,
The corpses blink in the rush of the river, and out of the water
    their chins they tip
And quaff the gush and lip the draught and crook their heads and
    crow,
Drowned and drunk with the cataract that carries them and
    buries them
And silts them over and covers them and lilts and chuckles over
    their bones;
The organ-tones that the winds raise will never pierce the water
    ways,
So all they will hear is the fall of hooves and the distant shake of
    harness,
And the beat of the bells on the horses' heads and the undertaker's
    laughter,
And the murmur that will lose its strength and blur at length to
    quietness,
And afterwards the minute heard descending, never ending
    heard,
And then the minute after and the minute after the minute after.

CANDLE POEMS

I

I have no clock, yet I can hear
The minutes pass while I sit here
Tired but free from tedium
And mark the waning cylinder.

To-morrow will be another day,
And to-day will then be yesterday,
To click the bonds of business
From Saturday to Saturday.

Another night will follow, but
My candle will then be a candle butt

[62]

And the door that is day and day's division
Will have opened once and shut.

Close your armoured books and mark
The waning cylinder that drips
Fluid time from pallid lips,
Making an island in the dark.

This island is too small, I fear;
Dark horses fret away the shore,
And I can build no breakwater
But only close a desperate ear
And mark the waning cylinder.

II

The candle in his white grave-clothes, always turning his cowled
     head,
Stood in his own shadow at the foot of my grave-bed,
Ho, said the candle with his rich dark beard,
How they howl like the dead!
And wagging his cowled head,
Ho, said the candle, they would make a body afeard.

NOCTURNE

The dark blood of night-time
Foams among the ivy,
And leaps toward the lunelet
Of sea-chawn ivory,
And nowhere finds an outlet.

The wind goes fingering
His lantern. The wind goes
In his glistening oil-cape
Knocking at the windows,
Slouching round the landscape.

Sinisterly bend and dip
Those hulks of cloud canvas,
Probing through the elm-trees,
Past the house; and then pass
To a larger emptiness.

THE LUGUBRIOUS, SALUBRIOUS
SEASIDE

The dogs' tails tick like metronomes,
Their barks encore the sticks you throw,
The sallow clouds yawn overhead,
The sagging deck-chairs yawn below.
I wish I had my marble clock
To race those minatory tails,
Or the fire-buckets at the Bank
To shame those proud enamelled pails,
Those wooden spades that dig the mind,
Unearthing memories of spades
When we were the protagonists
Flaunting down juvenile parades.
I hide my face in magazines
While children patronise the grave
Of mariners, while bathing girls
Deign to illuminate the wave.
That never-satisfied old maid, the sea,
Rehangs her white lace curtains ceaselessly.

HAPPY FAMILIES

The room is all a stupid quietness,
Cajoled only by the fire's caress;
We loll severally about and sit
Severally and do our business severally,
For there's a little bit for everybody;
But that's not all there is to it.

Crusted in sandstone, while the wooden clock
Places two doctor fingers on his mouth,
We seem fossils in rock,
Or leaves turned mummies in drouth,
And garnered into a mouldy shrubbery corner
Where the wind has done with us. When we are old
The gardener will use us for leaf-mould.

Dutifully sitting on chair, lying on sofa,
Standing on hearth-rug, here we are again,
John caught the bus, Joshua caught the train,

And I took a taxi, so we all got somewhere;
No one deserted, no one was a loafer,
Nobody disgraced us, luckily for us
No one put his foot in it or missed the bus.

But the wind is a beggar and always
Raps at front door, back door, side door;
In spite of the neat placard that says
"No Hawkers Here" he knocks the more,
He blows loose paper into petulance
And ruffles the brazier's fiery hair; and once
He caught me suddenly surreptitiously
And heft me out of my shell. We'll pass that over
And forget about it and quietly sit
Knitting close, sitting close under cover.

Snuff out the candle, for the cap, I think,
Seems to fit, excellently fit.
Te saluto—in a fraction, half a wink—
But that's not all there is to it.

BREAKING WEBS

The spider pendulously waits
Stranded in the unroaded air,
The spider's belly-mind creates
Thoroughfare on thoroughfare.

The fatally inquisitive moth
Wakes to ambition with a quiver,
Leaves its bed and board of cloth:
Wings of moth go flit and shiver.

And all the time on the window-pane
Shadow fingers of the trees
Wistfully grope and grope again
After the indoor mysteries.

Over asphalt, tar, and gravel
My racing model happily purrs,
Each charted road I yet unravel
Out of my mind's six cylinders.

Shutters of light, green and red,
Slide up and down. Like mingled cries,
Wind and sunlight clip and wed
Behind the canopy of my eyes.

. . . . . .

Yet all the time on the window-pane
Shadow fingers of the trees
Grope, grope, grope again
After unseen fatalities.

MAHAVVERAY

(SCENE: *The corner of a great many streets, all very long, high, and ugly, with windows boarded up; all quite empty; 2 policemen, A and B, on point duty.*)

A. Turn off the tap, Mahavveray, it's too cold here;
Icicles all over the shop, it's no joke here.
It's a bloody long time I've been waiting,
For they all let me down and left me waiting.

B. You've been here a dozen and a half year
Under the gutter and the grating. . . .

A. Turn off the tap, Mahavveray, it's too cold here.
No one comes along this beat at all,
With my baton and white gloves and all.

B. And no one will, never you fear;
It's not their affair to loiter
And patch up romances under a gutter;
People might think they were queer. . . .

A. Turn off the tap, Mahavveray; it's cold here.

B. If they came along, what would You say,
You old spec. of law and order?
I bet you don't know how to look a bit gay,
No one ever thought you were that sort of
Fellow with his phiz out for the day.

[66]

A. That old woman in the pawnshop said
   She can't keep the drum-sticks off her head
   For the crossbones beat it about so. . . .

B. There was an old woman and she didn't know what to do,
   So she bought boots that cripples left off,
   She sold them to army majors for wagers,
   And when they died with the whooping-cough
   She stole the boots from their great cold feet
   And sold them to army majors for charity.

A. That old woman is doing her bit.

B. And she sold them to ladies of delicate distinction
   Saying they were a sure fit.

A. But all the time she throbbed like parchment,
   For she can't keep the crossbones off her skull. . . .

B. There was an old woman and she didn't know what to do,
   So she went out into the garden-plot to pull
   Dried peas for dinner, and she mixed them with buttons
   And stirred them up well and poured them down the sink,
   And when the family came home for supper they said, "Well,
      well,
   There's not very much to eat or drink
   So you may go to Heaven."

A. But that old woman was doing her bit
   To provide for the family in such a delicate position
   That they all broke down in a red fit.

B. There was an old woman and she didn't know what to do,
   She said, "I'm going in for the beauty comp."
   All the princes west o' the moon came to that show,
   And the Pope came with a certain amount of pomp,
   And they looked at her through field-glasses as she sat on a
      table,
   And the Pope said to the princes, "What do you think of it?"
   And the princes said all at once, as well as they were able,
   "That old woman is doing her bit."

[67]

SPRING SUNSHINE

In a between world, a world of amber,
The old cat on the sand-warm window-sill
Sleeps on the verge of nullity.

Spring sunshine has a quality
Transcending rooks and the hammering
Of those who hang new pictures,
Asking if it is worth it
To clamour and caw, to add stick to stick for ever.

If it is worth while really
To colonise any more the already populous
Tree of knowledge, to portion and reportion
Bits of broken knowledge brittle and dead,
Whether it would not be better
To hide one's head in the warm sand of sleep
And be embalmed without hustle or bother.

The rooks bicker heckle bargain always
And market carts lumber—
Let me in the calm of the all-humouring sun
Also indulge my humour
And bury myself beyond creaks and cawings
In a below world, a bottom world of amber.

CRADLE SONG FOR MIRIAM

The clock's untiring fingers wind the wool of darkness
And we all lie alone, having long outgrown our cradles
(Sleep, sleep, Miriam)
And the flames like faded ladies always unheeded simper
And all is troubledness.

Soft the wool, dark the wool
Is gathered slowly, wholly up
Into a ball, all of it.

And yet in the back of the mind, lulled all else,
There is something unsleeping, un-tamperable-with

Something that whines and scampers
And like the ladies in the grate will not sleep nor forget itself,
Clawing at the wool like a kitten.

Sleep, sleep, Miriam.
And as for this animal of yours
He must be cradled also.
That he may not unravel this handiwork of forgetfulness,
That he may not philander with the flames before they die.

The world like a cradle rises and falls
On a wave of confetti and funerals
And sordor and stinks and stupid faces
And the deity making bored grimaces.

Oh what a muddle he has made of the wool,
(God will to-morrow have his hands full),
You must muzzle your beast, you must fasten him
For the whole of life—the interim.

Through the interim we pass
Everyone under an alias
Till they gather the strands of us together
And wind us up for ever and ever.

The clock's fingers wind, wind the wool of Lethe,
(Sleep, sleep, Miriam)
It glides across the floor drawn by hidden fingers
And the beast droops his head
And the fire droops its flounces
And winks a final ogle out of the fading embers
But no one pays attention;

This is too much, the flames say, insulted,
We who were once the world's beauties and now
No one pays attention
No one remembers us.

MAYFLY

Barometer of my moods today, mayfly,
Up and down one among a million, one

The same at best as the rest of the jigging mayflies,
One only day of May alive beneath the sun.

The yokels tilt their pewters and the foam
Flowers in the sun beside the jewelled water.
Daughter of the South, call the sunbeams home
To nest between your breasts. The kingcups
Ephemeral are gay gulps of laughter.

Gulp of yellow merriment; cackle of ripples;
Lips of the river that pout and whisper round the reeds.
The mayfly flirting and posturing over the water
Goes up and down in the lift so many times for fun.

'When we are grown up we are sure to alter
Much for the better, to adopt solider creeds
The kingcup will cease proffering his cup
And the foam will have blown from the beer and the heat no
        longer dance
And the lift lose fascination and the May
Change her tune to June—but the trouble with us mayflies
Is that we never have the chance to be grown up.'

They never have the chance, but what of time they have
They stretch out taut and thin and ringing clear;
So we, whose strand of life is not much more,
Let us too make our time elastic and
Inconsequently dance above the dazzling wave.

Nor put too much on the sympathy of things,
The dregs of drink, the dried cups of flowers,
The pathetic fallacy of the passing hours
When it is we who pass them—hours of stone,
Long rows of granite sphinxes looking on.

It is we who pass them, we the circus masters
Who make the mayflies dance, the lapwings lift their crests .
The show will soon shut down, its gay-rags gone,
But when this summer is over let us die together,
I want always to be near your breasts.

III

1931—1935

III

1911—1915

BELFAST

The hard cold fire of the northerner
Frozen into his blood from the fire in his basalt
Glares from behind the mica of his eyes
And the salt carrion water brings him wealth.

Down there at the end of the melancholy lough
Against the lurid sky over the stained water
Where hammers clang murderously on the girders
Like crucifixes the gantries stand.

And in the marble stores rubber gloves like polyps
Cluster; celluloid, painted ware, glaring
Metal patents, parchment lampshades, harsh
Attempts at buyable beauty.

In the porch of the chapel before the garish Virgin
A shawled factory-woman as if shipwrecked there
Lies a bunch of limbs glimpsed in the cave of gloom
By us who walk in the street so buoyantly and glib.

Over which country of cowled and haunted faces
The sun goes down with a banging of Orange drums
While the male kind murders each its woman
To whose prayer for oblivion answers no Madonna.

BIRMINGHAM

Smoke from the train-gulf hid by hoardings blunders upward,
        the brakes of cars
Pipe as the policeman pivoting round raises his flat hand, bars
With his figure of a monolith Pharaoh the queue of fidgety
        machines
(Chromium dogs on the bonnet, faces behind the triplex screens).
Behind him the streets run away between the proud glass of
        shops,
Cubical scent-bottles artificial legs arctic foxes and electric mops,
But beyond this centre the slumward vista thins like a diagram:
There, unvisited, are Vulcan's forges who doesn't care a tinker's
        damn.

Splayed outwards through the suburbs houses, houses for rest
Seducingly rigged by the builder, half-timbered houses with lips
    pressed
So tightly and eyes staring at the traffic through bleary haws
And only a six-inch grip of the racing earth in their concrete
    claws;
In these houses men as in a dream pursue the Platonic Forms
With wireless and cairn terriers and gadgets approximating to the
    fickle norms
And endeavour to find God and score one over the neighbour
By climbing tentatively upward on jerry-built beauty and
    sweated labour.

The lunch hour: the shops empty, shopgirls' faces relax
Diaphanous as green glass, empty as old almanacs
As incoherent with ticketed gewgaws tiered behind their heads
As the Burne-Jones windows in St. Philip's broken by crawling
    leads;
Insipid colour, patches of emotion, Saturday thrills
(This theatre is sprayed with 'June')—the gutter take our old
    playbills,
Next week-end it is likely in the heart's funfair we shall pull
Strong enough on the handle to get back our money; or at any
    rate it is possible.

On shining lines the trams like vast sarcophagi move
Into the sky, plum after sunset, merging to duck's egg, barred
    with mauve
Zeppelin clouds, and Pentecost-like the cars' headlights bud
Out from sideroads and the traffic signals, crême-de-menthe or
    bull's blood,
Tell one to stop, the engine gently breathing, or to go on
To where like black pipes of organs in the frayed and fading
    zone
Of the West the factory chimneys on sullen sentry will all night
    wait
To call, in the harsh morning, sleep-stupid faces through the
    daily gate.

[74]

TURF-STACKS

Among these turf-stacks graze no iron horses
Such as stalk, such as champ in towns and the soul of crowds,
Here is no mass-production of neat thoughts
No canvas shrouds for the mind nor any black hearses:
The peasant shambles on his boots like hooves
Without thinking at all or wanting to run in grooves.

But those who lack the peasant's conspirators,
The tawny mountain, the unregarded buttress,
Will feel the need of a fortress against ideas and against the
Shuddering insidious shock of the theory-vendors,
The little sardine men crammed in a monster toy
Who tilt their aggregate beast against our crumbling Troy.

For we are obsolete who like the lesser things
Who play in corners with looking-glasses and beads;
It is better we should go quickly, go into Asia
Or any other tunnel where the world recedes,
Or turn blind wantons like the gulls who scream
And rip the edge off any ideal or dream.

UPON THIS BEACH

Upon this beach the falling wall of the sea
Explodes its drunken marble
Amid gulls' gaiety.

Which ever-crumbling masonry, cancelling sum,
No one by any device can represent
In any medium.

Turn therefore inland, tripper, foot on the sea-holly,
Forget those waves' monstrous fatuity
And boarding bus be jolly.

[75]

CIRCE
'. . . vitreamque Circen'

Something of glass about her, of dead water,
Chills and holds us,
Far more fatal than painted flesh or the lodestone of live hair
This despair of crystal brilliance.
Narcissus' error
Enfolds and kills us—
Dazed with gazing on that unfertile beauty
Which is our own heart's thought.
Fled away to the beasts
One cannot stop thinking; Timon
Kept on finding gold.
In parrot-ridden forest or barren coast
A more importunate voice than bird or wave
Escutcheoned on the air with ice letters
Seeks and, of course, finds us
(Of course, being our echo).

Be brave, my ego, look into your glass
And realise that that never-to-be-touched
Vision is your mistress.

SPRING VOICES

The small householder now comes out warily
Afraid of the barrage of sun that shouts cheerily,
Spring is massing forces, birds wink in air,
The battlemented chestnuts volley green fire,
The pigeons banking on the wind, the hoots of cars,
Stir him to run wild, gamble on horses, buy cigars;
Joy lies before him to be ladled and lapped from his hand—
Only that behind him, in the shade of his villa, memories stand
Breathing on his neck and muttering that all this has happened
    before,
Keep the wind out, cast no clout, try no unwarranted jaunts
    untried before,
But let the spring slide by nor think to board its car
For it rides West to where the tangles of scrap-iron are;

Do not walk, these voices say, between the bucking clouds alone
Or you may loiter into a suddenly howling crater, or fall, jerked
  back, garrotted by the sun.

MUSEUMS

Museums offer us, running from among the buses,
A centrally heated refuge, parquet floors and sarcophaguses,
Into whose tall fake porches we hurry without a sound
Like a beetle under a brick that lies, useless, on the ground.
Warmed and cajoled by the silence the cowed cypher revives,
Mirrors himself in the cases of pots, paces himself by marble lives,
Makes believe it was he that was the glory that was Rome,
Soft on his cheek the nimbus of other people's martyrdom,
And then returns to the street, his mind an arena where sprawls
Any number of consumptive Keatses and dying Gauls.

A CONTACT

The trains pass and the trains pass, chains of lighted windows,
A register in an unknown language
For these are the trains in which one never goes.

The familiar rhythm but the unknown implications
Delight like a dead language
Which never shocks us by banal revelations.

So listening for the night express coming down the way
I receive the expected whistle of the engine
Sharp and straight on the ear like stigmata.

NATURE MORTE

(Even so it is not so easy to be dead)

As those who are not athletic at breakfast day by day
Employ and enjoy the sinews of others vicariously,
Shielded by the upheld journal from their dream-puncturing
  wives
And finding in the printed word a multiplication of their lives,

[77]

So we whose senses give us things misfelt and misheard
Turn also, for our adjustment, to the pretentious word
Which stabilises the light on the sun-fondled trees
And, by photographing our ghosts, claims to put us at our ease;
Yet even so, no matter how solid and staid we contrive
Our reconstructions, even a still life is alive
And in your Chardin the appalling unrest of the soul
Exudes from the dried fish and the brown jug and the bowl.

TO A COMMUNIST

Your thoughts make shape like snow; in one night only
The gawky earth grows breasts,
Snow's unity engrosses
Particular pettiness of stones and grasses.
But before you proclaim the millennium, my dear,
Consult the barometer—
This poise is perfect but maintained
For one day only.

THE INDIVIDUALIST SPEAKS

We with our Fair pitched among the feathery clover
Are always cowardly and never sober,
Drunk with steam-organs, thigh-rub and cream-soda
—We cannot remember enemies in this valley.

As chestnut candles turn to conkers, so we
Knock our brains together extravagantly
Instead of planting them to make more trees
—Who have not as yet sampled God's malice.

But to us urchins playing with paint and filth
A prophet scanning the road on the hither hills
Might utter the old warning of the old sin
—Avenging youth threatening an old war.

Crawling down like lava or termites
Nothing seduces, nothing dissolves, nothing affrights
You who scale off masks and smash the purple lights
—But I will escape, with my dog, on the far side of the Fair.

[78]

SUNDAY MORNING

Down the road someone is practising scales,
The notes like little fishes vanish with a wink of tails,
Man's heart expands to tinker with his car
For this is Sunday morning, Fate's great bazaar;
Regard these means as ends, concentrate on this Now,
And you may grow to music or drive beyond Hindhead anyhow,
Take corners on two wheels until you go so fast
That you can clutch a fringe or two of the windy past,
That you can abstract this day and make it to the week of time
A small eternity, a sonnet self-contained in rhyme.

But listen, up the road, something gulps, the church spire
Opens its eight bells out, skulls' mouths which will not tire
To tell how there is no music or movement which secures
Escape from the weekday time. Which deadens and endures.

AUGUST

The shutter of time darkening ceaselessly
Has whisked away the foam of may and elder
And I realise how now, as every year before,
Once again the gay months have eluded me.

For the mind, by nature stagey, welds its frame
Tomb-like around each little world of a day;
We jump from picture to picture and cannot follow
The living curve that is breathlessly the same.

While the lawn-mower sings moving up and down
Spirting its little fountain of vivid green,
I, like Poussin, make a still-bound fête of us
Suspending every noise, of insect or machine.

Garlands at a set angle that do not slip,
Theatrically (and as if for ever) grace
You and me and the stone god in the garden
And Time who also is shown with a stone face.

But all this is a dilettante's lie,
Time's face is not stone nor still his wings,
Our mind, being dead, wishes to have time die
For we being ghosts cannot catch hold of things.

THE GLACIER

Just as those who gaze get higher than those who climb
A paradox unfolds on any who can tamper with time.
Where bus encumbers upon bus and fills its slot
Speed up the traffic in a quick motion film of thought
Till bus succeeds bus so identically sliding through
That you cannot catch the fraction of a chink between the two;
But they all go so fast, bus after bus, day after day,
Year after year, that you cannot mark any headway,
But the whole stream of traffic seems to crawl
Carrying its dead boulders down a glacier wall
And we who have always been haunted by the fear of becoming
      stone
Cannot bear to watch that catafalque creep down
And therefore turn away to seemingly slower things
And rejoice there to have found the speed of fins and wings
In the minnow-twisting of the latinist who alone
Nibbles and darts through the shallows of the lexicon
Or among plate-glass cases in sombre rooms where
Eyes appraise the glazen life of majolica ware
Or where a gardener with trowel and rheumatic pains
Pumps up the roaring sap of vegetables through their veins.

PERSEUS

Borrowed wings on his ankles,
Carrying a stone death,
The hero entered the hall,
All in the hall looked up,
Their breath frozen on them,
And there was no more shuffle or clatter in the hall at all

So a friend of a man comes in
And leaves a book he is lending or flowers

And goes again, alive but as good as dead,
And you are left alive, no better than dead,
And you dare not turn the leaden pages of the book or touch the
  flowers, the hooded and arrested hours.

Close your eyes,
There are suns beneath your lids,
Or look in the looking-glass in the end room—
You will find it full of eyes,
The ancient smiles of men cut out with scissors and kept in
  mirrors.

Ever to meet me comes, in sun or dull,
The gay hero swinging the Gorgon's head
And I am left, with the dull drumming of the sun, suspended and
  dead,
Or the dumb grey-brown of the day is a leper's cloth,
And one feels the earth going round and round the globe of the
  blackening mantle, a mad moth.

AN APRIL MANIFESTO

Our April must replenish the delightful wells,
Bucket's lip dipping, light on the sleeping cells,
Man from his vigil in the wintry chapel
Will card his skin with accurate strigil.
O frivolous and astringent spring
We never come full circle, never remember
Self behind self years without number,
A series of dwindling mirrors, but take a tangent line
And start again. Our April must replenish
Our bank-account of vanity and give our doors a coat of varnish.
Leave the tedium of audits and of finding correct
For the gaiety of places where people collect
For the paper rosettes of the stadium and the plaudits.
And you, let you paint your face and sleek your leg with silk
Which is your right to do
As gay trams run on rails and cows give milk.
Sharp sun-strop, surface-gloss, and momentary caprice

These are what we cherish
Caring not if the bridges and the embankments
Of past and future perish and cease;
Before the leaves grow heavy and the good days vanish
Hold out your glasses which our April must replenish.

MORNING SUN

Shuttles of trains going north, going south, drawing threads of
 blue,
The shining of the lines of trams like swords,
Thousands of posters asserting a monopoly of the good, the
 beautiful, the true,
Crowds of people all in the vocative, you and you,
The haze of the morning shot with words.

Yellow sun comes white off the wet streets but bright
Chromium yellows in the gay sun's light,
Filleted sun streaks the purple mist,
Everything is kissed and reticulated with sun
Scooped-up and cupped in the open fronts of shops
And bouncing on the traffic which never stops.

And the street fountain blown across the square
Rainbow-trellises the air and sunlight blazons
The red butcher's and scrolls of fish on marble slabs,
Whistled bars of music crossing silver sprays
And horns of cars, touché, touché, rapiers' retort, a moving cage,
A turning page of shine and sound, the day's maze.

But when the sun goes out, the streets go cold, the hanging meat
And tiers of fish are colourless and merely dead,
And the hoots of cars neurotically repeat and the tiptoed feet
Of women hurry and falter whose faces are dead;
And I see in the air but not belonging there
The blown grey powder of the fountain grey as the ash
That forming on a cigarette covers the red.

[82]

CUCKOO

Cuckoo across the poppies
    Making myth—
Simeon on his pillar
    Stands in the air alone

Without context
    Not looking down,
Personification
    Of distance.

Nothing to be seen
    But a stone posture,
The shape of the song
    Of the cuckoo.

TRAIN TO DUBLIN

Our half-thought thoughts divide in sifted wisps
Against the basic facts repatterned without pause,
I can no more gather my mind up in my fist
Than the shadow of the smoke of this train upon the grass—
This is the way that animals' lives pass.

The train's rhythm never relents, the telephone posts
Go striding backwards like the legs of time to where
In a Georgian house you turn at the carpet's edge
Turning a sentence while, outside my window here,
The smoke makes broken queries in the air.

The train keeps moving and the rain holds off,
I count the buttons on the seat, I hear a shell
Held hollow to the ear, the mere
Reiteration of integers, the bell
That tolls and tolls, the monotony of fear.

At times we are doctrinaire, at times we are frivolous,
Plastering over the cracks, a gesture making good,
But the strength of us does not come out of us.
It is we, I think, are the idols and it is God
Has set us up as men who are painted wood,

[83]

And the trains carry us about. But not consistently so,
For during a tiny portion of our lives we are not in trains,
The idol living for a moment, not muscle-bound
But walking freely through the slanting rain,
Its ankles wet, its grimace relaxed again.

All over the world people are toasting the King,
Red lozenges of light as each one lifts his glass,
But I will not give you any idol or idea, creed or king,
I give you the incidental things which pass
Outward through space exactly as each was.

I give you the disproportion between labour spent
And joy at random; the laughter of the Galway sea
Juggling with spars and bones irresponsibly,
I give you the toy Liffey and the vast gulls,
I give you fuchsia hedges and whitewashed walls.

I give you the smell of Norman stone, the squelch
Of bog beneath your boots, the red bog-grass,
The vivid chequer of the Antrim hills, the trough of dark
Golden water for the cart-horses, the brass
Belt of serene sun upon the lough.

And I give you the faces, not the permanent masks,
But the faces balanced in the toppling wave—
His glint of joy in cunning as the farmer asks
Twenty per cent too much, or a girl's, forgetting to be suave,
A tiro choosing stuffs, preferring mauve.

And I give you the sea and yet again the sea's
Tumultuous marble,
With Thor's thunder or taking his ease akimbo
Lumbering torso, but finger-tips a marvel
Of surgeon's accuracy.

I would like to give you more but I cannot hold
This stuff within my hands and the train goes on;
I know that there are further syntheses to which,
As you have perhaps, people at last attain
And find that they are rich and breathing gold.

INTIMATIONS OF MORTALITY

The shadows of the banisters march march,
The lovers linger under the arch,
On the beach the waves creep,
The little boy cannot go to sleep.

He is afraid of God and the Devil—
If he shuts his eyes they will draw level,
So he watches the half-open door and waits
For people on the stairs carrying lights.

Someone comes, carrying a lamp,
The shadows of the banisters march march,
All is above board, order is restored,
Time on horseback under a Roman arch.

Then the final darkness for eight hours
The murderous grin of toothy flowers,
The tick of his pulse in the pillow, the sick
Vertigo of falling in a fanged pit.

After one perfunctory kiss
His parents snore in conjugal bliss.
The night watchman with crossed thumbs
Grows an idol. The Kingdom comes. . . .

WOLVES

I do not want to be reflective any more
Envying and despising unreflective things
Finding pathos in dogs and undeveloped handwriting
And young girls doing their hair and all the castles of sand
Flushed by the children's bedtime, level with the shore.

The tide comes in and goes out again, I do not want
To be always stressing either its flux or its permanence,
I do not want to be a tragic or philosophic chorus
But to keep my eye only on the nearer future
And after that let the sea flow over us.

Come then all of you, come closer, form a circle,
Join hands and make believe that joined
Hands will keep away the wolves of water
Who howl along our coast. And be it assumed
That no one hears them among the talk and laughter.

AUBADE

Having bitten on life like a sharp apple
Or, playing it like a fish, been happy,

Having felt with fingers that the sky is blue,
What have we after that to look forward to?

Not the twilight of the gods but a precise dawn
Of sallow and grey bricks, and newsboys crying war.

SNOW

The room was suddenly rich and the great bay-window was
Spawning snow and pink roses against it
Soundlessly collateral and incompatible:
World is suddener than we fancy it.

World is crazier and more of it than we think,
Incorrigibly plural. I peel and portion
A tangerine and spit the pips and feel
The drunkenness of things being various.

And the fire flames with a bubbling sound for world
Is more spiteful and gay than one supposes—
On the tongue on the eyes on the ears in the palms of one's
    hands—
There is more than glass between the snow and the huge roses.

IV

1936—1938

VI

1919-1929

CARRICKFERGUS

I was born in Belfast between the mountain and the gantries
  To the hooting of lost sirens and the clang of trams:
Thence to Smoky Carrick in County Antrim
  Where the bottle-neck harbour collects the mud which jams

The little boats beneath the Norman castle,
  The pier shining with lumps of crystal salt;
The Scotch Quarter was a line of residential houses
  But the Irish Quarter was a slum for the blind and halt.

The brook ran yellow from the factory stinking of chlorine,
  The yarn-mill called its funeral cry at noon;
Our lights looked over the lough to the lights of Bangor
  Under the peacock aura of a drowning moon.

The Norman walled this town against the country
  To stop his ears to the yelping of his slave
And built a church in the form of a cross but denoting
  The list of Christ on the cross in the angle of the nave.

I was the rector's son, born to the anglican order,
  Banned for ever from the candles of the Irish poor;
The Chichesters knelt in marble at the end of a transept
  With ruffs about their necks, their portion sure.

The war came and a huge camp of soldiers
  Grew from the ground in sight of our house with long
Dummies hanging from gibbets for bayonet practice
  And the sentry's challenge echoing all day long;

A Yorkshire terrier ran in and out by the gate-lodge
  Barred to civilians, yapping as if taking affront:
Marching at ease and singing 'Who Killed Cock Robin?'
  The troops went out by the lodge and off to the Front.

The steamer was camouflaged that took me to England—
  Sweat and khaki in the Carlisle train;
I thought that the war would last for ever and sugar
  Be always rationed and that never again

Would the weekly papers not have photos of sandbags
   And my governess not make bandages from moss
And people not have maps above the fireplace
   With flags on pins moving across and across—

Across the hawthorn hedge the noise of bugles,
   Flares across the night,
Somewhere on the lough was a prison ship for Germans,
   A cage across their sight.

I went to school in Dorset, the world of parents
   Contracted into a puppet world of sons
Far from the mill girls, the smell of porter, the salt-mines
   And the soldiers with their guns.

ICELAND

No shields now
   Cross the knoll,
The hills are dull
   With leaden shale,
Whose arms could squeeze
   The breath from time
And the climb is long
   From cairn to cairn.

Houses are few
   But decorous
In a ruined land
   Of sphagnum moss;
Corrugated iron
   Farms inherit
The spirit and phrase
   Of ancient sagas.

Men have forgotten
   Anger and ambush,
To make ends meet
   Their only business:
The lover riding
   In the lonely dale

[90]

Hears the plover's
   Single pipe

And feels perhaps
   But undefined
The drift of death
   In the sombre wind
Deflating the trim
   Balloon of lust
In a grey storm
   Of dust and grit.

So we who have come
   As trippers North
Have minds no match
   For this land's girth;
The glacier's licking
   Tongues deride
Our pride of life,
   Our flashy songs.

But the people themselves
   Who live here
Ignore the brooding
   Fear, the sphinx;
And the radio
   With tags of tune
Defies their pillared
   Basalt crags.

Whose ancestors
   Thought that at last
The end would come
   To a blast of horns
And gods would face
   The worst in fight,
Vanish in the night
   The last, the first

Night which began
   Without device

In ice and rocks,
    No shade or shape;
Grass and blood,
    The strife of life,
Were an interlude
    Which soon must pass

And all go back
    Relapse to rock
Under the shawl
    Of the ice-caps,
The cape which night
    Will spread to cover
The world when the living
    Flags are furled.

PASSAGE STEAMER

Upon the decks they take beef tea
    Who are so free, so free, so free,
But down the ladder in the engine-room
    (Doom, doom, doom, doom)
The great cranks rise and fall, repeat,
The great cranks plod with their Assyrian feet
    To match the monotonous energy of the sea.

Back from a journey I require
    Some new desire, desire, desire
But find in the open sea and sun
    None, none, none, none;
The gulls that bank around the mast
Insinuate that nothing we pass is past,
    That all our beginnings were long since begun.

And when I think of you, my dear,
    Who were so near, so near, so near,
The barren skies from wall to wall
    Appal, appal, pall, pall,
The spray no longer gilds the wave,
The sea looks nothing more nor less than a grave
    And the world and the day are grey and that is all.

POSTSCRIPT TO ICELAND

for W. H. Auden

Now the winter nights begin
Lonely comfort walls me in;
So before the memory slip
I review our Iceland trip—

Not for me romantic nor
Idyll on a mythic shore
But a fancy turn, you know,
Sandwiched in a graver show.

Down in Europe Seville fell,
Nations germinating hell,
The Olympic games were run—
Spots upon the Aryan sun.

And the don in me set forth
How the landscape of the north
Had educed the saga style
Plodding forward mile by mile.

And the don in you replied
That the North begins inside,
Our ascetic guts require
Breathers from the Latin fire.

So although no ghost was scotched
We were happy while we watched
Ravens from their walls of shale
Cruise around the rotting whale,

Watched the sulphur basins boil,
Loops of steam uncoil and coil,
While the valley fades away
To a sketch of Judgment Day.

So we rode and joked and smoked
With no miracles evoked,
With no levitations won
In the thin unreal sun;

[93]

In that island never found
Visions blossom from the ground,
No conversions like St. Paul,
No great happenings at all.

Holidays should be like this,
Free from over-emphasis,
Time for soul to stretch and spit
Before the world comes back on it,

Before the chimneys row on row
Sneer in smoke, 'We told you so'
And the fog-bound sirens call
Ruin to the long sea-wall.

Rows of books around me stand,
Fence me round on either hand;
Through that forest of dead words
I would hunt the living birds—

Great black birds that fly alone
Slowly through a land of stone,
And the gulls who weave a free
Quilt of rhythm on the sea.

Here in Hampstead I sit late
Nights which no one shares and wait
For the 'phone to ring or for
Unknown angels at the door;

Better were the northern skies
Than this desert in disguise—
Rugs and cushions and the long
Mirror which repeats the song.

For the litany of doubt
From these walls comes breathing out
Till the room becomes a pit
Humming with the fear of it

With the fear of loneliness
And uncommunicableness;

All the wires are cut, my friends
Live beyond the severed ends.

So I write these lines for you
Who have felt the death-wish too,
But your lust for life prevails—
Drinking coffee, telling tales.

Our prerogatives as men
Will be cancelled who knows when;
Still I drink your health before
The gun-butt raps upon the door.

SAND IN THE AIR

Books, do not look at me,
    Clock, do not stare;
The fire's ashes fidget,
    There is sand in the air;
Drums tell its coming—
    The sandstorm that blows
From the desert of darkness—
    O in the desert of darkness
        Where is she walking?

Otherwise regular
    Quickening their beat
The marchers of madness
    Pick up their feet,
Make for my table
    And the empty chair
That faces me—Where,
    Where and why is she absent
        Leaving it empty?

Dial her number,
    None will reply;
In the shrivelled world
    There is only I;
Her voice is frozen,

Hangs in my brain
On the crags of memory—
O my dear, go away
From the crags of memory.

NOW THAT THE SHAPES OF MIST

Now that the shapes of mist like hooded beggar-children
Slink quickly along the middle of the road
And the lamps draw trails of milk in ponds of lustrous lead
I am decidedly pleased not to be dead.

Or when wet roads at night reflect the clutching
Importunate fingers of trees and windy shadows
Lunge and flounce on the windscreen as I drive
I am glad of the accident of being alive.

There are so many nights with stars or close-
ly interleaved with battleship-grey or plum,
So many visitors whose Buddha-like palms are pressed
Against the windowpanes where people take their rest.

Whose favour now is yours to screen your sleep—
You need not hear the strings that are tuning for the dawn—
Mingling, my dear, your breath with the quiet breath
Of sleep whom the old writers called the brother of Death.

HIDDEN ICE

There are few songs for domesticity
For routine work, money-making or scholarship
Though these are apt for eulogy or for tragedy.

And I would praise our adaptability
Who can spend years and years in offices and beds
Every morning twirling the napkin ring,
A twitter of inconsequent vitality.

And I would praise our inconceivable stamina
Who work to the clock and calendar and maintain
The equilibrium of nerves and notions,
Our mild bravado in the face of time.

Those who ignore disarm. The domestic ambush
The pleated lampshade the defeatist clock
May never be consummated and we may never
Strike on the rock beneath the calm upholstering.

But some though buoyed by habit, though convoyed
By habitual faces and hands that help the food
Or help one with one's coat, have lost their bearings
Struck hidden ice or currents no one noted.

One was found like Judas kissing flowers
And one who sat between the clock and the sun
Lies like a Saint Sebastian full of arrows
Feathered from his own hobby, his pet hours.

From OUT OF THE PICTURE

I

The Oracle

The oracle
  High betweeen the cliffs,
The tripod over
  The mephitic cleft,
Or the sybil's cave
  Where the winds blow
The dead leaf answers
  To and fro:
Where shall we find truth in an oracle?

The oracle
  Among the talking oaks,
The flight of birds,
  The examination of guts,
Luck of the cards,
  Lines of the hand,
Call of the raven
  In a sallow land:
Where shall we find truth in an oracle?

II
Riding in Cars

Riding in cars
  On tilting roads
We have left behind
  Our household gods,
We have left behind
  The cautious clause,
The laws of the over-
  rational mind.

Frost on the window,
  Skater's figures,
Gunmen fingering
  Anxious triggers,
Stocks and shares
  (The ribbon of the rich)
The favourite down
  At the blind ditch.

Forgotten now
  The early days,
Youth's idyllic
  And dawdling ways;
Cruising along
  On the long road
We do not notice
  The limping god.

Swinging between
  Crutches he comes
To an overture
  Of buried drums;
His eyes will turn
  Our hands to stone,
His name is Time,
  He walks alone.

III

War Heroes

When the heroes came back from the ten years' war
(But no war now will last ten years)
They struck a port they seemed to have seen before.
There were old men sitting on the bollards
Puffing smoke across the sea,
There were dead men hanging in the gantries,
There was a lame bird limping on the quay.
When were we here before? one of them said.
The captain answered: This is where we were born
And where we have now returned. Dead to the Dead.

IV

Pindar is Dead

There are hikers on all the roads—
    Pindar is dead—
The petrol pumps are doing a roaring business,
Motors are tuning up for the Easter races,
Building companies are loaning to the newly married—
    Pindar is dead and that's no matter.

There are climbers on all the hills—
    Pindar is dead—
With oiled boots and ropes they are tackling Snowdon,
The swimming baths are filled for Easter Monday,
Doctored with chlorine to prevent infection—
    Pindar is dead and that's no matter.

There is money on all the horses—
    Pindar is dead—
One belongs to a proud and a plethoric peer,
One to a maharajah, one to a midland magnate,
One to a dago count and one to a tweeded spinster—
    Pindar is dead and that's no matter.

[99]

There are flowers in all the markets—
   Pindar is dead—
Daffodils, tulips, and forced roses,
New potatoes and green peas for Easter,
Wreaths of moss and primrose for the churches
But no wreaths for runners, whether of olive or laurel—
   Pindar is dead and that's no matter.

V

Les Neiges D'Antan

What's become of all the glory and the grandeur of the gold-men
      and the gunmen,
The long breakers topped with silver of expanding power and
      profits,
Of the well-upholstered mansion, seven flights of stairs for the
      servants
Carrying coal from six in the morning?
What's become of the squadron of butlers, valets, grooms and
      second housemaids?
Gone like the carriage-horse and cabhorse that once dunged the
      streets of London.
What's become of the oracles in beards and whiskers, beauty in
      bustles?
What's become of Mr. Gladstone or of grandpa's roll-top desk,
Waterloo Bridge and General Gordon?
What's become of them? What's becoming of us?
Look ahead, Long-Sighted Jim,
What do you see in the future dim?
   I look ahead and what do I see?
   I see a pageant, a Lord Mayor's procession,
   The Aldermen and the flunkeys, the carnival giants,
   The tableaux on lorries, the flags and the coaches,
   And every single one of the people who make that procession
   Carries a white stick to show that he is blind.
What's become of the light of day, the golden spokes of the sun's
      wheels,
What's become of the fingers of light that picked the locks of the
      dark places,
What's become of all our private sentinels?

[100]

Answer: The sentry has gone.
He will not come back.
The pavement was worn by his feet
But moss will grow over the tracks.
Anyone now can approach
The door of your house without fear.
The burglar, the beggar, the drunk,
The murdering madman, the whore,
The prophet in sackcloth, the priest,
The jackal, the tiger, the snake,
All have their eye on your door.
Close all the doors, bar all the shutters,
Be ready with revolver and electric torch,
Fire extinguisher and telephone directory,
Bible, cheque book and *savoir faire:*
The vultures are gathered together,
Their hooked wings carve the urban air.
When the golden cycle is over, the wise men said,
Fire will consume the lot, the game resume,
And feathers of the birds of prey will singe as they tear the prey,
And the corpses roast where they fell
And the small blue flames will play
Like kittens with a ball of wool . . .
  FIRE FIRE FIRE FIRE . . .
Fire in Troy, fire in Babylon, fire in Nineveh, fire in London,
  FIRE FIRE FIRE FIRE
The buckets are empty of water, the hoses are punctured,
The city main is cut off, the holy well is dry,
There is no succour in the dusty ground, the metallic sky,
No rock will spout with water at the prophet's rod,
Nor fate repeat the legendary flood,
There is nothing to stem the mechanical march of fire,
Nothing to assuage the malice of the drunken fire.
  FIRE FIRE FIRE FIRE

VI

Empty Shoes

  Some one said that shoes had personality,
  That when you die your shoes. . . .
  That the frozen overflow of personality

Hangs on in jags after the general thaw
When a man has died.
Icicles, acroteria.
In a corner, in a cloakroom, among rackets and rods
An old pair of brogues
With criss-cross wrinkles like an old man's face.
Or when a girl has died
Her shoes are lined up, spruce as soldiers,
Waiting for the word Dismiss.
And in hotels at night passing from door to door
There is something terrible in all those empty shoes.

VII

The Jingles of the Morning

Shall we remember the jingles of the morning,
The pipers the pedlars and the brass farthings,
The buds of music, the imagined darlings?
    No, we shall *not* remember.

Shall we remember the games with puffball and plantain,
Searching for the lost handle to the silent fountain,
Hiding in the shrubbery, shutting our eyes and counting?

Shall we remember the marigolds parading,
Smell of grass and noise of the corncrake railing
And the fun of dragging a stick along the paling?

And after that shall we remember the races,
The broken tape, the clamour of companions' voices,
The schoolboy's callow joys in smut and curses?

And shall we remember our early adult pleasure,
The dive in love's lagoons of brilliant azure,
The gay martyrdom, the brave fantasia?

Shall we remember the kick of inspired religion,
The visions in drink, the feel of the homing pigeon
Drawn by a magnet to an intuited region?

Shall we remember the noise of the moving nations
Or shall we remember the gusty sun's creations,
The night and the never-to-be-climbed-to constellations?
    No, we shall *not* remember.

VIII

Finale

It is not enough
To have winning ways,
    The trimmed wick burns clear,
To follow with an indolent eye
The flicker-pattern of the days,
    For here ends our hoarded oil.

The acquisitive arts
Are not enough,
    The trimmed wick burns clear,
It is a little and a tired time
To be making money or love,
    Here ends our hoarded oil.

A kiss, a cuddle,
A crossed cheque,
    The trimmed wick burns clear,
Walk among statues in the dark,
The odds are you will break your neck—
    Here ends our hoarded oil.

TAKEN FOR GRANTED

Taken for granted
    The household orbit in childhood
The punctual sound of the gong
    The round of domestic service.

The lamps were trimmed at six,
    Sticks were lavish for firewood,
The cat made bread of my knees,
    The housewife shopped in the morning.

The shops were fragrant, the blistered
  Vagrant peered in the windows
At tripes like deep-sea plants,
  Sausages in ropes of marble.

On the knees of bountiful gods
  We lived in the ease of acceptance
Taking until we were twenty
  God's plenty for granted.

THE BRANDY GLASS

Only let it form within his hands once more—
The moment cradled like a brandy glass.
Sitting alone in the empty dining hall . . .
From the chandeliers the snow begins to fall
Piling around carafes and table legs
And chokes the passage of the revolving door.
The last diner, like a ventriloquist's doll
Left by his master, gazes before him, begs:
'Only let it form within my hands once more.'

THE SUNLIGHT ON THE GARDEN

The sunlight on the garden
Hardens and grows cold,
We cannot cage the minute
Within its nets of gold,
When all is told
We cannot beg for pardon.

Our freedom as free lances
Advances towards its end;
The earth compels, upon it
Sonnets and birds descend;
And soon, my friend,
We shall have no time for dances.

The sky was good for flying
Defying the church bells
[104]

And every evil iron
Siren and what it tells:
The earth compels,
We are dying, Egypt, dying

And not expecting pardon,
Hardened in heart anew,
But glad to have sat under
Thunder and rain with you,
And grateful too
For sunlight on the garden.

JUNE THUNDER

The Junes were free and full, driving through tiny
Roads, the mudguards brushing the cowparsley,
Through fields of mustard and under boldly embattled
   Mays and chestnuts

Or betweeen beeches verdurous and voluptuous
Or where broom and gorse beflagged the chalkland—
All the flare and gusto of the unenduring
   Joys of a season

Now returned but I note as more appropriate
To the maturer mood impending thunder
With an indigo sky and the garden hushed except for
   The treetops moving.

Then the curtains in my room blow suddenly inward,
The shrubbery rustles, birds fly heavily homeward,
The white flowers fade to nothing on the trees and rain comes
   Down like a dropscene.

Now there comes the catharsis, the cleansing downpour
Breaking the blossoms of our overdated fancies
Our old sentimentality and whimsicality
   Loves of the morning.

Blackness at half-past eight, the night's precursor,
Clouds like falling masonry and lightning's lavish

Annunciation, the sword of the mad archangel
Flashed from the scabbard.

If only you would come and dare the crystal
Rampart of rain and the bottomless moat of thunder,
If only now you would come I should be happy
  Now if now only.

THE HEATED MINUTES

The heated minutes climb
The anxious hill,
The tills fill up with cash,
The tiny hammers chime
The bells of good and ill,
And the world piles with ash
From fingers killing time.

If you were only here
Among these rocks,
I should not feel the dull
The taut and ticking fear
That hides in all the clocks
And creeps inside the skull—
If you were here, my dear.

LEAVING BARRA

The dazzle on the sea, my darling,
Leads from the western channel
A carpet of brilliance taking
My leave for ever of the island.

I never shall visit that island
Again with its easy tempo—
The seal sunbathing, the circuit
Of gulls on the wing for garbage.

I go to a different garbage
And scuffle for scraps of notice,

Pretend to ignore the stigma
That stains my life and my leisure.

For fretful even in leisure
I fidget for different values,
Restless as a gull and haunted
By a hankering after Atlantis.

I do not know that Atlantis
Unseen and uncomprehended,
Dimly divined but keenly
Felt with a phantom hunger.

If only I could crush the hunger
If only I could lay the phantom
Then I should no doubt be happy
Like a fool or a dog or a buddha.

O the self-abnegation of Buddha
The belief that is disbelieving
The denial of chiaroscuro
Not giving a damn for existence!

But I would cherish existence
Loving the beast and the bubble
Loving the rain and the rainbow,
Considering philosophy alien.

For all the religions are alien
That allege that life is a fiction,
And when we agree in denial
The cock crows in the morning.

If only I could wake in the morning
And find I had learned the solution,
Wake with the knack of knowledge
Who as yet have only an inkling.

Though some facts foster the inkling—
The beauty of the moon and music,
The routine courage of the worker,
The gay endurance of women,

And you who to me among women
Stand for so much that I wish for,
I thank you, my dear, for the example
Of living like a fugue and moving.

For few are able to keep moving,
They drag and flag in the traffic;
While you are alive beyond question
Like the dazzle on the sea, my darling

TRILOGY FOR X

I

When clerks and navvies fondle
    Beside canals their wenches,
In rapture or in coma
    The haunches that they handle,
And the orange moon sits idle
    Above the orchard slanted—
Upon such easy evenings
    We take our loves for granted.

But when, as now, the creaking
    Trees on the hills of London
Like bison charge their neighbours
    In wind that keeps us waking
And in the draught the scalloped
    Lampshade swings a shadow,
We think of love bound over—
    The mortgage on the meadow.

And one lies lonely, haunted
    By limbs he half remembers,
And one, in wedlock, wonders
    Where is the girl he wanted;
And some sit smoking, flicking
    The ash away and feeling
For love gone up like vapour
    Between the floor and ceiling.

But now when winds are curling
    The trees do you come closer,
Close as an eyelid fasten
    My body in darkness, darling;
Switch the light off and let me
    Gather you up and gather
The power of trains advancing
    Further, advancing further.

II

And love hung still as crystal over the bed
    And filled the corners of the enormous room;
The boom of dawn that left her sleeping, showing
    The flowers mirrored in the mahogany table.

O my love, if only I were able
    To protract this hour of quiet after passion,
Not ration happiness but keep this door for ever
    Closed on the world, its own world closed within it.

But dawn's waves trouble with the bubbling minute,
    The names of books come clear upon their shelves,
The reason delves for duty and you will wake
    With a start and go on living on your own.

The first train passes and the windows groan,
    Voices will hector and your voice become
A drum in tune with theirs, which all last night
    Like sap that fingered through a hungry tree
Asserted our one night's identity.

III

March gave clear days,
    Gave unaccustomed sunshine,
Prelude to who knows
    What dead end or downfall;
O my love, to
    Browse in the painted prelude.

Regent's Park was
　Gay with ducks and deck-chairs,
Omens were absent,
　Cooks bought cloves and parsley;
O my love, to
　Stop one's ear to omens.

Pigeons courting, the cock
　Like an eighteenth-century marquis
Puffing his breast and dragging
　His fantail waltzwise;
O my love, the
　Southward trains are puffing.

Nursemaids gossiped,
　Sun was bright on pram-paint,
Gold in the breeze the arrow
　Swivelled on church-tops;
But Living drains the living
　Sieve we catch our gold in.

Toy sail skidding on Whitestone
　Pond at the peak of London,
Challenge of bells at morning,
　Crocus and almond;
O my love, my
　Thoughts avoid the challenge

But the rumbling summer rolls
　A register behind us—
March to April to May
　To denser summer—
And the road is dusty, the goal
　Unknown we march to.

Rampant on Europe headlines
　Herald beasts of fable;
Backward the eyes to ancient
　Codes—vellum and roseleaf;
From the moving train of time the
　Fields move backward.

And now the searchlights
    Play their firemen's hoses,
Evil their purport
    Though their practice lovely,
Defence and death being always
    Collateral, coæval.

And now the soldier
    Tightens belt and outlook,
Eyes on the target,
    Mind in the trigger-finger,
And a flight of lead connecting
    Self and horizon.

And now, and last, in London
    Poised on the edge of absence
I ask for a moment's mention
    Of days the days will cancel,
Though the long run may also
    Bring what we ask for.

Summer, 1938

CHESS

At the penultimate move, their saga nearly sung,
They have worked so hard to prove what lads they were when
        young,
Have looked up every word in order to be able to say
The gay address unheard when they were dumb and gay.
Your Castle to King's Fourth under your practised hand!
What is the practice worth, so few being left to stand?
Better the raw levies jostling in the square
Than two old men in a crevice sniping at empty air;
The veterans on the pavement puff their cheeks and blow
The music of enslavement that echoes back 'I told you so';
The chapped hands fumble flutes, the tattered posters cry
Their craving for recruits who have not had time to die.
While our armies differ they move and feel the sun,
The victor is a cypher once the war is won.
Choose your gambit, vary the tactics of your game,
You move in a closed ambit that always ends the same.

[111]

CIRCUS

I

Trapezists

Intricacy of engines,
Delicacy of darkness;
They rise into the tent's
Top like deep-sea divers

And hooked from the mouth like fish
Frame their frolic
Above the silent music
And the awed audience,

Hang by their teeth
Beneath the cone of canvas,
The ring beneath them
An eye that is empty

Who live in a world
Of aery technic
Like dolls or angels
Sexless and simple

Our fear their frame,
Hallowed by handclaps,
Honoured by eyes
Upward in incense.

On the tent's walls
Fourfold shadowed
In a crucifixion's
Endless moment

Intricacy of,
Delicacy of,
Darkness and engines.

II

Horses

The long whip lingers,
Toys with the sawdust;
The horses amble
On a disc of dreams.

The drumsticks flower
In pink percussion
To mix with the metal
Petals of brass.

The needle runs
In narrower circles;
The long whip leaps
And leads them inward.

Piebald horses
And ribald music
Circle around
A spangled lady.

III

Clowns

Clowns, Clowns and
Clowns
A firm that furthers
Nobody's business

Zanies by royal
Charter and adept
At false addition
And gay combustion

With bladders for batons
And upright eyebrows
Flappers for feet
And figs for no one.

The child's face pops
Like ginger beer
To see the air
Alive with bowlers.

Bric-a-brac
Pick-a-back
Spillbucket
Splits.

IV

Elephants

Tonnage of instinctive
Wisdom in tinsel,
Trunks like questions
And legs like tree trunks

On each forehead
A buxom blonde
And round each leg
A jangle of bells,

Deep in each brain
A chart of tropic
Swamp and twilight
Of creepered curtains,

Shamble in shoddy
Finery forward
And make their salaams
To the tiers of people—

Dummies with a reflex
Muscle of laughter
When they see the mountains
Come to Mahomet . . .

Efficacy of engines,
Obstinacy of darkness.

CHRISTMAS SHOPPING

Spending beyond their income on gifts for Christmas—
Swing doors and crowded lifts and draperied jungles—
What shall we buy for our husbands and sons
   Different from last year?

Foxes hang by their noses behind plate glass—
Scream of macaws across festoons of paper—
Only the faces on the boxes of chocolates are free
   From boredom and crowsfeet.

Sometimes a chocolate box girl escapes in the flesh,
Lightly manoeuvres the crowd, trilling with laughter;
After a couple of years her feet and her brain will
   Tire like the others.

The great windows marshal their troops for assault on the purse,
Something-and-eleven the yard, hoodwinking logic,
The eleventh hour draining the gurgling pennies
   Down to the conduits

Down to the sewers of money—rats and marshgas—
Bubbling in maundering music under the pavement;
Here go the hours of routine, the weight on our eyelids—
   Pennies on corpses'.

While over the street in the centrally heated public
Library dwindling figures with sloping shoulders
And hands in pockets, weighted in the boots like chessmen,
   Stare at the printed

Columns of ads, the quickset road to riches,
Starting at a little and temporary but once we're
Started who knows whether we shan't continue,
   Salaries rising,

Rising like a salmon against the bullnecked river,
Bound for the spawning-ground of care-free days—
Good for a fling before the golden wheels run
   Down to a standstill.

And Christ is born—The nursery glad with baubles,
Alive with light and washable paint and children's
Eyes expects as its due the accidental
　　Loot of a system.

Smell of the South—oranges in silver paper,
Dates and ginger, the benison of firelight,
The blue flames dancing round the brandied raisins,
　　Smiles from above them,

Hands from above them as of gods but really
These their parents, always seen from below, them-
Selves are always anxious looking across the
　　Fence to the future—

Out there lies the future gathering quickly
Its blank momentum; through the tubes of London
The dead winds blow the crowds like beasts in flight from
　　Fire in the forest.

The little firtrees palpitate with candles
In hundreds of chattering households where the suburb
Straggles like nervous handwriting, the margin
　　Blotted with smokestacks.

Further out on the coast the lighthouse moves its
Arms of light through the fog that wads our welfare,
Moves its arms like a giant at Swedish drill whose
　　Mind is a vacuum.

BAGPIPE MUSIC

It's no go the merrygoround, it's no go the rickshaw,
All we want is a limousine and a ticket for the peepshow.
Their knickers are made of crêpe-de-chine, their shoes are made
　　of python,
Their halls are lined with tiger rugs and their walls with heads of
　　bison.

John MacDonald found a corpse, put it under the sofa,
Waited till it came to life and hit it with a poker,

Sold its eyes for souvenirs, sold its blood for whiskey,
Kept its bones for dumb-bells to use when he was fifty.

It's no go the Yogi-Man, it's no go Blavatsky,
All we want is a bank balance and a bit of skirt in a taxi.

Annie MacDougall went to milk, caught her foot in the heather,
Woke to hear a dance record playing of Old Vienna.
It's no go your maidenheads, it's no go your culture,
All we want is a Dunlop tyre and the devil mend the puncture.

The Laird o' Phelps spent Hogmanay declaring he was sober,
Counted his feet to prove the fact and found he had one foot over.
Mrs. Carmichael had her fifth, looked at the job with repulsion,
Said to the midwife 'Take it away; I'm through with over-
    production'.

It's no go the gossip column, it's no go the Ceilidh,
All we want is a mother's help and a sugar-stick for the baby.

Willie Murray cut his thumb, couldn't count the damage,
Took the hide of an Ayrshire cow and used it for a bandage.
His brother caught three hundred cran when the seas were lavish,
Threw the bleeders back in the sea and went upon the parish.

It's no go the Herring Board, it's no go the Bible,
All we want is a packet of fags when our hands are idle.

It's no go the picture palace, it's no go the stadium,
It's no go the country cot with a pot of pink geraniums,
It's no go the Government grants, it's no go the elections,
Sit on your arse for fifty years and hang your hat on a pension.

It's no go my honey love, it's no go my poppet;
Work your hands from day to day, the winds will blow the profit.
The glass is falling hour by hour, the glass will fall for ever,
But if you break the bloody glass you won't hold up the weather.

V

1938

V

AUTUMN JOURNAL

I

Close and slow, summer is ending in Hampshire,
    Ebbing away down ramps of shaven lawn where close-clipped
        yew
Insulates the lives of retired generals and admirals
    And the spyglasses hung in the hall and the prayer-books
        ready in the pew
And August going out to the tin trumpets of nasturtiums
    And the sunflowers' Salvation Army blare of brass
And the spinster sitting in a deck-chair picking up stitches
    Not raising her eyes to the noise of the 'planes that pass
Northward from Lee-on-Solent. Macrocarpa and cypress
    And roses on a rustic trellis and mulberry trees
And bacon and eggs in a silver dish for breakfast
    And all the inherited assets of bodily ease
And all the inherited worries, rheumatism and taxes,
    And whether Stella will marry and what to do with Dick
And the branch of the family that lost their money in Hatry
    And the passing of the *Morning Post* and of life's climacteric
And the growth of vulgarity, cars that pass the gate-lodge
    And crowds undressing on the beach
And the hiking cockney lovers with thoughts directed
    Neither to God nor Nation but each to each.
But the home is still a sanctum under the pelmets,
    All quiet on the Family Front,
Farmyard noises across the fields at evening
    While the trucks of the Southern Railway dawdle . . . shunt
Into poppy sidings for the night—night which knows no passion
    No assault of hands or tongue
For all is old as flint or chalk or pine-needles
    And the rebels and the young
Have taken the train to town or the two-seater
    Unravelling rails or road,
Losing the thread deliberately behind them—
    Autumnal palinode.
And I am in the train too now and summer is going
    South as I go north
Bound for the dead leaves falling, the burning bonfire,
    The dying that brings forth

The harder life, revealing the trees' girders,
   The frost that kills the germs of *laissez-faire*;
West Meon, Tisted, Farnham, Woking, Weybridge,
   Then London's packed and stale and pregnant air.
My dog, a symbol of the abandoned order,
   Lies on the carriage floor,
Her eyes inept and glamorous as a film star's,
   Who wants to live, i.e. wants more
Presents, jewellery, furs, gadgets, solicitations
   As if to live were not
Following the curve of a planet or controlled water
   But a leap in the dark, a tangent, a stray shot.
It is this we learn after so many failures,
   The building of castles in sand, of queens in snow,
That we cannot make any corner in life or in life's beauty,
   That no river is a river which does not flow.
Surbiton, and a woman gets in, painted
   With dyed hair but a ladder in her stocking and eyes
Patient beneath the calculated lashes,
   Inured for ever to surprise;
And the train's rhythm becomes the *ad nauseam* repetition
   Of every tired aubade and maudlin madrigal,
The faded airs of sexual attraction
   Wandering like dead leaves along a warehouse wall:
'I loved my love with a platform ticket,
   A jazz song,
A handbag, a pair of stockings of Paris Sand—
   I loved her long.
I loved her between the lines and against the clock,
   Not until death
But till life did us part I loved her with paper money
   And with whisky on the breath.
I loved her with peacock's eyes and the wares of Carthage,
   With glass and gloves and gold and a powder puff
With blasphemy, camaraderie, and bravado
   And lots of other stuff.
I loved my love with the wings of angels
   Dipped in henna, unearthly red,
With my office hours, with flowers and sirens,
   With my budget, my latchkey, and my daily bread.'
And so to London and down the ever-moving
   Stairs

Where a warm wind blows the bodies of men together
And blows apart their complexes and cares.

II

Spider, spider, twisting tight—
  But the watch is wary beneath the pillow—
I am afraid in the web of night
  When the window is fingered by the shadows of branches,
When the lions roar beneath the hill
  And the meter clicks and the cistern bubbles
And the gods are absent and the men are still—
  Noli me tangere, my soul is forfeit.
Some now are happy in the hive of home,
  Thigh over thigh and a light in the night nursery,
And some are hungry under the starry dome
  And some sit turning handles.
Glory to God in the Lowest, peace beneath the earth,
  Dumb and deaf at the nadir;
I wonder now whether anything is worth
  The eyelid opening and the mind recalling.
And I think of Persephone gone down to dark,
  No more a virgin, gone the garish meadow,
But why must she come back, why must the snowdrop mark
  That life goes on for ever?
There are nights when I am lonely and long for love
  But to-night is quintessential dark forbidding
Anyone beside or below me; only above
  Pile high the tumulus, good-bye to starlight.
Good-bye the Platonic sieve of the Carnal Man
  But good-bye also Plato's philosophising;
I have a better plan
  To hit the target straight without circumlocution.
If you can equate Being in its purest form
  With denial of all appearance,
Then let me disappear—the scent grows warm
  For pure Not-Being, Nirvana.
Only the spider spinning out his reams
  Of colourless thread says Only there are always
Interlopers, dreams,
  Who let no dead dog lie nor death be final;
Suggesting, while he spins, that to-morrow will outweigh

[123]

To-night, that Becoming is a match for Being,
That to-morrow is also a day,
    That I must leave my bed and face the music.
As all the others do who with a grin
    Shake off sleep like a dog and hurry to desk or engine
And the fear of life goes out as they clock in
    And history is reasserted.
Spider, spider, your irony is true;
    Who am I—or I—to demand oblivion?
I must go out to-morrow as the others do
    And build the falling castle;
Which has never fallen, thanks
    Not to any formula, red tape or institution,
Not to any creeds or banks,
    But to the human animal's endless courage.
Spider, spider, spin
    Your register and let me sleep a little,
Not now in order to end but to begin
    The task begun so often.

III

August is nearly over, the people
    Back from holiday are tanned
With blistered thumbs and a wallet of snaps and a little
    Joie de vivre which is contraband;
Whose stamina is enough to face the annual
    Wait for the annual spree,
Whose memories are stamped with specks of sunshine
    Like faded *fleurs de lys*.
Now the till and the typewriter call the fingers,
    The workman gathers his tools
For the eight-hour day but after that the solace
    Of films or football pools
Or of the gossip or cuddle, the moments of self-glory
    Or self-indulgence, blinkers on the eyes of doubt,
The blue smoke rising and the brown lace sinking
    In the empty glass of stout.
Most are accepters, born and bred to harness,
    And take things as they come,
But some refusing harness and more who are refused it
    Would pray that another and a better Kingdom come,

Which now is sketched in the air or travestied in slogans
    Written in chalk or tar on stucco or plaster-board
But in time may find its body in men's bodies,
    Its law and order in their heart's accord,
Where skill will no longer languish nor energy be trammelled
    To competition and graft,
Exploited in subservience but not allegiance
    To an utterly lost and daft
System that gives a few at fancy prices
    Their fancy lives
While ninety-nine in the hundred who never attend the banquet
    Must wash the grease of ages off the knives.
And now the tempter whispers 'But you also
    Have the slave-owner's mind,
Would like to sleep on a mattress of easy profits,
    To snap your fingers or a whip and find
Servants or houris ready to wince and flatter
    And build with their degradation your self-esteem;
What you want is not a world of the free in function
    But a niche at the top, the skimmings of the cream.'
And I answer that that is largely so for habit makes me
    Think victory for one implies another's defeat,
That freedom means the power to order, and that in order
    To preserve the values dear to the élite
The élite must remain a few. It is so hard to imagine
    A world where the many would have their chance without
A fall in the standard of intellectual living
    And nothing left that the highbrow cared about.
Which fears must be suppressed. There is no reason for thinking
    That, if you give a chance to people to think or live,
The arts of thought or life will suffer and become rougher
    And not return more than you could ever give.
And now I relapse to sleep, to dreams perhaps and reaction
    Where I shall play the gangster or the sheikh,
Kill for the love of killing, make the world my sofa,
    Unzip the women and insult the meek.
Which fantasies no doubt are due to my private history,
    Matter for the analyst,
But the final cure is not in his past-dissecting fingers
    But in a future of action, the will and fist
Of those who abjure the luxury of self-pity
    And prefer to risk a movement without being sure

[125]

If movement would be better or worse in a hundred
    Years or a thousand when their heart is pure.
None of our hearts are pure, we always have mixed motives,
    Are self deceivers, but the worst of all
Deceits is to murmur 'Lord, I am not worthy'
    And, lying easy, turn your face to the wall.
But may I cure that habit, look up and outwards
    And may my feet follow my wider glance
First no doubt to stumble, then to walk with the others
    And in the end—with time and luck—to dance.

IV

September has come and I wake
    And I think with joy how whatever, now or in future, the
        system
Nothing whatever can take
    The people away, there will always be people
For friends or for lovers though perhaps
    The conditions of love will be changed and its vices diminished
And affection not lapse
    To narrow possessiveness, jealousy founded on vanity.
September has come, it is *hers*
    Whose vitality leaps in the autumn,
Whose nature prefers
    Trees without leaves and a fire in the fire-place;
So I give her this month and the next
    Though the whole of my year should be hers who has
        rendered already
So many of its days intolerable or perplexed
    But so many more so happy;
Who has left a scent on my life and left my walls
    Dancing over and over with her shadow,
Whose hair is twined in all my waterfalls
    And all of London littered with remembered kisses.
So I am glad
    That life contains her with her moods and moments
More shifting and more transient than I had
    Yet thought of as being integral to beauty;
Whose mind is like the wind on a sea of wheat,
    Whose eyes are candour,
And assurance in her feet

Like a homing pigeon never by doubt diverted.
To whom I send my thanks
    That the air has become shot silk, the streets are music,
And that the ranks
    Of men are ranks of men, no more of cyphers.
So that if now alone
    I must pursue this life, it will not be only
A drag from numbered stone to numbered stone
    But a ladder of angels, river turning tidal.
Off hand, at times hysterical, abrupt,
    You are one I always shall remember,
Whom cant can never corrupt
        Nor argument disinherit.
Frivolous, always in a hurry, forgetting the address,
    Frowning too often, taking enormous notice
Of hats and backchat—how could I assess
    The thing that makes you different?
You whom I remember glad or tired,
    Smiling in drink or scintillating anger,
Inopportunely desired
    On boats, on trains, on roads when walking.
Sometimes untidy, often elegant,
    So easily hurt, so readily responsive,
To whom a trifle could be an irritant
    Or could be balm and manna.
Whose words would tumble over each other and pelt
    From pure excitement,
Whose fingers curl and melt
    When you were friendly.
I shall remember you in bed with bright
    Eyes or in a café stirring coffee
Abstractedly and on your plate the white
    Smoking stub your lips had touched with crimson.
And I shall remember how your words could hurt
    Because they were so honest
And even your lies were able to assert
    Integrity of purpose.
And it is on the strength of knowing you
    I reckon generous feeling more important
Than the mere deliberating what to do
    When neither the pros nor cons affect the pulses.
And though I have suffered from your special strength

[127]

Who never flatter for points nor fake responses
I should be proud if I could evolve at length
  An equal thrust and pattern.

V

To-day was a beautiful day, the sky was a brilliant
  Blue for the first time for weeks and weeks
But posters flapping on the railings tell the fluttered
  World that Hitler speaks, that Hitler speaks
And we cannot take it in and we go to our daily
  Jobs to the dull refrain of the caption 'War'
Buzzing around us as from hidden insects
  And we think 'This must be wrong, it has happened before,
Just like this before, we must be dreaming;
  It was long ago these flies
Buzzed like this, so why are they still bombarding
  The ears if not the eyes?'
And we laugh it off and go round town in the evening
  And this, we say, is on me;
Something out of the usual, a Pimm's Number One, a Picon—
  But did you see
The latest? You mean whether Cobb has bust the record
  Or do you mean the Australians have lost their last by ten
Wickets or do you mean that the autumn fashions—
  No, we don't mean anything like that again.
No, what we mean is Hodza, Henlein, Hitler,
  The Maginot Line,
The heavy panic that cramps the lungs and presses
  The collar down the spine.
And when we go out into Piccadilly Circus
  They are selling and buying the late
Special editions snatched and read abruptly
  Beneath the electric signs as crude as Fate.
And the individual, powerless, has to exert the
  Powers of will and choice
And choose between enormous evils, either
  Of which depends on somebody else's voice.
The cylinders are racing in the presses,
  The mines are laid,
The ribbon plumbs the fallen fathoms of Wall Street,
  And you and I are afraid.

To-day they were building in Oxford Street, the mortar
    Pleasant to smell,
But now it seems futility, imbecility,
    To be building shops when nobody can tell
What will happen next. What will happen
    We ask and waste the question on the air;
Nelson is stone and Johnnie Walker moves his
    Legs like a cretin over Trafalgar Square.
And in the Corner House the carpet-sweepers
    Advance between the tables after crumbs
Inexorably, like a tank battalion
    In answer to the drums.
In Tottenham Court Road the tarts and negroes
    Loiter beneath the lights
And the breeze gets colder as on so many other
    September nights.
A smell of French bread in Charlotte Street, a rustle
    Of leaves in Regent's Park
And suddenly from the Zoo I hear a sea-lion
    Confidently bark.
And so to my flat with the trees outside the window
    And the dahlia shapes of the lights on Primrose Hill
Whose summit once was used for a gun emplacement
    And very likely will
Be used that way again. The bloody frontier
    Converges on our beds
Like jungle beaters closing in on their destined
    Trophy of pelts and heads.
And at this hour of the day it is no good saying
    'Take away this cup';
Having helped to fill it ourselves it is only logic
    That now we should drink it up.
Nor can we hide our heads in the sands, the sands have
    Filtered away;
Nothing remains but rock at this hour, this zero
    Hour of the day.
Or that is how it seems to me as I listen
    To a hooter call at six
And then a woodpigeon calls and stops but the wind continues
    Playing its dirge in the trees, playing its tricks.
And now the dairy cart comes clopping slowly—
    Milk at the doors—

I   [129]   M.C.P.

And factory workers are on their way to factories
    And charwomen to chores.
And I notice feathers sprouting from the rotted
    Silk of my black
Double eiderdown which was a wedding
    Present eight years back.
And the linen which I lie on came from Ireland
    In the easy days
When all I thought of was affection and comfort,
    Petting and praise.
And now the woodpigeon starts again denying
    The values of the town
And a car having crossed the hill accelerates, changes
    Up, having just changed down.
And a train begins to chug and I wonder what the morning
    Paper will say,
And decide to go quickly to sleep for the morning already
    Is with us, the day is to-day.

VI

And I remember Spain
    At Easter ripe as an egg for revolt and ruin
Though for a tripper the rain
    Was worse than the surly or the worried or the haunted faces
With writings on the walls—
    Hammer and sickle, Boicot, Viva, Muerra;
With café-au-lait brimming the waterfalls,
    With sherry, shellfish, omelettes.
With fretted stone the Moor
    Had chiselled for effects of sun and shadow;
With shadows of the poor,
    The begging cripples and the children begging.
The churches full of saints
    Tortured on racks of marble—
The old complaints
    Covered with gilt and dimly lit with candles.
With powerful or banal
    Monuments of riches or repression
And the Escorial
    Cold for ever within like the heart of Philip.
With ranks of dominoes

Deployed on café tables the whole of Sunday
With cabarets that call the tourist, shows
    Of thighs and eyes and nipples.
With slovenly soldiers, nuns,
    And peeling posters from the last elections
Promising bread or guns
    Or an amnesty or another
Order or else the old
    Glory veneered and varnished
As if veneer could hold
    The rotten guts and crumbled bones together.
And a vulture hung in air
    Below the cliffs of Ronda and below him
His hook-winged shadow wavered like despair
    Across the chequered vineyards.
And the boot-blacks in Madrid
    Kept us half an hour with polish and pincers
And all we did
    In that city was drink and think and loiter.
And in the Prado half-
    wit princes looked from the canvas they had paid for
(Goya had the laugh—
    But can what is corrupt be cured by laughter?)
And the day at Aranjuez
    When the sun came out for once on the yellow river
With Valdepeñas burdening the breath
    We slept a royal sleep in the royal gardens;
And at Toledo walked
    Around the ramparts where they throw the garbage
And glibly talked
    Of how the Spaniards lack all sense of business.
And Avila was cold
    And Segovia was picturesque and smelly
And a goat on the road seemed old
    As the rocks or the Roman arches.
And Easter was wet and full
    In Seville and in the ring on Easter Sunday
A clumsy bull and then a clumsy bull
    Nodding his banderillas died of boredom.
And the standard of living was low
    But that, we thought to ourselves, was not our business;
All that the tripper wants is the *status quo*

[131]

Cut and dried for trippers.
And we thought the papers a lark
    With their party politics and blank invective;
And we thought the dark
    Women who dyed their hair should have it dyed more often
And we sat in trains all night
    With the windows shut among civil guards and peasants
And tried to play piquet by a tiny light
    And tried to sleep bolt upright;
And cursed the Spanish rain
    And cursed their cigarettes which came to pieces
And caught heavy colds in Cordova and in vain
    Waited for the right light for taking photos.
And we met a Cambridge don who said with an air
    'There's going to be trouble shortly in this country,'
And ordered anis, pudgy and debonair,
    Glad to show off his mastery of the language.
But only an inch behind
    This map of olive and ilex, this painted hoarding,
Careless of visitors the people's mind
    Was tunnelling like a mole to day and danger.
And the day before we left
    We saw the mob in flower at Algeciras
Outside a toothless door, a church bereft
    Of its images and its aura.
And at La Linea while
    The night put miles between us and Gibraltar
We heard the blood-lust of a drunkard pile
    His heaven high with curses;
And next day took the boat
    For home, forgetting Spain, not realising
That Spain would soon denote
    Our grief, our aspirations;
Not knowing that our blunt
    Ideals would find their whetstone, that our spirit
Would find its frontier on the Spanish front,
    Its body in a rag-tag army.

VII

Conferences, adjournments, ultimatums,
    Flights in the air, castles in the air,
[132]

The autopsy of treaties, dynamite under the bridges,
  The end of *laissez faire*.
After the warm days the rain comes pimpling
  The paving stones with white
And with the rain the national conscience, creeping,
  Seeping through the night.
And in the sodden park on Sunday protest
  Meetings assemble not, as so often, now
Merely to advertise some patent panacea
  But simply to avow
The need to hold the ditch; a bare avowal
  That may perhaps imply
Death at the doors in a week but perhaps in the long run
  Exposure of the lie.
Think of a number, double it, treble it, square it,
  And sponge it out
And repeat *ad lib*. and mark the slate with crosses;
  There is no time to doubt
If the puzzle really has an answer. Hitler yells on the wireless,
  The night is damp and still
And I hear dull blows on wood outside my window;
  They are cutting down the trees on Primrose Hill.
The wood is white like the roast flesh of chicken,
  Each tree falling like a closing fan;
No more looking at the view from seats beneath the branches,
  Everything is going to plan;
They want the crest of this hill for anti-aircraft,
  The guns will take the view
And searchlights probe the heavens for bacilli
  With narrow wands of blue.
And the rain came on as I watched the territorials
  Sawing and chopping and pulling on ropes like a team
In a village tug-of-war; and I found my dog had vanished
  And thought 'This is the end of the old régime,'
But found the police had got her at St. John's Wood station
  And fetched her in the rain and went for a cup
Of coffee to an all-night shelter and heard a taxi-driver
  Say 'It turns me up
When I see these soldiers in lorries'—rumble of tumbrils
  Drums in the trees
Breaking the eardrums of the ravished dryads—
  It turns me up; a coffee, please.

[133]

And as I go out I see a windscreen-wiper
    In an empty car
Wiping away like mad and I feel astounded
    That things have gone so far.
And I come back here to my flat and wonder whether
    From now on I need take
The trouble to go out choosing stuff for curtains
    As I don't know anyone to make
Curtains quickly. Rather one should quickly
    Stop the cracks for gas or dig a trench
And take one's paltry measures against the coming
    Of the unknown Uebermensch.
But one—meaning I—is bored, am bored, the issue
    Involving principle but bound in fact
To squander principle in panic and self-deception—
    Accessories after the act,
So that all we foresee is rivers in spate sprouting
    With drowning hands
And men like dead frogs floating till the rivers
    Lose themselves in the sands.
And we who have been brought up to think of 'Gallant Belgium'
    As so much blague
Are now preparing again to essay good through evil
    For the sake of Prague;
And must, we suppose, become uncritical, vindictive,
    And must, in order to beat
The enemy, model ourselves upon the enemy,
    A howling radio for our paraclete.
The night continues wet, the axe keeps falling,
    The hill grows bald and bleak
No longer one of the sights of London but maybe
    We shall have fireworks here by this day week.

VIII

Sun shines easy, sun shines gay
    On bug-house, warehouse, brewery, market,
On the chocolate factory and the B.S.A.,
    On the Greek town hall and Josiah Mason;
On the Mitchells and Butlers Tudor pubs,
    On the white police and the one-way traffic
And glances off the chromium hubs

[134]

And the metal studs in the sleek macadam.
  Eight years back about this time
    I came to live in this hazy city
  To work in a building caked with grime
    Teaching the classics to Midland students;
Virgil, Livy, the usual round,
    Principal parts and the lost digamma;
And to hear the prison-like lecture room resound
    To Homer in a Dudley accent.
But Life was comfortable, life was fine
    With two in a bed and patchwork cushions
And checks and tassels on the washing-line,
    A gramophone, a cat, and the smell of jasmine.
The steaks were tender, the films were fun,
    The walls were striped like a Russian ballet,
There were lots of things undone
    But nobody cared, for the days were early.
Nobody niggled, nobody cared,
    The soul was deaf to the mounting debit,
The soul was unprepared
    But the firelight danced on the ply-wood ceiling.
We drove round Shropshire in a bijou car—
    Bewdley, Cleobury Mortimer, Ludlow—
And the map of England was a toy bazaar
    And the telephone wires were idle music.
And sun shone easy, sun shone hard
    On quickly dropping pear-tree blossom
And pigeons courting in the cobbled yard
    With flashing necks and notes of thunder.
We slept in linen, we cooked with wine,
    We paid in cash and took no notice
Of how the train ran down the line
    Into the sun against the signal.
We lived in Birmingham through the slump—
    Line your boots with a piece of paper—
Sunlight dancing on the rubbish dump,
    On the queues of men and the hungry chimneys.
And the next election came—
    Labour defeats in Erdington and Aston;
And life went on—for us went on the same;
    Who were we to count the losses?
Some went back to work and the void

Took on shape while others climbing
The uphill nights of the unemployed
    Woke in the morning to factory hooters.
Little on the plate and nothing in the post;
    Queue in the rain or try the public
Library where the eye may coast
    Columns of print for a hopeful harbour.
But roads ran easy, roads ran gay
    Clear of the city and we together
Could put on tweeds for a getaway
    South or west to Clee or the Cotswolds;
Forty to the gallon; into the green
    Fields in the past of English history;
Flies in the bonnet and dust on the screen
    And no look back to the burning city.
That was then and now is now,
    Here again on a passing visit,
Passing through but how
    Memory blocks the passage.
Just as in Nineteen-Thirty-One
    Sun shines easy but I no longer
Docket a place in the sun—
    No wife, no ivory tower, no funk-hole.
The night grows purple, the crisis hangs
    Over the roofs like a Persian army
And all of Xenophon's parasangs
    Would take us only an inch from danger.
Black-out practice and A.R.P.,
    Newsboys driving a roaring business,
The flapping paper snatched to see
    If anything has, or has not, happened.
And I go to the Birmingham Hippodrome
    Packed to the roof and primed for laughter
And beautifully at home
    With the ukulele and the comic chestnuts;
'As pals we meet, as pals we part'—
    Embonpoint and a new tiara;
The comedian spilling the apple-cart
    Of doubles entendres and doggerel verses
And the next day begins
    Again with alarm and anxious
Listening to bulletins

From distant, measured voices
Arguing for peace
    While the zero hour approaches,
While the eagles gather and the petrol and oil and grease
    Have all been applied and the vultures back the eagles.
But once again
    The crisis is put off and things look better
And we feel negotiation is not vain—
    Save my skin and damn my conscience.
And negotiation wins,
    If you can call it winning,
And here we are—just as before—safe in our skins;
    Glory to God for Munich.
And stocks go up and wrecks
    Are salved and politicians' reputations
Go up like Jack-on-the-Beanstalk; only the Czechs
    Go down and without fighting.

IX

Now we are back to normal, now the mind is
    Back to the even tenor of the usual day
Skidding no longer across the uneasy camber
    Of the nightmare way.
We are safe though others have crashed the railings
    Over the river ravine; their wheel-tracks carve the bank
But after the event all we can do is argue
    And count the widening ripples where they sank.
October comes with rain whipping around the ankles
    In waves of white at night
And filling the raw clay trenches (the parks of London
    Are a nasty sight).
In a week I return to work, lecturing, coaching,
    As impresario of the Ancient Greeks
Who wore the chiton and lived on fish and olives
    And talked philosophy or smut in cliques;
Who believed in youth and did not gloze the unpleasant
    Consequences of age;
What is life, one said, or what is pleasant
    Once you have turned the page
Of love? The days grow worse, the dice are loaded
    Against the living man who pays in tears for breath;

[137]

Never to be born was the best, call no man happy
  This side death.
Conscious—long before Engels—of necessity
  And therein free
They plotted out their life with truism and humour
  Between the jealous heaven and the callous sea.
And Pindar sang the garland of wild olive
  And Alcibiades lived from hand to mouth
Double-crossing Athens, Persia, Sparta,
  And many died in the city of plague, and many of drouth
In Sicilian quarries, and many by the spear and arrow
  And many more who told their lies too late
Caught in the eternal factions and reactions
  Of the city-state.
And free speech shivered on the pikes of Macedonia
  And later on the swords of Rome
And Athens became a mere university city
  And the goddess born of the foam
Became the kept hetaera, heroine of Menander,
  And the philosopher narrowed his focus, confined
His efforts to putting his own soul in order
  And keeping a quiet mind.
And for a thousand years they went on talking,
  Making such apt remarks,
A race no longer of heroes but of professors
  And crooked business men and secretaries and clerks
Who turned out dapper little elegiac verses
  On the ironies of fate, the transience of all
Affections, carefully shunning an over-statement
  But working the dying fall.
The Glory that was Greece: put it in a syllabus, grade it
  Page by page
To train the mind or even to point a moral
  For the present age:
Models of logic and lucidity, dignity, sanity,
  The golden mean between opposing ills
Though there were exceptions of course but only exceptions—
  The bloody Bacchanals on the Thracian hills.
So the humanist in his room with Jacobean panels
  Chewing his pipe and looking on a lazy quad
Chops the Ancient World to turn a sermon
  To the greater glory of God.

[138]

But I can do nothing so useful or so simple;
  These dead are dead
And when I should remember the paragons of Hellas
  I think instead
Of the crooks, the adventurers, the opportunists,
  The careless athletes and the fancy boys,
The hair-splitters, the pedants, the hard-boiled sceptics
  And the Agora and the noise
Of the demagogues and the quacks; and the women pouring
  Libations over graves
And the trimmers at Delphi and the dummies at Sparta and lastly
  I think of the slaves.
And how one can imagine oneself among them
  I do not know;
It was all so unimaginably different
  And all so long ago.

                    X
And so return to work—the M.A. gown,
  Alphas and Betas, central heating, floor-polish,
Demosthenes on the Crown
  And Oedipus at Colonus.
And I think of the beginnings of other terms
  Coming across the sea to unknown England
And memory reaffirms
  That alarm and exhilaration of arrival:
White wooden boxes, clatter of boots, a smell
  Of changing-rooms—Lifebuoy soap and muddy flannels—
And over all a bell
  Dragooning us to dormitory or classroom,
Ringing with a tongue of frost across the bare
  Benches and desks escutcheoned with initials;
We sat on the hot pipes by the wall, aware
  Of the cold in our bones and the noise and the bell impending.
A fishtail gas-flare in the dark latrine;
  Chalk and ink and rows of pegs and lockers;
The War was on—maize and margarine
  And lessons on the map of Flanders.
But we had our toys—our electric torches, our glass
  Dogs and cats, and plasticine and conkers,
And we had our games, we learned to dribble and pass

In jerseys striped like tigers.
And we had our makebelieve, we had our mock
    Freedom in walks by twos and threes on Sunday,
We dug out fossils from the yellow rock
    Or drank the Dorset distance.
And we had our little tiptoe minds, alert
    To jump for facts and fancies and statistics
And our little jokes of Billy Bunter dirt
    And a heap of home-made dogma.
The Abbey chimes varnished the yellow street,
    The water from the taps in the bath was yellow,
The trees were full of owls, the sweets were sweet
    And life an expanding ladder.
And reading romances we longed to be grown up,
    To shoot from the hip and marry lovely ladies
And smoke cigars and live on claret cup
    And lie in bed in the morning;
Taking it for granted that things would still
    Get better and bigger and better and bigger and better,
That the road across the hill
    Led to the Garden of Eden;
Everything to expect and nothing to deplore,
    Cushy days beyond the dumb horizon
And nothing to doubt about, to linger for
    In the halfway house of childhood.
And certainly we did not linger, we went on
    Growing and growing, gluttons for the future,
And four foot six was gone
    And we found it was time to be leaving
To be changing school, sandstone changed for chalk
    And ammonites for the flinty husks of sponges,
Another lingo to talk
    And jerseys in other colours.
And still the acquiring of unrelated facts,
    A string of military dates for history,
And the Gospels and the Acts
    And logarithms and Greek and the Essays of Elia;
And still the exhilarating rhythm of free
    Movement swimming or serving at tennis,
The fives-courts' tattling repartee
    Or rain on the sweating body.
But life began to narrow to what was done—

The dominant gerundive—
And number Two must mimic Number One
   In bearing, swearing, attitude and accent.
And so we jettisoned all
   Our childish fantasies and anarchism;
The weak must go to the wall
   But strength implies the system;
You must lose your soul to be strong, you cannot stand
   Alone on your own legs or your own ideas;
The order of the day is complete conformity and
   An automatic complacence.
Such was the order of the day; only at times
   The Fool among the yes-men flashed his motley
To prick their pseudo-reason with his rhymes
   And drop his grain of salt on court behaviour.
And sometimes a whisper in books
   Would challenge the code, or a censored memory sometimes,
Sometimes the explosion of rooks,
   Sometimes the mere batter of light on the senses.
And the critic jailed in the mind would peep through the grate
   And husky from long silence, murmur gently
That there is something rotten in the state
   Of Denmark but the state is not the whole of Denmark,
And a spade is still a spade
   And the difference is not final between a tailored
Suit and a ready-made
   And knowledge is not—necessarily—wisdom;
And a cultured accent alone will not provide
   A season ticket to the Vita Nuova;
And there are many better men outside
   Than ever answered roll-call.
But the critic did not win, has not won yet
   Though always reminding us of points forgotten;
We hasten to forget
   As much as he remembers.
And school was what they always said it was,
   An apprenticeship to life, an initiation,
And all the better because
   The initiates were blindfold;
The reflex action of a dog or sheep
   Being enough for normal avocations
And life rotating in an office sleep

[141]

As long as things are normal.
Which it was assumed that they would always be;
   On that assumption terms began and ended;
And now, in Nineteen-Thirty-Eight A.D.,
   Term is again beginning.

XI

But work is alien; what do I care for the Master
   Of those who know, of those who know too much?
I am too harassed by my familiar devils,
   By those I cannot see, by those I may not touch;
Knowing perfectly well in the mind, on paper,
   How wasteful and absurd
Are personal fixations but yet the pulse keeps thrumming
   And her voice is faintly heard
Through walls and walls of indifference and abstraction
   And across the London roofs
And every so often calls up hopes from nowhere,
   A distant clatter of hoofs,
And my common sense denies she is returning
   And says, if she does return, she will not stay;
And my pride, in the name of reason, tells me to cut my losses
   And call it a day.
Which, if I had the cowardice of my convictions,
   I certainly should do
But doubt still finds a loophole
   To gamble on another rendezvous.
And I try to feel her in fancy but the fancy
   Dissolves in curls of mist
And I try to summarise her but how can hungry
   Love be a proper analyst?
For suddenly I hate her and would murder
   Her memory if I could
And then of a sudden I see her sleeping gently
   Inaccessible in a sleeping wood
But thorns and thorns around her
   And the cries of night
And I have no knife or axe to hack my passage
   Back to the lost delight.
And then I think of the others and jealousy riots
   In impossible schemes

[142]

To kill them with all the machinery of fact and with all the
    Tortures of dreams.
But yet, my dear, if only for my own distraction,
    I have to try to assess
Your beauty of body, your paradoxes of spirit,
    Even your taste in dress.
Whose emotions are an intricate dialectic,
    Whose eagerness to live
A many-sided life might be deplored as fickle,
    Unpractical, or merely inquisitive.
A superficial comment; for your instinct
    Sanctions all you do,
Who know that truth is nothing in abstraction,
    That action makes both wish and principle come true;
Whose changes have the logic of a prism,
    Whose moods create,
Who never linger haggling on the threshold,
    To weigh the pros and cons until it is too late.
At times intractable, virulent, hypercritical,
    With a bitter tongue;
Over-shy at times, morose, defeatist,
    At times a token that the world is young;
Given to over-statement, careless of caution,
    Quick to sound the chimes
Of delicate intuition, at times malicious
    And generous at times.
Whose kaleidoscopic ways are all authentic,
    Whose truth is not of a statement but of a dance
So that even when you deceive your deceits are merely
    Technical and of no significance.
And so, when I think of you, I have to meet you
    In thought on your own ground;
To apply to you my algebraic canons
    Would merely be unsound;
And, having granted this, I cannot balance
    My hopes or fears of you in pros and cons;
It has been proved that Achilles cannot catch the Tortoise,
    It has been proved that men are automatons,
Everything wrong has been proved. I will not bother
    Any more with proof;
I see the future glinting with your presence
    Like moon on a slate roof,

[143]

And my spirits rise again. It is October,
    The year-god dying on the destined pyre
With all the colours of a scrambled sunset
    And all the funeral elegance of fire
In the grey world to lie cocooned but shaping
    His gradual return;
No one can stop the cycle;
    The grate is full of ash but fire will always burn.
Therefore, listening to the taxis
    (In which you never come) so regularly pass,
I wait content, banking on the spring and watching
    The dead leaves canter over the dowdy grass.

XII

These days are misty, insulated, mute
    Like a faded tapestry and the soft pedal
Is down and the yellow leaves are falling down
    And we hardly have the heart to meddle
Any more with personal ethics or public calls;
    People have not recovered from the crisis,
Their faces are far away, the tone of the words
    Belies their thesis.
For they say that now it is time unequivocally to act,
    To let the pawns be taken,
That criticism, a virtue previously,
    Now can only weaken
And that when we go to Rome
    We must do as the Romans do, cry out together
For bread and circuses; put on your togas now
    For this is Roman weather.
Circuses of death and from the topmost tiers
    A cataract of goggling, roaring faces;
On the arena sand
    Those who are about to die try out their paces.
Now it is night, a cold mist creeps, the night
    Is still and damp and lonely;
Sitting by the fire it is hard to realise
    That the legions wait at the gates and that there is only
A little time for rest though not by rights for rest,
    Rather for whetting the will, for calculating
A compromise between necessity and wish,

[144]

Apprenticed late to learn the trade of hating.
Remember the sergeant barking at bayonet practice
    When you were small;
To kill a dummy you must act a dummy
    Or you cut no ice at all.
Now it is morning again, the 25th of October,
    In a white fog the cars have yellow lights;
The chill creeps up the wrists, the sun is sallow,
    The silent hours grow down like stalactites.
And reading Plato talking about his Forms
    To damn the artist touting round his mirror,
I am glad that I have been left the third best bed
    And live in a world of error.
His world of capital initials, of transcendent
    Ideas is too bleak;
For me there remain to all intents and purposes
    Seven days in the week
And no one Tuesday is another and you destroy it
    If you subtract the difference and relate
It merely to the Form of Tuesday. This is Tuesday
    The 25th of October, 1938.
Aristotle was better who watched the insect breed,
    The natural world develop,
Stressing the function, scrapping the Form in Itself,
    Taking the horse from the shelf and letting it gallop.
Education gives us too many labels
    And clichés, cuts too many Gordian knots;
Trains us to keep the roads nor reconnoitre
    Any of the beauty-spots or danger-spots.
Not that I would rather be a peasant; the Happy Peasant
    Like the Noble Savage is a myth;
I do not envy the self-possession of an elm-tree
    Nor the aplomb of a granite monolith.
All that I would like to be is human, having a share
    In a civilised, articulate and well-adjusted
Community where the mind is given its due
    But the body is not distrusted.
As it is, the so-called humane studies
    May lead to cushy jobs
But leave the men who land them spiritually bankrupt
    Intellectual snobs.
Not but what I am glad to have my comforts,

K   [145]   M.C.P.

Better authentic mammon than a bogus god;
If it were not for Lit.Hum. I might be climbing
  A ladder with a hod.
And seven hundred a year
  Will pay the rent and the gas and the 'phone and the grocer;
(The Emperor takes his seat beneath the awning,
  Those who are about to die . . .) Come, pull the curtains closer.

XIII

Which things being so, as we said when we studied
  The classics, I ought to be glad
That I studied the classics at Marlborough and Merton,
  Not everyone here having had
The privilege of learning a language
  That is incontrovertibly dead,
And of carting a toy-box of hall-marked marmoreal phrases
  Around in his head.
We wrote compositions in Greek which they said was a lesson
  In logic and good for the brain;
We marched, counter-marched to the field-marshal's blue-pencil
    baton,
  We dressed by the right and we wrote out the sentence again.
We learned that a gentleman never misplaces his accents,
  That nobody knows how to speak, much less how to write
English who has not hob-nobbed with the great-grandparents of
    English,
  That the boy on the Modern Side is merely a parasite
But the classical student is bred to the purple, his training in
    syntax
  Is also a training in thought
And even in morals; if called to the bar or the barracks
  He always will do what he ought.
And knowledge, besides, should be prized for the sake of
    knowledge:
  Oxford crowded the mantelpiece with gods—
Scaliger, Heinsius, Dindorf, Bentley and Wilamowitz—
  As we learned our genuflexions for Honour Mods.
And then they taught us philosophy, logic and metaphysics,
  The Negative Judgment and the Ding an Sich,
And every single thinker was powerful as Napoleon
  And crafty as Metternich.

[146]

And it really was very attractive to be able to talk about tables
    And to ask if the table *is*,
And to draw the cork out of an old conundrum
    And watch the paradoxes fizz.
And it made one confident to think that nothing
    Really was what it seemed under the sun,
That the actual was not real and the real was not with us
    And all that mattered was the One.
And they said 'The man in the street is so naïve, he never
    Can see the wood for the trees;
He thinks he knows he sees a thing but cannot
    Tell you how he knows the thing he thinks he sees.'
And oh how much I liked the Concrete Universal,
    I never thought that I should
Be telling them vice-versa
    That they can't see the trees for the wood.
But certainly it was fun while it lasted
    And I got my honours degree
And was stamped as a person of intelligence and culture
    For ever wherever two or three
Persons of intelligence and culture
    Are gathered together in talk
Writing definitions on invisible blackboards
    In non-existent chalk.
But such sacramental occasions
    Are nowadays comparatively rare;
There is always a wife or a boss or a dun or a client
    Disturbing the air.
Barbarians always, life in the particular always,
    Dozens of men in the street,
And the perennial if unimportant problem
    Of getting enough to eat.
So blow the bugles over the metaphysicians,
    Let the pure mind return to the Pure Mind;
I must be content to remain in the world of Appearance
    And sit on the mere appearance of a behind.
But in case you should think my education was wasted
    I hasten to explain
That having once been to the University of Oxford
    You can never really again
Believe anything that anyone says and that of course is an asset
    In a world like ours;

Why bother to water a garden
  That is planted with paper flowers?
O the Freedom of the Press, the Late Night Final,
  To-morrow's pulp;
One should not gulp one's port but as it isn't
  Port, I'll gulp it if I want to gulp
But probably I'll just enjoy the colour
  And pour it down the sink
For I don't call advertisement a statement
  Or any quack medicine a drink.
Good-bye now, Plato and Hegel,
  The shop is closing down;
They don't want any philosopher-kings in England,
  There ain't no universals in this man's town.

XIV

The next day I drove by night
  Among red and amber and green, spears and candles,
Corkscrews and slivers of reflected light
  In the mirror of the rainy asphalt
Along the North Circular and the Great West roads
  Running the gauntlet of impoverished fancy
Where housewives bolster up their jerry-built abodes
  With *amour propre* and the habit of Hire Purchase.
The wheels whished in the wet, the flashy strings
  Of neon lights unravelled, the windscreen-wiper
Kept at its job like a tiger in a cage or a cricket that sings
  All night through for nothing.
Factory, a site for a factory, rubbish dumps,
  Bungalows in lath and plaster, in brick, in concrete,
And shining semi-circles of petrol pumps
  Like intransigent gangs of idols.
And the road swings round my head like a lassoo
  Looping wider and wider tracts of darkness
And the country succeeds the town and the country too
  Is damp and dark and evil.
And coming over the Chilterns the dead leaves leap
  Charging the windscreen like a barrage of angry
Birds as I take the steep
  Plunge to Henley or Hades.
And at the curves of the road the telephone wires

Shine like strands of silk and the hedge solicits
My irresponsible tyres
    To an accident, to a bed in the wet grasses.
And in quiet crooked streets only the village pub
    Spills a golden puddle
Over the pavement and trees bend down and rub
    Unopened dormer windows with their knuckles.
Nettlebed, Shillingford, Dorchester—each unrolls
    The road to Oxford; *Qu'allais-je faire* to-morrow
Driving voters to the polls
    In that home of lost illusions?
And what am I doing it for?
    Mainly for fun, partly for a half-believed-in
Principle, a core
    Of fact in a pulp of verbiage,
Remembering that this crude and so-called obsolete
    Top-heavy tedious parliamentary system
Is our only ready weapon to defeat
    The legions' eagles and the lictors' axes;
And remembering that those who by their habit hate
    Politics can no longer keep their private
Values unless they open the public gate
    To a better political system.
That Rome was not built in a day is no excuse
    For *laissez-faire*, for bowing to the odds against us;
What is the use
    Of asking what is the use of one brick only?
The perfectionist stands for ever in a fog
    Waiting for the fog to clear; better to be vulgar
And use your legs and leave a blank for Hogg
    And put a cross for Lindsay.
There are only too many who say 'What difference does it make
    One way or the other?
To turn the stream of history will take
    More than a by-election.'
So Thursday came and Oxford went to the polls
    And made its coward vote and the streets resounded
To the triumphant cheers of the lost souls—
    The profiteers, the dunderheads, the smarties.
And I drove back to London in the dark of the morning, the trees
    Standing out in the headlights cut from cardboard;
Wondering which disease

Is worse—the Status Quo or the Mere Utopia.
For from now on
    Each occasion must be used, however trivial,
To rally the ranks of those whose chance will soon be gone
    For even guerrilla warfare.
The nicest people in England have always been the least
    Apt to solidarity or alignment
But all of them must now align against the beast
    That prowls at every door and barks in every headline
Dawn and London and daylight and last the sun:
    I stop the car and take the yellow placard
Off the bonnet; that little job is done
    Though without success or glory.
The plane-tree leaves come sidling down
    (Catch my guineas, catch my guineas)
And the sun caresses Camden Town,
    The barrows of oranges and apples.

XV

Shelley and jazz and lieder and love and hymn-tunes
    And day returns too soon;
We'll get drunk among the roses
    In the valley of the moon.
Give me an aphrodisiac, give me lotus,
    Give me the same again;
Make all the erotic poets of Rome and Ionia
    And Florence and Provence and Spain
Pay a tithe of their sugar to my potion
    And ferment my days
With the twang of Hawaii and the boom of the Congo;
    Let the old Muse loosen her stays
Or give me a new Muse with stockings and suspenders
    And a smile like a cat,
With false eyelashes and finger-nails of carmine
    And dressed by Schiaparelli, with a pill-box hat.
Let the aces run riot round Brooklands,
    Let the tape-machines go drunk,
Turn on the purple spotlight, pull out the Vox Humana,
    Dig up somebody's body in a cloakroom trunk.
Give us sensations and then again sensations—
    Strip-tease, fireworks, all-in wrestling, gin;

[150]

Spend your capital, open your house and pawn your padlocks,
  Let the critical sense go out and the Roaring Boys come in.
Give me a houri but houris are too easy,
  Give me a nun;
We'll rape the angels off the golden reredos
  Before we're done.
Tiger-women and Lesbos, drums and entrails,
  And let the skies rotate,
We'll play roulette with the stars, we'll sit out drinking
  At the Hangman's Gate.
O look who comes here. I cannot see their faces
  Walking in file, slowly in file;
They have no shoes on their feet, the knobs of their ankles
  Catch the moonlight as they pass the stile
And cross the moor among the skeletons of bog-oak
  Following the track from the gallows back to the town;
Each has the end of a rope around his neck. I wonder
  Who let these men come back, who cut them down—
And now they reach the gate and line up opposite
  The neon lights on the medieval wall
And underneath the sky-signs
  Each one takes his cowl and lets it fall
And we see their faces, each the same as the other,
  Men and women, each like a closed door,
But something about their faces is familiar;
  Where have we seen them before?
Was it the murderer on the nursery ceiling
  Or Judas Iscariot in the Field of Blood
Or someone at Gallipoli or in Flanders
  Caught in the end-all mud.
But take no notice of them, out with the ukulele,
  The saxophone and the dice;
They are sure to go away if we take no notice;
  Another round of drinks or make it twice.
That was a good one, tell us another, don't stop talking,
  Cap your stories; if
You haven't any new ones tell the old ones,
  Tell them as often as you like and perhaps those horrible stiff
People with blank faces that are yet familiar
  Won't be there when you look again, but don't
Look just yet, just give them time to vanish. I said to vanish;
  What do you mean—they won't?

[151]

Give us the songs of Harlem or Mitylene—
    Pearls in wine—
There can't be a hell unless there is a heaven
    And a devil would have to be divine
And there can't be such things one way or the other;
    That we know;
You can't step into the same river twice so there can't be
    Ghosts; thank God that rivers always flow.
Sufficient to the moment is the moment;
    Past and future merely don't make sense
And yet I thought I had seen them . . .
    But *how*, if there is only a present tense?
Come on, boys, we aren't afraid of bogies,
    Give us another drink;
This little lady has a fetish,
    She goes to bed in mink.
This little pig went to market—
    Now I think you may look, I think the coast is clear.
Well, why don't you answer?
    I can't answer because they are still there.

XVI

Nightmare leaves fatigue:
    We envy men of action
Who sleep and wake, murder and intrigue
    Without being doubtful, without being haunted.
And I envy the intransigence of my own
    Countrymen who shoot to kill and never
See the victim's face become their own
    Or find his motive sabotage their motives.
So reading the memoirs of Maud Gonne,
    Daughter of an English mother and a soldier father
I note how a single purpose can be founded on
    A jumble of opposites:
Dublin Castle, the vice-regal ball,
    The embassies of Europe,
Hatred scribbled on a wall,
    Gaols and revolvers.
And I remember, when I was little, the fear
    Bandied among the servants
That Casement would land at the pier

With a sword and a horde of rebels;
And how we used to expect, at a later date,
  When the wind blew from the west, the noise of shooting
Starting in the evening at eight
  In Belfast in the York Street district;
And the voodoo of the Orange bands
  Drawing an iron net through darkest Ulster,
Flailing the limbo lands—
  The linen mills, the long wet grass, the ragged hawthorn.
And one read black where the other read white, his hope
  The other man's damnation:
Up the Rebels, To Hell with the Pope,
  And God Save—as you prefer—the King or Ireland.
The land of scholars and saints:
  Scholars and saints my eye, the land of ambush,
Purblind manifestoes, never-ending complaints,
  The born martyr and the gallant ninny;
The grocer drunk with the drum,
  The land-owner shot in his bed, the angry voices
Piercing the broken fanlight in the slum,
  The shawled woman weeping at the garish altar.
Kathaleen ni Houlihan! Why
  Must a country, like a ship or a car, be always female,
Mother or sweetheart? A woman passing by,
  We did but see her passing.
Passing like a patch of sun on the rainy hill
  And yet we love her for ever and hate our neighbour
And each one in his will
  Binds his heirs to continuance of hatred.
Drums on the haycock, drums on the harvest, black
  Drums in the night shaking the windows:
King William is riding his white horse back
  To the Boyne on a banner.
Thousands of banners, thousands of white
  Horses, thousands of Williams
Waving thousands of swords and ready to fight
  Till the blue sea turns to orange.
Such was my country and I thought I was well
  Out of it, educated and domiciled in England,
Though yet her name keeps ringing like a bell
  In an under-water belfry.
Why do we like being Irish? Partly because

It gives us a hold on the sentimental English
As members of a world that never was,
  Baptised with fairy water;
And partly because Ireland is small enough
  To be still thought of with a family feeling,
And because the waves are rough
  That split her from a more commercial culture;
And because one feels that here at least one can
  Do local work which is not at the world's mercy
And that on this tiny stage with luck a man
  Might see the end of one particular action.
It is self-deception of course;
  There is no immunity in this island either;
A cart that is drawn by somebody else's horse
  And carrying goods to somebody else's market.
The bombs in the turnip sack, the sniper from the roof,
  Griffith, Connolly, Collins, where have they brought us?
Ourselves alone! Let the round tower stand aloof
  In a world of bursting mortar!
Let the school-children fumble their sums
  In a half-dead language;
Let the censor be busy on the books; pull down the Georgian
      slums;
  Let the games be played in Gaelic.
Let them grow beet-sugar; let them build
  A factory in every hamlet;
Let them pigeon-hole the souls of the killed
  Into sheep and goats, patriots and traitors.
And the North, where I was a boy,
  Is still the North, veneered with the grime of Glasgow,
Thousands of men whom nobody will employ
  Standing at the corners, coughing.
And the street-children play on the wet
  Pavement—hopscotch or marbles;
And each rich family boasts a sagging tennis-net
  On a spongy lawn beside a dripping shrubbery.
The smoking chimneys hint
  At prosperity round the corner
But they make their Ulster linen from foreign lint
  And the money that comes in goes out to make more money.
A city built upon mud;
  A culture built upon profit;

Free speech nipped in the bud,
    The minority always guilty.
Why should I want to go back
    To you, Ireland, my Ireland?
The blots on the page are so black
    That they cannot be covered with shamrock.
I hate your grandiose airs,
    Your sob-stuff, your laugh and your swagger,
Your assumption that everyone cares
    Who is the king of your castle.
Castles are out of date,
    The tide flows round the children's sandy fancy;
Put up what flag you like, it is too late
    To save your soul with bunting.
Odi atque amo:
    Shall we cut this name on trees with a rusty dagger?
Her mountains are still blue, her rivers flow
    Bubbling over the boulders.
She is both a bore and a bitch;
    Better close the horizon,
Send her no more fantasy, no more longings which
    Are under a fatal tariff.
For common sense is the vogue
    And she gives her children neither sense nor money
Who slouch around the world with a gesture and a brogue
    And a faggot of useless memories.

XVII

From the second floor up, looking north, having breakfast
    I see the November sun at nine o'clock
Gild the fusty brickwork of rows on rows of houses
    Like animals asleep and breathing smoke,
And savouring Well-being
    I light my first cigarette, grow giddy and blink,
Glad of this titillation, this innuendo,
    This make-believe of standing on a brink;
For all our trivial daily acts are altered
    Into heroic or romantic make-believe
Of which we are hardly conscious—Who is it calls me
    When the cold draught picks my sleeve?
Or sneezing in the morning sunlight or smelling the bonfire

Over the webbed lawn and the naked cabbage plot?
Or stepping into a fresh-filled bath with strata
    Of cold water and hot?
We lie in the bath between tiled walls and under
    Ascending scrolls of steam
And feel the ego merge as the pores open
    And we lie in the bath and dream;
And responsibility dies and the thighs are happy
    And the body purrs like a cat
But this lagoon grows cold, we have to leave it, stepping
    On to a check rug on a cork mat.
The luxury life is only to be valued
    By those who are short of money or pressed for time
As the cinema gives the poor their Jacob's ladder
    For Cinderellas to climb.
And Plato was right to define the bodily pleasures
    As the pouring water into a hungry sieve
But wrong to ignore the rhythm which the intercrossing
    Coloured waters permanently give.
And Aristotle was right to posit the Alter Ego
    But wrong to make it only a halfway house:
Who could expect—or want—to be spiritually self-supporting,
    Eternal self-abuse?
Why not admit that other people are always
    Organic to the self, that a monologue
Is the death of language and that a single lion
    Is less himself, or alive, than a dog and another dog?
Virtue going out of us always; the eyes grow weary
    With vision but it is vision builds the eye;
And in a sense the children kill their parents
    But do the parents die?
And the beloved destroys like fire or water
    But water scours and sculps and fire refines
And if you are going to read the testaments of cynics,
    You must read between the lines.
A point here and a point there: the current
    Jumps the gaps, the ego cannot live
Without becoming other for the Other
    Has got yourself to give.
And even the sense of taste provides communion
    With God as plant or beast;
The sea in fish, the field in a salad of endive,

A sacramental feast.
The soul's long searchlight hankers for a body,
    The single body hungers for its kind,
The eye demands the light at the risk of blindness
    And the mind that did not doubt would not be mind
And discontent is eternal. In luxury or business,
    In family or sexual love, in purchases or prayers,
Our virtue is invested, the self put out at interest,
    The returns are never enough, the fact compares
So badly with the fancy yet fancy itself is only
    A divination of fact
And if we confine the world to the prophet's tripod
    The subjects of our prophecy contract.
Open the world wide, open the senses,
    Let the soul stretch its blind enormous arms,
There is vision in the fingers only needing waking,
    Ready for light's alarms.
O light, terror of light, hoofs and ruthless
    Wheels of steel and brass
Dragging behind you lacerated captives
    Who also share your triumph as you pass.
Light which is time, belfry of booming sunlight,
    The ropes run up and down,
The whole town shakes with the peal of living people
    Who break and build the town.
Aristotle was right to think of man-in-action
    As the essential and really existent man
And man means men in action; try and confine your
    Self to yourself if you can.
Nothing is self-sufficient, pleasure implies hunger
    But hunger implies hope:
I cannot lie in this bath for ever, clouding
    The cooling water with rose geranium soap.
I cannot drug my life with the present moment;
    The present moment may rape—but all in vain—
The future, for the future remains a virgin
    Who must be tried again.

XVIII

In the days that were early the music came easy
    On cradle and coffin, in the corn and the barn

[157]

Songs for the reaping and spinning and only the shepherd
    Then as now was silent beside the tarn:
Cuffs of foam around the beer-brown water,
    Crinkled water and a mackerel sky;
It is all in the day's work—the grey stones and heather
    And the sheep that breed and break their legs and die.
The uplands now as then are fresh but in the valley
    Polluted rivers run—the Lethe and the Styx;
The soil is tired and the profit little and the hunchback
    Bobs on a carthorse round the sodden ricks.
Sing us no more idylls, no more pastorals,
    No more epics of the English earth;
The country is a dwindling annexe to the factory,
    Squalid as an after-birth.
This England is tight and narrow, teeming with unwanted
    Children who are so many, each is alone;
Niobe and her children
    Stand beneath the smokestack turned to stone.
And still the church-bells brag above the empty churches
    And the Union Jack
Thumps the wind above the law-courts and the barracks
    And in the allotments the black
Scarecrow holds a fort of grimy heads of cabbage
    Besieged by grimy birds
Like a hack politician fighting the winged aggressor
    With yesterday's magic coat of ragged words.
Things were different when men felt their programme
    In the bones and pulse, not only in the brain,
Born to a trade, a belief, a set of affections;
    That instinct for belief may sprout again,
There are some who have never lost it
    And some who foster or force it into growth
But most of us lack the right discontent, contented
    Merely to cavil. Spiritual sloth
Creeps like lichen or ivy over the hinges
    Of the doors which never move;
We cannot even remember who is behind them
    Nor even, soon, shall have the chance to prove
If anyone at all is behind them—
    The Sleeping Beauty or the Holy Ghost
Or the greatest happiness of the greatest number;
    All we can do at most

Is press an anxious ear against the keyhole
  To hear the Future breathing; softly tread
In the outer porch beneath the marble volutes—
  Who knows if God, as Nietzsche said, is dead?
There is straw to lay in the streets; call the hunchback,
  The gentleman farmer, the village idiot, the Shropshire Lad,
To insulate us if they can with coma
  Before we all go mad.
What shall we pray for, Lord? Whom shall we pray to?
  Shall we give like decadent Athens the benefit of the doubt
To the Unknown God or smugly pantheistic
  Assume that God is everywhere round about?
But if we assume such a God, then who the devil
  Are these with empty stomachs or empty smiles?
The blind man's stick goes tapping on the pavement
  For endless glittering miles
Beneath the standard lights; the paralytic winding
  His barrel-organ sprays the passers-by
With April music; the many-ribboned hero
  With half a lung or a leg waits his turn to die.
God forbid an Indian acquiescence,
  The apotheosis of the status quo;
If everything that happens happens according
  To the nature and wish of God, then God must go:
Lay your straw in the streets and go about your business
  An inch at a time, an inch at a time,
We have not even an hour to spend repenting
  Our sins; the quarters chime
And every minute is its own alarum clock
  And what we are about to do
Is of vastly more importance
  Than what we have done or not done hitherto.
It is December now, the trees are naked
  As the three crosses on the hill;
Through the white fog the face of the orange sun is cryptic
  Like a lawyer making the year's will.
The year has little to show, will leave a heavy
  Overdraft to its heir;
Shall we try to meet the deficit or passing
  By on the other side continue *laissez-faire*?
International betrayals, public murder,
  The devil quoting scripture, the traitor, the coward, the thug

Eating dinner in the name of peace and progress,
    The doped public sucking a dry dug;
Official recognition of rape, revival of the ghetto
    And free speech gagged and free
Energy scrapped and dropped like surplus herring
    Back into the barren sea;
Brains and beauty festering in exile,
    The shadow of bars
Falling across each page, each field, each raddled sunset,
    The alien lawn and the pool of nenuphars;
And hordes of homeless poor running the gauntlet
    In hostile city streets of white and violet lamps
Whose flight is without a terminus but better
    Than the repose of concentration camps.
Come over, they said, into Macedonia and help us
    But the chance is gone;
Now we must help ourselves, we can leave the vulture
    To pick the corpses clean in Macedon.
No wonder many would renounce their birthright,
    The responsibility of moral choice,
And sit with a mess of pottage taking orders
    Out of a square box from a mad voice—
Lies on the air endlessly repeated
    Turning the air to fog,
Blanket on blanket of lie, no room to breathe or fidget
    And nobody to jog
Your elbow and say 'Up there the sun is rising;
    Take it on trust, the sun will always shine.'
The sun may shine no doubt but how many people
    Will see it with their eyes in Nineteen-Thirty-Nine?
Yes, the earlier days had their music,
    We have some still to-day,
But the orchestra is due for the bonfire
    If things go on this way.
Still there are still the seeds of energy and choice
    Still alive even if forbidden, hidden,
And while a man has voice
    He may recover music.

XIX

The pigeons riddle the London air,
  The shutter slides from the chain-store window .
The frock-coat statue stands in the square
  Caring for no one, caring for no one.
The night-shift men go home to bed,
  The kettle sings and the bacon sizzles;
Some are hungry and some are dead—
  A wistful face in a faded photo.
Under the stairs is a khaki cap;
  That was Dad's, Dad was a plumber—
You hear that dripping tap?
  He'd have had it right in no time.
No time now; Dad is dead,
  He left me five months gone or over;
Tam cari capitis, for such a well-loved head
  What shame in tears, what limit?
It is the child I mean,
  Born prematurely, strangled;
Dad was off the scene,
  He would have made no difference.
The stretchers run from ward to ward,
  The telephone rings in empty houses,
The torn shirt soaks on the scrubbing board,
  O what a busy morning.
Baby Croesus crawls in a pen
  With alphabetical bricks and biscuits;
The doll-dumb file of sandwichmen
  Carry lies from gutter to gutter.
The curate buys his ounce of shag,
  The typist tints her nails with coral,
The housewife with her shopping bag
  Watches the cleaver catch the naked
New Zealand sheep between the legs—
  What price now New Zealand?
The cocker spaniel sits and begs
  With eyes like a waif on the movies.
O what a busy morning,
  Engines start with a roar,
All the wires are buzzing,
  The tape-machines vomit on the floor.

And I feel that my mind once again is open,
  The lady is gone who stood in the way so long,
The hypnosis is over and no one
  Calls encore to the song.
When we are out of love, how were we ever in it?
  Where are the mountains and the mountain skies,
That heady air instinct with
  A strange sincerity which winged our lies?
The peaks have fallen in like dropping pastry:
  Now I could see her come
Around the corner without the pulse responding,
  The flowery orator in the heart is dumb,
His bag of tricks is empty, his over-statements,
  Those rainbow bubbles, have burst:
When we meet, she need not feel embarrassed,
  The cad with the golden tongue has done his worst
And has no orders from me to mix his phrases rich,
  To make the air a carpet
For her to walk on; I only wonder which
  Day, which hour, I found this freedom.
But freedom is not so exciting,
  We prefer to be drawn
In the rush of the stars as they circle—
  A traffic that ends with dawn.
Now I am free of the stars
  And the word 'love' makes no sense, this history is almost
Ripe for the mind's museum—broken jars
  That once held wine or perfume.
Yet looking at their elegance on the stands
  I feel a certain pride that only lately
(And yet so long ago) I held them in my hands
  While they were full and fragrant.
So on this busy morning I hope, my dear,
  That you are also busy
With another vintage of another year;
  I wish you luck and I thank you for the party—
A good party though at the end my thirst
  Was worse than at the beginning
But never to have drunk no doubt would be the worst;
  Pain, they say, is always twin to pleasure.
Better to have these twins
  Than no children at all, very much better

[162]

To act for good and bad than have no sins
    And take no action either.
You were my blizzard who had been my bed
    But taking the whole series of blight and blossom
I would not choose a simpler crop instead;
    Thank you, my dear—dear against my judgment.

XX

Nelson stands on a black pillar,
    The electric signs go off and on—
Distilleries and life insurance companies—
    The traffic circles, coming and gone,
Past the National Gallery closed and silent
    Where in their frames
Other worlds persist, the passions of the artist
    Caught like frozen flames:
The Primitives distilling from the cruel
    Legend a faith that is almost debonair,
Sebastian calmly waiting the next arrow,
    The crucifixion in the candid air:
And Venice lolling in wealth for ever under glass,
    Pearls in her hair, panther and velvet:
And the rococo picnic on the grass
    With wine and lutes and banter:
And the still life proclaiming with aplomb
    The self-content of bread or fruit or vases
And personality like a silent bomb
    Lurking in the formal portrait.
Here every day the visitors walk slowly
    Rocking along the parquet as if on a ship's deck
Feeling a vague affinity with the pictures
    Yet wary of these waves which gently peck
The side of the boat in passing; they are anxious
    To end the voyage, to land in their own time;
The sea of the past glimmers with white horses,
    A paradigm
Of life's successions, treacheries, recessions;
    The unfounded confidence of the dead affronts
Our own system of values
    Like airmen doing their stunts
Over our private garden; these arrogant Old Masters

Swoop and loop and lance us with a quick
Shadow; we only want to cultivate our garden,
    Not for us the virtuoso, slick
Tricks of the airy region,
    For our part our feet are on the ground,
They should not be allowed to fly so low above us,
    Their premises are unsound
And history has refuted them and yet
    They cast their shadows on us like aspersions;
Propellers and white horses,
    Movement, movement, can we never forget
The movements of the past which should be dead?
    The mind of Socrates still clicks like scissors
And Christ who should lie quiet in the garden
    Flowered in flame instead.

        .   .   .   .

A week to Christmas, cards of snow and holly,
    Gimcracks in the shops,
Wishes and memories wrapped in tissue paper,
    Trinkets, gadgets and lollipops
And as if through coloured glasses
    We remember our childhood's thrill
Waking in the morning to the rustling of paper,
    The eiderdown heaped in a hill
Of wogs and dogs and bears and bricks and apples
    And the feeling that Christmas Day
Was a coral island in time where we land and eat our lotus
    But where we can never stay.
There was a star in the East, the magi in their turbans
    Brought their luxury toys
In homage to a child born to capsize their values
    And wreck their equipoise.
A smell of hay like peace in the dark stable—
    Not peace however but a sword
To cut the Gordian knot of logical self-interest,
    The fool-proof golden cord;
For Christ walked in where no philosopher treads
    But armed with more than folly,
Making the smooth place rough and knocking the heads
    Of Church and State together.
In honour of whom we have taken over the pagan
    Saturnalia for our annual treat

[164]

Letting the belly have its say, ignoring
    The spirit while we eat.
And Conscience still goes crying through the desert
    With sackcloth round his loins:
A week to Christmas—hark the herald angels
    Beg for copper coins.

XXI

And when we clear away
    All this debris of day-by-day experience,
What comes out to light, what is there of value
    Lasting from day to day?
I sit in my room in comfort
    Looking at enormous flowers—
Equipment purchased with my working hours,
    A daily mint of perishable petals.
The figures of the dance repeat
    The unending cycle of making and spending money,
Eating our daily bread in order to earn it
    And earning in order to eat.
And is that all the story,
    The mainspring and the plot,
Or merely a mechanism without which not
    Any story could be written?
Sine qua non!
    Sine qua non indeed, we cannot ever
Live by soul alone; the soul without the stomach
    Would find its glory gone.
But the total cause outruns the mere condition,
    There is more to it than that;
Life would be (as it often seems) flat
    If it were merely a matter of not dying.
For each individual then
    Would be fighting a losing battle
But with life as collective creation
    The rout is rallied, the battle begins again.
Only give us the courage of our instinct,
    The will to truth and love's initiative,
Then we could hope to live
    A life beyond the self but self-completing.
And, as the emperor said, What is the use

Of the minor loyalty—'Dear city of Cecrops',
Unless we have also the wider franchise, can answer
    'Dear city of Zeus'?
And so when the many regrets
    Trouble us for the many lost affections,
Let us take the wider view before we count them
    Hopelessly bad debts.
For Cecrops has his rights as Zeus has his
    And every tree is a tree of branches
And every wood is a wood of trees growing
    And what has been contributes to what is.
So I am glad to have known them,
    The people or events apparently withdrawn;
The world is round and there is always dawn
    Undeniably somewhere.
'Praised be thou, O Lord, for our brother the sun'
    Said the grey saint, laving his eyes in colour;
Who creates and destroys for ever
    And his cycle is never done.
In this room chrysanthemums and dahlias
    Like brandy hit the heart; the fire,
A small wild animal, furthers its desire
    Consuming fuel, self-consuming.
And flames are the clearest cut
    Of shapes and the most transient:
O fire, my spendthrift,
    May I spend like you, as reckless but
Giving as good return—burn the silent
    Into running sound, deride the dark
And jump to glory from a single spark
    And purge the world and warm it.
The room grows cold, the flicker fades,
    The sinking ashes whisper, the fickle
Eye forgets but later will remember
    The radiant cavalcades.
The smoke has gone from the chimney,
    The water has flowed away under the bridge,
The silhouetted lovers have left the ridge,
    The flower has closed its calyx.
The crow's-feet have come to stay,
    The jokes no longer amuse, the palate
Rejects milk chocolate and Benedictine—

Yesterday and the day before yesterday.
But oh, not now my love, but oh my friend,
    Can you not take it merely on trust that life is
The only thing worth living and that dying
    Had better be left to take care of itself in the end?
For to have been born is in itself a triumph
    Among all that waste of sperm
And it is gratitude to wait the proper term
    Or, if not gratitude, duty.
I know that you think these phrases high falutin
    And, when not happy, see no claim or use
For staying alive; the quiet hands seduce
    Of the god who is god of nothing.
And while I sympathise
    With the wish to quit, to make the great refusal,
I feel that such a defeat is also treason,
    That deaths like these are lies.
A fire should be left burning
    Till it burns itself out:
We shan't have another chance to dance and shout
    Once the flames are silent.

XXII

December the nineteenth: over the black roofs
    And the one black paint-brush poplar
The white steam rises and deploys in puffs
    From the house-hidden railway, a northern
Geyser erupting in a land of lava,
    But white can be still whiter for now
The dun air starts to jig with specks that circle
    Like microbes under a lens; this is the first snow;
And soon the specks are feathers blandly sidling
    Inconsequent as the fancies of young girls
And the air has filled like a dance-hall,
    A waltz of white dresses and strings of pearls.
And the papers declare the snow has come to stay,
    A new upholstery on roof and garden
Refining, lining, underlining the day,
    And the sombre laurels break parole and blossom
In enormous clumps of peonies; and the cars
    Turn animal, moving slowly

In their white fur like bears,
    And the white trees fade into the hill behind them
As negroes' faces fade in a dark background,
    Our London world
Grown all of a piece and peaceful like the Arctic,
    The sums all cancelled out and the flags furled.
At night we sleep behind stockades of frost,
    Nothing alive in the streets to run the gauntlet
Of this unworldly cold except the lost
    Wisps of steam from the gratings of the sewers.
It is holiday time, time for the morning snack,
    Time to be leaving the country:
I have taken my ticket south, I will not look back,
    The pipes may burst for all I care, the gutter
Dribble with dirty snow, the Christmas party
    Be ruined by catarrh;
Let us flee this country and leave its complications
    Exactly where they (the devil take them) are.
So Dover to Dunkerque:
    The Land of Cockayne begins across the Channel.
The hooter cries to hell with the year's work,
    The snowflakes flirt with the steam of the steamer.
But the train in France is cold, the window
    Frosted with patterns of stars and fern,
And when we scrape a peephole on the window
    There is nothing new to learn;
Nothing but snow and snow all the way to Paris,
    No roast pigs walk this way
And any snatched half-hour of self-indulgence
    Is an intercalary day.
Sweet, my love, my dear, whoever you are or were,
    I need your company on this excursion
For, where there is the luxury of leisure, there
    There should also be the luxury of women.
I do not need you on my daily job
    Nor yet on any spiritual adventure,
Not when I earn my keep but when I rob
    Time of his growth of tinsel:
No longer thinking you or any other
    Essential to my life—soul-mate or dual star:
All I want is an elegant and witty playmate
    At the perfume counter or the cocktail bar.

So here where tourist values are the only
   Values, where we pretend
That eating and drinking are more important than thinking
   And looking at things than action and a casual friend
Than a colleague and that work is a dull convenience
   Designed to provide
Money to spend on amusement and that amusement
   Is an eternal bride
Who will never sink to the level of a wife, that gossip
   Is the characteristic of art
And that the sensible man must keep his æsthetic
   And his moral standards apart—
Here, where we think all this, I need you badly,
   Whatever your name or age or the colour of your hair;
I need your surface company (what happens
   Below the surface is my own affair).
And I feel a certain pleasurable nostalgia
   In sitting alone, drinking, wondering if you
Will suddenly thread your way among these vulcanite tables
   To a mutually unsuspected rendezvous
Among these banal women with feathers in their hats and halos
   Of evanescent veils
And these bald-at-thirty Englishmen whose polished
   Foreheads are the tombs of record sales;
Where alcohol, anchovies and shimmying street-lamps
   Knock the stolid almanac cock-a-hoop,
Where reason drowns and the senses
   Foam, flame, tingle and loop the loop.
And striking red or green matches to light these loose
   Cigarettes of black tobacco I need you badly—
The age-old woman apt for all misuse
   Whose soul is out of the picture.
How I enjoy this bout of cynical self-indulgence,
   Of glittering and hard-boiled make-believe;
The cynic is a creature of over-statements
   But an overstatement is something to achieve.
And how (with a grain of salt) I enjoy hating
   The world to which for ever I belong,
This hatred, this escape, being equally factitious—
   A passing song.
For I cannot stay in Paris
   And, if I did, no doubt I should soon be bored

For what I see is not the intimate city
  But the brittle dance of lights in the Place de la Concorde.
So much for Christmas: I must go further south
  To see the New Year in on hungry faces
But where the hungry mouth
  Refuses to deny the heart's allegiance.
Look: the road winds up among the prickly vineyards
  And naked winter trees;
Over there are pain and pride beyond the snow-lit
  Sharp annunciation of the Pyrenees.

XXIII

The road ran downhill into Spain,
  The wind blew fresh on bamboo grasses,
The white plane-trees were bone-naked
  And the issues plain:
We have come to a place in space where shortly
  All of us may be forced to camp in time:
The slender searchlights climb,
  Our sins will find us out, even our sins of omission.
When I reached the town it was dark,
  No lights in the streets but two and a half millions
Of people in circulation
  Condemned like the beasts in the ark
With nothing but water around them:
  Will there ever be a green tree or a rock that is dry?
The shops are empty and in Barceloneta the eye-
  Sockets of the houses are empty.
But still they manage to laugh
  Though they have no eggs, no milk, no fish, no fruit, no
      tobacco, no butter,
Though they live upon lentils and sleep in the Metro,
  Though the old order is gone and the golden calf
Of Catalan industry shattered;
  The human values remain, purged in the fire,
And it appears that every man's desire
  Is life rather than victuals.
Life being more, it seems, than merely the bare
  Permission to keep alive and receive orders,
Humanity being more than a mechanism
  To be oiled and greased and for ever unaware

[170]

O the work it is turning out, of why the wheels keep turning;
    Here at least the soul has found its voice
Though not indeed by choice;
    The cost was heavy.
They breathe the air of war and yet the tension
    Admits, beside the slogans it evokes,
An interest in philately or pelota
    Or private jokes.
And the sirens cry in the dark morning
    And the lights go out and the town is still
And the sky is pregnant with ill-will
    And the bombs come foxing the fated victim
As pretty as a Guy Fawkes show—
    Silver sprays and tracer bullets—
And in the pauses of destruction
    The cocks in the centre of the town crow.
The cocks crow in Barcelona
    Where clocks are few to strike the hour;
Is it the heart's reveille or the sour
    Reproach of Simon Peter?
The year has come to an end,
    Time for resolutions, for stock-taking;
Felice Nuevo Año!
    May God, if there is one, send
As much courage again and greater vision
    And resolve the antinomies in which we live
Where man must be either safe because he is negative
    Or free on the edge of a razor.
Give those who are gentle strength,
    Give those who are strong a generous imagination,
And make their half-truth true and let the crooked
    Footpath find its parent road at length.
I admit that for myself I cannot straiten
    My broken rambling track
Which reaches so irregularly back
    To burning cities and rifled rose-bushes
And cairns and lonely farms
    Where no one lives, makes love or begets children,
All my heredity and my upbringing
    Having brought me only to the Present's arms—
The arms not of a mistress but of a wrestler,
    Of a God who straddles over the night sky;

[171]

No wonder Jacob halted on his thigh—
    The price of a drawn battle.
For never to begin
    Anything new because we know there is nothing
New, is an academic sophistry—
    The original sin.
I have already had friends
    Among things and hours and people
But taking them one by one—odd hours and passing people;
    Now I must make amends
And try to correlate event with instinct
    And me with you or you and you with all,
No longer think of time as a waterfall
    Abstracted from a river.
I have loved defeat and sloth,
    The tawdry halo of the idle martyr;
I have thrown away the roots of will and conscience,
    Now I must look for both,
Not any longer act among the cushions
    The Dying Gaul;
Soon or late the delights of self-pity must pall
    And the fun of cursing the wicked
World into which we were born
    And the cynical admission of frustration
('Our loves are not full measure,
    There are blight and rooks on the corn').
Rather for any measure so far given
    Let us be glad
Nor wait on purpose to be wisely sad
    When doing nothing we find we have gained nothing.
For here and now the new valkyries ride
    The Spanish constellations
As over the Plaza Cataluña
    Orion lolls on his side;
Droning over from Majorca
    To maim or blind or kill
The bearers of the living will,
    The stubborn heirs of freedom
Whose matter-of-fact faith and courage shame
    Our niggling equivocations—
We who play for safety,
    A safety only in name.

Whereas these people contain truth, whatever
    Their nominal façade.
Listen: a whirr, a challenge, an aubade—
    It is the cock crowing in Barcelona.

XXIV

Sleep, my body, sleep, my ghost,
    Sleep, my parents and grand-parents,
And all those I have loved most:
    One man's coffin is another's cradle.
Sleep, my past and all my sins,
    In distant snow or dried roses
Under the moon for night's cocoon will open
    When day begins.
Sleep, my fathers, in your graves
    On upland bogland under heather;
What the wind scatters the wind saves,
    A sapling springs in a new country.
Time is a country, the present moment
    A spotlight roving round the scene;
We need not chase the spotlight,
    The future is the bride of what has been.
Sleep, my fancies and my wishes,
    Sleep a little and wake strong,
The same but different and take my blessing—
    A cradle-song.
And sleep, my various and conflicting
    Selves I have so long endured,
Sleep in Asclepius' temple
    And wake cured.
And you with whom I shared an idyll
    Five years long,
Sleep beyond the Atlantic
    And wake to a glitter of dew and to bird-song.
And you whose eyes are blue, whose ways are foam,
    Sleep quiet and smiling
And do not hanker
    For a perfection which can never come.
And you whose minutes patter
    To crowd the social hours,
Curl up easy in a placid corner

[173]

And let your thoughts close in like flowers.
And you, who work for Christ, and you, as eager
      For a better life, humanist, atheist,
And you, devoted to a cause, and you, to a family,
      Sleep and may your beliefs and zeal persist.
Sleep quietly, Marx and Freud,
      The figure-heads of our transition.
Cagney, Lombard, Bing and Garbo,
      Sleep in your world of celluloid.
Sleep now also, monk and satyr,
      Cease your wrangling for a night.
Sleep, my brain, and sleep, my senses,
      Sleep, my hunger and my spite.
Sleep, recruits to the evil army,
      Who, for so long misunderstood,
Took to the gun to kill your sorrow;
      Sleep and be damned and wake up good.
While we sleep, what shall we dream?
      Of Tir nan Og or South Sea islands,
Of a land where all the milk is cream
      And all the girls are willing?
Or shall our dream be earnest of the real
      Future when we wake,
Design a home, a factory, a fortress
      Which, though with effort, we can really make?
What is it we want really?
      For what end and how?
If it is something feasible, obtainable,
      Let us dream it now,
And pray for a possible land
      Not of sleep-walkers, not of angry puppets,
But where both heart and brain can understand
      The movements of our fellows;
Where life is a choice of instruments and none
      Is debarred his natural music,
Where the waters of life are free of the ice-blockade of hunger
      And thought is free as the sun,
Where the altars of sheer power and mere profit
      Have fallen to disuse,
Where nobody sees the use
      Of buying money and blood at the cost of blood and money,
Where the individual, no longer squandered

In self-assertion, works with the rest, endowed
With the split vision of a juggler and the quick lock of a taxi,
    Where the people are more than a crowd.
So sleep in hope of this—but only for a little;
    Your hope must wake
While the choice is yours to make,
    The mortgage not foreclosed, the offer open.
Sleep serene, avoid the backward
    Glance; go forward, dreams, and do not halt
(Behind you in the desert stands a token
    Of doubt—a pillar of salt).
Sleep, the past, and wake, the future,
    And walk out promptly through the open door;
But you, my coward doubts, may go on sleeping,
    You need not wake again—not any more.
The New Year comes with bombs, it is too late
    To dose the dead with honourable intentions:
If you have honour to spare, employ it on the living;
    The dead are dead as Nineteen-Thirty-Eight.
Sleep to the noise of running water
    To-morrow to be crossed, however deep;
This is no river of the dead or Lethe,
    To-night we sleep
On the banks of Rubicon—the die is cast;
    There will be time to audit
The accounts later, there will be sunlight later
    And the equation will come out at last.

VI

1939—1940

IV

PROGNOSIS

Goodbye, Winter,
The days are getting longer,
The tea-leaf in the teacup
Is herald of a stranger.

Will he bring me business
Or will he bring me gladness
Or will he come for cure
Of his own sickness?

With a pedlar's burden
Walking up the garden
Will he come to beg
Or will he come to bargain?

Will he come to pester,
To cringe or to bluster,
A promise in his palm
Or a gun in his holster?

Will his name be John
Or will his name be Jonah
Crying to repent
On the Island of Iona?

Will his name be Jason
Looking for a seaman
Or a mad crusader
Without rhyme or reason?

What will be his message—
War or work or marriage?
News as new as dawn
Or an old adage?

Will he give a champion
Answer to my question
Or will his words be dark
And his ways evasion?

[179]

Will his name be Love
And all his talk be crazy?
Or will his name be Death
And his message easy?

STYLITE

The saint on the pillar stands,
The pillar is alone,
He has stood so long
That he himself is stone;
Only his eyes
Range across the sand
Where no one ever comes
And the world is banned.

Then his eyes close,
He stands in his sleep,
Round his neck there comes
The conscience of a rope,
And the hangman counting
Counting to ten—
At nine he finds
He has eyes again.

The saint on the pillar stands,
The pillars are two,
A young man opposite
Stands in the blue,
A white Greek god,
Confident, with curled
Hair above the groin
And his eyes on the world.

ENTIRELY

If we could get the hang of it entirely
    It would take too long;
All we know is the splash of words in passing
    And falling twigs of song,

And when we try to eavesdrop on the great
    Presences it is rarely
That by a stroke of luck we can appropriate
    Even a phrase entirely.

If we could find our happiness entirely
    In somebody else's arms
We should not fear the spears of the spring nor the city's
    Yammering fire alarms
But, as it is, the spears each year go through
    Our flesh and almost hourly
Bell or siren banishes the blue
    Eyes of Love entirely.

And if the world were black or white entirely
    And all the charts were plain
Instead of a mad weir of tigerish waters,
    A prism of delight and pain,
We might be surer where we wished to go
    Or again we might be merely
Bored but in brute reality there is no
    Road that is right entirely.

PLANT AND PHANTOM

Man: a flutter of pages,
Leaves in the Sibyl's cave,
Shadow changing from dawn to twilight,
Murmuration of corn in the wind,
A shaking of hands with hallucinations,
Hobnobbing with ghosts, a pump of blood,
Mirage, a spider dangling
Over chaos and man a chaos.

Who cheats the pawky Fates
By what he does, not is,
By what he makes, imposing
On flux an architectonic—
Cone of marble, calyx of ice,
Spandrel and buttress, iron
Loops across the void,
Stepping stones in the random.

[181]

Man: a dance of midges,
Gold glass in the sunlight,
Prattle of water, palaver
Of starlings in a disused
Chimney, a gimcrack castle,
Seaweed tugging the rocks,
Guttering candles, the Northern
Lights and the Seventh Wave.

Whose life is a bluff, professing
To follow the laws of Nature,
In fact a revolt, a mad
Conspiracy and usurpation,
Smuggling over the frontier
Of fact a sense of value,
Metabolism of death,
Re-orchestration of world.

Man: a riot of banners,
Bulge in the wind, a prism,
Organ-pipes in the sunset,
Orgy of brains and glands,
Thunder-crackle and the bounce of hail,
Wink of wings and fog's delusion,
A rampant martyr, a midnight
Echo, a forest fire.

Who felt with his hands in empty
Air for the Word and did not
Find it but felt the aura,
Dew on the skin, could not forget it.
Ever since has fumbled, intrigued,
Clambered behind and beyond, and learnt
Words of blessing and cursing, hoping
To find in the end the Word Itself.

THE BRITISH MUSEUM READING ROOM

Under the hive-like dome the stooping haunted readers
Go up and down the alleys, tap the cells of knowledge—
Honey and wax, the accumulation of years—

Some on commission, some for the love of learning,
Some because they have nothing better to do
Or because they hope these walls of books will deaden
  The drumming of the demon in their ears.

Cranks, hacks, poverty-stricken scholars,
In pince-nez, period hats or romantic beards
  And cherishing their hobby or their doom
Some are too much alive and some are asleep
Hanging like bats in a world of inverted values,
Folded up in themselves in a world which is safe and silent:
  This is the British Museum Reading Room.

Out on the steps in the sun the pigeons are courting,
Puffing their ruffs and sweeping their tails or taking
  A sun-bath at their ease
And under the totem poles—the ancient terror—
Between the enormous fluted Ionic columns
There seeps from heavily jowled or hawk-like foreign faces
  The guttural sorrow of the refugees.

LONDON RAIN

The rain of London pimples
The ebony street with white
And the neon-lamps of London
Stain the canals of night
And the park becomes a jungle
In the alchemy of night.

My wishes turn to violent
Horses black as coal—
The randy mares of fancy,
The stallions of the soul—
Eager to take the fences
That fence about my soul.

Across the countless chimneys
The horses ride and across
The country to the channel
Where warning beacons toss,

To a place where God and No-God
Play at pitch and toss.

Whichever wins I am happy
For God will give me bliss
But No-God will absolve me
From all I do amiss
And I need not suffer conscience
If the world was made amiss.

Under God we can reckon
On pardon when we fall
But if we are under No-God
Nothing will matter at all,
Adultery and murder
Will count for nothing at all.

So reinforced by logic
As having nothing to lose
My lust goes riding horseback
To ravish where I choose,
To burgle all the turrets
Of beauty as I choose.

But now the rain gives over
Its dance upon the town,
Logic and lust together
Come dimly tumbling down,
And neither God nor No-God
Is either up or down.

The argument was wilful,
The alternatives untrue,
We need no metaphysics
To sanction what we do
Or to muffle us in comfort
From what we did not do.

Whether the living river
Began in bog or lake,
The world is what was given,

The world is what we make.
And we only can discover
Life in the life we make.

So let the water sizzle
Upon the gleaming slates,
There will be sunshine after
When the rain abates
And rain returning duly
When the sun abates.

My wishes now come homeward,
Their gallopings in vain,
Logic and lust are quiet
And again it starts to rain;
Falling asleep I listen
To the falling London rain.

THE CLOSING ALBUM

I

Dublin

Grey brick upon brick,
Declamatory bronze
On sombre pedestals—
O'Connell, Grattan, Moore—
And the brewery tugs and the swans
On the balustraded stream
And the bare bones of a fanlight
Over a hungry door
And the air soft on the cheek
And porter running from the taps
With a head of yellow cream
And Nelson on his pillar
Watching his world collapse.

This was never my town,
I was not born nor bred
Nor schooled here and she will not
Have me alive or dead

But yet she holds my mind
With her seedy elegance,
With her gentle veils of rain
And all her ghosts that walk
And all that hide behind
Her Georgian façades—
The catcalls and the pain,
The glamour of her squalor,
The bravado of her talk.

The lights jig in the river
With a concertina movement
And the sun comes up in the morning
Like barley-sugar on the water
And the mist on the Wicklow hills
Is close, as close
As the peasantry were to the landlord,
As the Irish to the Anglo-Irish,
As the killer is close one moment
To the man he kills,
Or as the moment itself
Is close to the next moment.

She is not an Irish town
And she is not English,
Historic with guns and vermin
And the cold renown
Of a fragment of Church latin,
Of an oratorical phrase.
But O the days are soft,
Soft enough to forget
The lesson better learnt,
The bullet on the wet
Streets, the crooked deal,
The steel behind the laugh,
The Four Courts burnt.

Fort of the Dane,
Garrison of the Saxon,
Augustan capital
Of a Gaelic nation,
Appropriating all

The alien brought,
You give me time for thought
And by a juggler's trick
You poise the toppling hour—
O greyness run to flower,
Grey stone, grey water
And brick upon grey brick.

II

Cushendun

Fuchsia and ragweed and the distant hills
Made as it were out of clouds and sea:
All night the bay is plashing and the moon
   Marks the break of the waves.

Limestone and basalt and a whitewashed house
With passages of great stone flags
And a walled garden with plums on the wall
   And a bird piping in the night.

Forgetfulness: brass lamps and copper jugs
And home-made bread and the smell of turf or flax
And the air a glove and the water lathering easy
   And convolvulus in the hedge.

Only in the dark green room beside the fire
With the curtains drawn against the winds and waves
There is a little box with a well-bred voice:
   What a place to talk of War.

III

Sligo and Mayo

In Sligo the country was soft; there were turkeys
   Gobbling under sycamore trees
And the shadows of clouds on the mountains moving
   Like browsing cattle at ease.

And little distant fields were sprigged with haycocks
   And splashed against a white

Roadside cottage a welter of nasturtium
   Deluging the sight,

And pullets pecking the flies from around the eyes of heifers
   Sitting in farmyard mud
Among hydrangeas and the falling ear-rings
   Of fuchsias red as blood.

But in Mayo the tumbledown walls went leap-frog
   Over the moors,
The sugar and salt in the pubs were damp in the casters
   And the water was brown as beer upon the shores

Of desolate loughs, and stumps of hoary bog-oak
   Stuck up here and there
And as the twilight filtered on the heather
   Water-music filled the air,

And when the night came down upon the bogland
   With all-enveloping wings
The coal-black turfstacks rose against the darkness
   Like the tombs of nameless kings.

IV

Galway

   O the crossbones of Galway,
   The hollow grey houses,
   The rubbish and sewage,
   The grass-grown pier,
   And the dredger grumbling
   All night in the harbour:
   The war came down on us here.

   Salmon in the Corrib
   Gently swaying
   And the water combed out
   Over the weir
   And a hundred swans
   Dreaming on the harbour:
   The war came down on us here.

The night was gay
With the moon's music
But Mars was angry
On the hills of Clare
And September dawned
Upon willows and ruins:
The war came down on us here.

V

Why, now it has happened,
Should the clock go on striking to the firedogs
And why should the rooks be blown upon the evening
Like burnt paper in a chimney?

And why should the sea maintain its turbulence,
  Its elegance,
And draw a film of muslin down the sand
With each receding wave?

And why, now it has happened,
Should the atlas still be full of the maps of countries
We never shall see again?

And why, now it has happened,
And doom all night is lapping at the door,
Should I remember that I ever met you—
Once in another world?

August–September, 1939

MEETING POINT

Time was away and somewhere else
There were two glasses and two chair
And two people with the one pulse
(Somebody stopped the moving stairs):
Time was away and somewhere else.

And they were neither up nor down
The stream's music did not stop
Flowing through heather, limpid brown,

[189]

Although they sat in a coffee shop
And they were neither up nor down.

The bell was silent in the air
Holding its inverted poise—
Between the clang and clang a flower,
A brazen calyx of no noise:
The bell was silent in the air.

The camels crossed the miles of sand
That stretched around the cups and plates;
The desert was their own, they planned
To portion out the stars and dates:
The camels crossed the miles of sand.

Time was away and somewhere else.
The waiter did not come, the clock
Forgot them and the radio waltz
Came out like water from a rock:
Time was away and somewhere else.

Her fingers flicked away the ash
That bloomed again in tropic trees:
Not caring if the markets crash
When they had forests such as these,
Her fingers flicked away the ash.

God or whatever means the Good
Be praised that time can stop like this,
That what the heart has understood
Can verify in the body's peace
God or whatever means the Good.

Time was away and she was here
And life no longer what it was,
The bell was silent in the air
And all the room a glow because
Time was away and she was here.

A TOAST

The slurred and drawled and crooning sounds,
The blurred and suave and sidling smells,
The webs of dew, the bells of buds,
The sun going down in crimson suds—
    This is on me and these are yours.

The bland and sculped and urgent beasts,
The here and there and nowhere birds,
The tongues of fire, the words of foam,
The curdling stars in the night's dome—
    This is on me and these are yours.

The face and grace and muscle of man
The balance of his body and mind,
Who keeps a trump behind his brain
Till instinct flicks it out again—
    This is on me and these are yours.

The courage of eyes, the craft of hands,
The gay feet, the pulse of hope,
The will that flings a rope—though hard—
To catch the future off its guard—
    This is on me and these are yours.

The luck and pluck and plunge of blood,
The wealth and spilth and sport of breath,
And sleep come down like death above
The fever and the peace of love—
    This is on me and these are yours.

ORDER TO VIEW

It was a big house, bleak;
Grass on the drive;
We had been there before
But memory, weak in front of
A blistered door, could find
Nothing alive now;
The shrubbery dripped, a crypt

[191]

Of leafmould dreams; a tarnished
Arrow over an empty stable
Shifted a little in the almost wind,

And wishes were unable
To rise; on the garden wall
The pear trees had come loose
From rotten loops; one wish,
A rainbow bubble, rose,
Faltered, broke in the dull
Air—What was the use?
The bell-pull would not pull
And the whole place, one might
Have supposed, was deadly ill:
The world was closed,

And remained closed until
A sudden angry tree
Shook itself like a setter
Flouncing out of a pond
And beyond the sombre line
Of limes a cavalcade
Of clouds rose like a shout of
Defiance. Near at hand
Somewhere in a loose-box
A horse neighed
And all the curtains flew out of
The windows; the world was open.

NOVELETTES

I

The Old Story

The old story is true of charms fading;
He knew her first before her charm was mellow—
Slim; surprise in her eyes; like a woodland creature
Crept abroad who found the world amazing,

Who, afterwards maturing, yet was dainty,
Light on her feet and gentle with her fingers;

Put on a little flesh, became an easy
Spreadeagled beauty for Renaissance painters.

And then she went; he did not see her after
Until by the shore of a cold sea in winter
With years behind her and the waves behind her
Drubbing the memory up and down the pebbles.

Flotsam and wrack; the bag of old emotions;
Watch in the swirl her ten years back reflections—
White as a drowning hand, then gone for ever;
Here she stands who was twenty and is thirty.

The same but different and he found the difference
A surgeon's knife without an anaesthetic;
He had known of course that this happens
But had not guessed the pain of it or the panic,

And could not say 'My love', could hardly
Say anything at all, no longer knowing
Whom he was talking to but watched the water
Massing for action on the cold horizon.

II

Les Sylphides

Life in a day: he took his girl to the ballet;
Being shortsighted himself could hardly see it—
   The white skirts in the grey
   Glade and the swell of the music
   Lifting the white sails.

Calyx upon calyx, canterbury bells in the breeze
The flowers on the left mirror to the flowers on the right
   And the naked arms above
   The powdered faces moving
   Like seaweed in a pool.

Now, he thought, we are floating—ageless, oarless—
Now there is no separation, from now on
   You will be wearing white
   Satin and a red sash
   Under the waltzing trees.

But the music stopped, the dancers took their curtain,
The river had come to a lock—a shuffle of programmes—
    And we cannot continue down
    Stream unless we are ready
    To enter the lock and drop.

So they were married—to be the more together—
And found they were never again so much together,
    Divided by the morning tea,
    By the evening paper,
    By children and tradesmen's bills.

Waking at times in the night she found assurance
In his regular breathing but wondered whether
    It was really worth it and where
    The river had flowed away
    And where were the white flowers.

III

The Gardener

He was not able to read or write,
He did odd jobs on gentlemen's places
Cutting the hedge or hoeing the drive
    With the smile of a saint,
    With the pride of a feudal chief,
    For he was not quite all there.

Crippled by rheumatism
By the time his hair was white,
He would reach the garden by twelve
    His legs in soiled puttees,
    A clay pipe in his teeth,
    A tiny flag in his cap,
    A white cat behind him,
    And his eyes a cornflower blue.

And between the clack of the shears
Or the honing of the scythe
Or the rattle of the rake on the gravel
He would talk to amuse the children,

[194]

He would talk to himself or the cat
Or the robin waiting for worms
Perched on the handle of the spade;
Would remember snatches of verse
From the elementary school
About a bee and a wasp
Or the cat by the barndoor spinning;
And would talk about himself for ever—
You would never find his like—
Always in the third person;
And would level his stick like a gun
(With a glint in his eye)
Saying 'Now I'm a Frenchman'—
He was not quite right in the head.

He believed in God—
The Good Fellow Up There—
And he used a simile of Homer
Watching the falling leaves,
And every year he waited for the Twelfth of July,
Cherishing his sash and his fife
For the carnival of banners and drums.
He was always claiming but never
Obtaining his old age pension,
For he did not know his age.
And his rheumatism at last
Kept him out of the processions.
And he came to work in the garden
Later and later in the day,
Leaving later at night;
In the damp dark of the night
At ten o'clock or later
You could hear him mowing the lawn,
The mower moving forward,
And backward, forward and backward
For he mowed while standing still;
He was not quite up to the job.

But he took a pride in the job,
He kept a bowl of cold
Tea in the crotch of a tree,
Always enjoyed his food

And enjoyed honing the scythe
And making the potato drills
And putting the peasticks in;
And enjoyed the noise of the corncrake,
And the early hawthorn hedge
Peppered black and green,
And the cut grass dancing in the air—
Happy as the day was long.

Till his last sickness took him
And he could not leave his house
And his eyes lost their colour
And he sat by the little range
With a finch in a cage and a framed
Certificate of admission
Into the Orange Order,
And his speech began to wander
And memory ebbed
Leaving upon the shore
Odd shells and heads of wrack
And his soul went out on the ebbing
Tide in a trim boat
To find the Walls of Derry
Or the land of the Ever Young.

IV

Christina

It all began so easy
With bricks upon the floor
Building motley houses
And knocking down your houses
And always building more.

The doll was called Christina,
Her under-wear was lace,
She smiled while you dressed her
And when you then undressed her
She kept a smiling face.

Until the day she tumbled
And broke herself in two

And her legs and arms were hollow
And her yellow head was hollow
Behind her eyes of blue.

. . . . .

He went to bed with a lady
Somewhere seen before,
He heard the name Christina
And suddenly saw Christina
Dead on the nursery floor.

V

Provence

It is a decade now since he and she
Spent September in Provence: the vineyard
Was close about the house; mosquitoes and cicadas
Garrulous day and night; and by the sea
Thighs and shoulders tanning themselves and one
Gay old man in particular who never
Missed a day, a glutton for the sun,
But did not bathe. He and she with swimming
Every noon were wild for food; a Basque
Woman cooked on charcoal—aubergine with garlic,
And there were long green grapes exploding on the palate
And smelling of eau de Cologne. They had nothing to ask
Except that it should go on. Watching the vintage—
A file of bullock carts and the muzzle of each
Animal munching purple—he suddenly said
'We must get married soon.' Down on the beach
His wife and three of his three children dead,
An old man lay in the sun, perfectly happy.

VI

The Preacher

He carried a ball of darkness with him, unrolled it
To find his way by in streets and rooms,
Every train or boat he took was Charon's ferry,
He never left the Catacombs;

He never smiled but spun his strands of black
Among the secular crowd who, when he tripped their feet,
Saw their own faces in the wet street, saw
Their hell beneath the street.

Among old iron, cinders, sizzling dumps,
A world castrated, amputated, trepanned,
He walked in the lost acres crying 'Repent
For the Kingdom of Death is at hand'.

He took the books of pagan art and read
Between the lines or worked them out to prove
Humanism a palimpsest and God's
Anger a more primal fact than love.

And in the city at night where drunken song
Climbed the air like tendrils of vine
He bared a knife and slashed the roots and laid
Another curse on Cain. The sign

Of the cross between his eyes, his mouth drawn down,
He passed the flower-sellers and all
The roses reeked of an abattoir, the gardenias
Became the décor of a funeral.

His hands were always clenched, an eagle
Riveted on a world of vice;
Going upstairs he built, block upon block,
An Aztec pyramid of sacrifice.

Going upstairs to die in a bare room
He tried to square his accounts; lying in bed
He summoned home his deeds, drew back
Sixty years' expended thread,

Pulled it in through the chink beneath the door,
Wrapped it around him, all
His faith and his despair a ball of black
And he himself at the centre of the ball.

DÉBÂCLE

They had built it up—but not for this the lean
And divinatory years,
The red-eyed pioneers
Facing the dark and making the desert green.

Not for this the pale inventor's lamp
Alight till dawn, the hands
Weary with sifting sands,
The burst of nuggets on the miners' camp.

Vision and sinew made it of light and stone;
Not grateful nor enchanted
Their heirs took it for granted
Having a world—a world that was all their own.

At sundown now the windows had gone gold
For half an hour; a quick
Chill came off the brick
Walls and the flesh was suddenly old and cold.

Crumbling between the fingers, under the feet,
Crumbling behind the eyes,
Their world gives way and dies
And something twangs and breaks at the end of the street.

DEATH OF AN ACTRESS

I see from the paper that Florrie Forde is dead—
Collapsed after singing to wounded soldiers,
At the age of sixty-five. The American notice
Says no doubt all that need be said

About this one-time chorus girl; whose rôle
For more than forty stifling years was giving
Sexual, sentimental, or comic entertainment,
A gaudy posy for the popular soul.

Plush and cigars: she waddled into the lights,
Old and huge and painted, in velvet and tiara,

Her voice gone but around her head an aura
Of all her vanilla-sweet forgotten vaudeville nights.

With an elephantine shimmy and a sugared wink
She threw a trellis of Dorothy Perkins roses
Around an audience come from slum and suburb
And weary of the tea-leaves in the sink;

Who found her songs a rainbow leading west
To the home they never had, to the chocolate Sunday
Of boy and girl, to cowslip time, to the never-
Ending weekend Islands of the Blest.

In the Isle of Man before the war before
The present one she made a ragtime favourite
Of 'Tipperary', which became the swan-song
Of troop-ships on a darkened shore;

And during Munich sang her ancient quiz
Of *Where's Bill Bailey?* and the chorus answered,
Muddling through and glad to have no answer:
Where's Bill Bailey? How do *we* know where he is!

Now on a late and bandaged April day
In a military hospital Miss Florrie
Forde has made her positively last appearance
And taken her bow and gone correctly away.

Correctly. For she stood
For an older England, for children toddling
Hand in hand while the day was bright. Let the wren and robin
Gently with leaves cover the Babes in the Wood.

BAR-ROOM MATINS

Popcorn peanuts clams and gum:
We whose Kingdom has not come
Have mouths like men but still are dumb

Who only deal with Here and Now
As circumstances may allow:
The sponsored programme tells us how.

[200]

And yet the preachers tell the pews
What man misuses God can use:
Give us this day our daily news

That we may hear behind the brain
And through the sullen heat's migraine
The atavistic voice of Cain:

'Who entitled you to spy
From your easy heaven? Am I
My brother's keeper? Let him die.'

And God in words we soon forget
Answers through the radio set:
'The curse is on his forehead yet.'

Mass destruction, mass disease:
We thank thee, Lord, upon our knees
That we were born in times like these

When with doom tumbling from the sky
Each of us has an alibi
For doing nothing—Let him die.

Let him die, his death will be
A drop of water in the sea,
A journalist's commodity.

Pretzels crackers chips and beer:
Death is something that we fear
But it titillates the ear.

Anchovy almond ice and gin:
All shall die though none can win;
Let the Untergang begin—

Die the soldiers, die the Jews,
And all the breadless homeless queues.
Give us this day our daily news.

FLIGHT OF THE HEART

Heart, my heart, what will you do?
There are five lame dogs and one deaf-mute
All of them with demands on you.

I will build myself a copper tower
With four ways out and no way in
But mine the glory, mine the power.

And what if the tower should shake and fall
With three sharp taps and one big bang?
What would you do with yourself at all?

I would go in the cellar and drink the dark
With two quick sips and one long pull,
Drunk as a lord and gay as a lark.

But what when the cellar roof caves in
With one blue flash and nine old bones?
How, my heart, will you save your skin?

I will go back where I belong
With one foot first and both eyes blind,
I will go back where I belong
In the fore-being of mankind.

REFUGEES

With prune-dark eyes, thick lips, jostling each other
These, disinterred from Europe, throng the deck
To watch their hope heave up in steel and concrete
Powerful but delicate as a swan's neck,

Thinking, each of them, the worst is over
And we do not want any more to be prominent or rich,
Only to be ourselves, to be unmolested
And make ends meet—an ideal surely which

Here if anywhere is feasible. Their glances
Like wavering antennae feel

Around the sliding limber towers of Wall Street
And count the numbered docks and gingerly steal

Into the hinterland of their own future
Behind this excessive annunciation of towers,
Tracking their future selves through a continent of strangeness.
The liner moves to the magnet; the quay flowers

With faces of people's friends. But these are mostly
Friendless and all they look to meet
Is a secretary who holds his levée among ledgers,
Tells them to take a chair and wait . . .

And meanwhile the city will go on, regardless
Of any new arrival, trains like prayers
Radiating from stations haughty as cathedrals,
Tableaux of spring in milliners' windows, great affairs

Being endorsed on a vulcanite table, lines of washing
Feebly garish among grimy brick and dour
Iron fire-escapes; barrows of cement are rumbling
Up airy planks; a florist adds a flower

To a bouquet that is bound for somebody's beloved
Or for someone ill; in a sombre board-room great
Problems wait to be solved or shelved. The city
Goes on but you, you will probably find, must wait

Till something or other turns up. Something-or-Other
Becomes an expected angel from the sky;
But do not trust the sky, the blue that looks so candid
Is non-committal, frigid as a harlot's eye.

Gangways—the handclasp of the land. The resurrected,
The brisk or resigned Lazaruses, who want
Another chance, go trooping ashore. But chances
Are dubious. Fate is stingy, recalcitrant

And officialdom greets them blankly as they fumble
Their foreign-looking baggage; they still feel
The movement of the ship while through their imagination
The known and the unheard-of constellations wheel.

[203]

JEHU

Peace on New England, on the shingled white houses, on golden
Rod and the red Turkey carpet spikes of sumach. The little
American flags are flapping in the graveyard. Continuous
    Chorus of grasshoppers. Fleece
Of quiet around the mind. Honey-suckle, phlox and smoke-bush,
Hollyhocks and nasturtium and corn on the cob. And the pine
    wood
    Smelling of outmoded peace.

A king sat over the gate looking to the desert. A spiral
Of dust came toward him, a special messenger asking
Anxiously 'Is it peace?' The heavy eyebrows lowered,
    He answered 'What have I
To do with peace?' and the messenger mopped the sweat and
    obedient
Took his place behind the king who still sat scanning
    Miles of desert and sky.

Negative prospect; sand in the lungs; blood in the sand; deceiving
Mirage of what were once ideals or even motives
And in this desert even a ghost can hardly
    Live—but in the long run what
Have I to do with life? He got up blandly, harnessed his horses
And furiously drove, his eyeballs burning and the chariot's
    Axles burning hot.

Someone sat in a window with a new coiffure, her raddled
Face, a Muse's possibly once but now a harlot's,
Smirked at the charioteer who, looking past her, signalled
    To the maids to throw her down
And they threw her down and the wheels went over her ribs and
    the carcase,
The one-time inspiration of artists, the toast of kings, was
    abandoned
    To the scavenger dogs of the town.

And now the sand blows over Kent and Wales where we may
    shortly
Learn the secret of the desert's purge, of the mad driving,
The cautery of the gangrened soul, though we are not certain

[204]

Whether we shall stand beside
The charioteer, the surgeon, or shall be one with the pampered
Queen who tittered in the face of death, unable to imagine
    The meaning of the flood tide.

THE DEATH-WISH

It being in this life forbidden to move
Too lightly, people, over-cautious, contrive
To save their lives by weighting them with dead
Habits, hopes, beliefs, anything not alive,
Till all this ballast of unreality sinks
The boat and all our thinking gurgles down
Into the deep sea that never thinks.

Which being so, it is not surprising that
Some in their impatience jump the rails,
Refusing to wait the communal failure, preferring
The way the madman or the meteor fails,
Deceiving themselves to think their death uncommon,
And mad to possess the unpossessable sea
As a man in spring desires to die in woman.

AUTOBIOGRAPHY

In my childhood trees were green
And there was plenty to be seen.

Come back early or never come.

My father made the walls resound,
He wore his collar the wrong way round.

Come back early or never come.

My mother wore a yellow dress;
Gently, gently, gentleness.

Come back early or never come.

[205]

When I was five the black dreams came;
Nothing after was quite the same.

Come back early or never come.

The dark was talking to the dead;
The lamp was dark beside my bed.

Come back early or never come.

When I woke they did not care;
Nobody, nobody was there.

Come back early or never come.

When my silent terror cried,
Nobody, nobody replied.

Come back early or never come.

I got up; the chilly sun
Saw me walk away alone.

Come back early or never come.

CONVERSATION

Ordinary people are peculiar too:
Watch the vagrant in their eyes
Who sneaks away while they are talking with you
Into some black wood behind the skull,
Following un-, or other, realities,
Fishing for shadows in a pool.

But sometimes the vagrant comes the other way
Out of their eyes and into yours
Having mistaken you perhaps for yesterday
Or for tomorrow night, a wood in which
He may pick up among the pine-needles and burrs
The lost purse, the dropped stitch.

[206]

Vagrancy however is forbidden; ordinary men
Soon come back to normal, look you straight
In the eyes as if to say 'It will not happen again',
Put up a barrage of common sense to baulk
Intimacy but by mistake interpolate
Swear-words like roses in their talk.

THE EAR

There are many sounds which are neither music nor voice,
There are many visitors in masks or in black glasses
Climbing the spiral staircase of the ear. The choice
Of callers is not ours. Behind the hedge
Of night they wait to pounce. A train passes,
The thin and audible end of a dark wedge.

We should like to lie alone in a deaf hollow
Cocoon of self where no person or thing would speak;
In fact we lie and listen as a man might follow
A will o' the wisp in an endless eyeless bog,
Follow the terrible drone of a cock chafer, or the bleak
Oracle of a barking dog.

EVENING IN CONNECTICUT

Equipoise: becalmed
Trees, a dome of kindness;
Only the scissory noise of the grasshoppers;
Only the shadows longer and longer.

The lawn a raft
In a sea of singing insects,
Sea without waves or mines or   remonitions:
Life on a china cup.

But turning. The trees turn
Soon to brocaded autumn.
Fall. The fall of dynasties; the emergence
Of sleeping kings from caves—

[207]

Beard over the breastplate,
Eyes not yet in focus, red
Hair on the back of the hands, unreal
Heraldic axe in the hands.

Unreal but still can strike.
And in defence we cannot call on the evening
Or the seeming-friendly woods—
Nature is not to be trusted,

Nature whose falls of snow,
Falling softer than catkins,
Bury the lost and over their grave a distant
Smile spreads in the sun.

Not to be trusted, no,
Deaf at the best; she is only
And always herself, Nature is only herself,
Only the shadows longer and longer.

ENTERED IN THE MINUTES

I

Barcelona in Wartime

In the Paralelo a one-legged
Man sat on the ground,
His one leg out before him,
Smiling. A sudden sound

Of crazy laughter shivered
The sunlight; overhead
A parrot in a window of aspidistras
Was laughing like the dead.

II

Business Men

The two men talking business
So easily in the train
Project themselves upon me
Just as the window pane

[208]

Reflects their faces, and I
Find myself in a trance
To hear two strangers talking
The same language for once.

III
Night Club

After the legshows and the brandies
And all the pick-me-ups for tired
Men there is a feeling
Something more is required.

The lights go down and eyes
Look up across the room;
Salome comes in, bearing
The head of God knows whom.

IV
Didymus

Refusing to fall in love with God, he gave
Himself to the love of created things,
Accepting only what he could see, a river
Full of the shadows of swallows' wings

That dipped and skimmed the water; he would not
Ask where the water ran or why.
When he died a swallow seemed to plunge
Into the reflected, the wrong sky.

PLAIN SPEAKING

In the beginning and in the end the only decent
Definition is tautology: man is man,
Woman woman, and tree tree, and world world,
Slippery, self-contained; catch as catch can.

Which when caught between the beginning and end
Turn other than themselves, their entities unfurled,

o   [209]

Flapping and overlapping—a tree becomes
A talking tower, and a woman becomes world.

Catch them in nets, but either the thread is thin
Or the mesh too big or, thirdly, the fish die
And man from false communion dwindles back
Into a mere man under a mere sky.

But dream was dream and love was love and what
Happened happened—even if the judge said
It should have been otherwise—and glitter glitters
And I am I although the dead are dead.

PERDITA

The glamour of the end attic, the smell of old
Leather trunks—Perdita, where have you been
Hiding all these years? Somewhere or other a green
Flag is waving under an iron vault
And a brass bell is the herald of green country
And the wind is in the wires and the broom is gold.

Perdita, what became of all the things
We said that we should do? The cobwebs cover
The labels of Tyrol. The time is over-
Due and in some metropolitan station
Among the clank of cans and the roistering files
Of steam the caterpillars wait for wings.

THE DOWSER

An inkling only, whisper in the bones
Of strange weather on the way,
Twitch of the eyelid, shadow of a passing bird.
It is coming some time soon.

What? or who? An inkling only,
Adumbration of unknown glory
Drew to the feet of Saint Francis where the waves
Broke, an army of fish.

Humming wires; feel of a lost limb
Cut off in another life;
Trance on the tripod; effulgence
Of headlights beyond the rise in the road.

And the hazel rod bent, dipping, contorting,
Snake from sleep; they were right
Who remembered some old fellow
(Dead long ago) who remembered the well.

'Dig', he said, 'dig',
Holding the lantern, the rod bent double,
And we dug respecting his knowledge,
Not waiting for morning, keenly

Dug: the clay was heavy
Two hours heavy before
The clink of a spade revealed
What or whom? We expected a well—

A well? A mistake somewhere . . .
More of a tomb . . . Anyway we backed away
From the geyser suddenly of light that erupted, sprayed
Rocketing over the sky azaleas and gladioli.

THE RETURN

All the lost interpretations,
All the unconsummated consummations,
All the birds that flew and left the big sky empty
Come back throwing shadows on our patience.

Bethlehem is desolate and the stables
Cobwebbed, mute; below each Tower of Babel's
Sentrydom of night, inside the bleak
Glass of cafés chairs are piled on tables.

Notwithstanding which, notwithstanding
The hospital—the icicles round the landing—
Expecting Birth, we know that it will come
Sooner or later, banding

Together the good daemons, the defiance
And lolloping vulcanite of sea-lions,
The harlequinade of water through a sluice,
Tigers in the air, and in the teeth of science

The acclamation of earth's returning daughter,
Jonquils out of hell, and after
Hell the imperative of joy, the dancing
Fusillade of sunlight on the water.

CRADLE SONG FOR ELEANOR

Sleep, my darling, sleep;
    The pity of it all
Is all we compass if
    We watch disaster fall.
Put off your twenty-odd
    Encumbered years and creep
Into the only heaven,
    The robbers' cave of sleep.

The wild grass will whisper,
    Lights of passing cars
Will streak across your dreams
    And fumble at the stars;
Life will tap the window
    Only too soon again,
Life will have her answer—
    Do not ask her when.

When the winsome bubble
    Shivers, when the bough
Breaks, will be the moment
    But not here or now.
Sleep and, asleep, forget
    The watchers on the wall
Awake all night who know
    The pity of it all.

VII

1941—1944

TO HEDLI

Because the velvet image,
Because the lilting measure,
No more convey my meaning
I am compelled to use
Such words as disabuse
My mind of casual pleasure
And turn it towards a centre—
A zone which others too
And you
May choose to enter.

PRAYER BEFORE BIRTH

I am not yet born; O hear me.
Let not the bloodsucking bat or the rat or the stoat or the
    club-footed ghoul come near me.

I am not yet born, console me.
I fear that the human race may with tall walls wall me,
    with strong drugs dope me, with wise lies lure me,
        on black racks rack me, in blood-baths roll me.

I am not yet born; provide me
With water to dandle me, grass to grow for me, trees to talk
    to me, sky to sing to me, birds and a white light
        in the back of my mind to guide me.

I am not yet born; forgive me
For the sins that in me the world shall commit, my words
    when they speak me, my thoughts when they think me,
        my treason engendered by traitors beyond me,
            my life when they murder by means of my
                hands, my death when they live me.

I am not yet born; rehearse me
In the parts I must play and the cues I must take when
    old men lecture me, bureaucrats hector me, mountains
        frown at me, lovers laugh at me, the white
            waves call me to folly and the desert calls
                me to doom and the beggar refuses
                    my gift and my children curse me.

I am not yet born; O hear me,
Let not the man who is beast or who thinks he is God
    come near me.

I am not yet born; O fill me
With strength against those who would freeze my
    humanity, would dragoon me into a lethal automaton,
        would make me a cog in a machine, a thing with
            one face, a thing, and against all those
                who would dissipate my entirety, would
                    blow me like thistledown hither and

thither or hither and thither
like water held in the
hands would spill me.

Let them not make me a stone and let them not spill me.
Otherwise kill me.

PRECURSORS

O that the rain would come—the rain in big battalions—
Or thunder flush the hedge a more clairvoyant green
Or wind walk in and whip us and strip us or booming
Harvest moon transmute this muted scene.

But all is flat, matt, mute, unlivened, unexpectant,
And none but insects dare to sing or pirouette;
That Man is a dancer is an anachronism—
Who has forgotten his steps or hardly learnt them yet.

Yet one or two we have known who had the gusto
Of wind or water-spout, and one or two
Who carry an emerald lamp behind their faces
And—during thunder-storms—the light comes shining through.

EXPLORATIONS

The whale butting through scarps of moving marble,
The tapeworm probing the intestinal darkness,
The swallows drawn collectively to their magnet,
    These are our prototypes and yet,
Though we may envy them still, they are merely patterns
    To wonder at—and forget.

For the ocean-carver, cumbrous but unencumbered,
Who tired of land looked for his freedom and frolic in water,
Though he succeeded, has failed; it is only instinct
    That plots his graph and he,
Though appearing to us a free and a happy monster, is merely
    An appanage of the sea.

[216]

And the colourless blind worm, triumphantly self-degraded,
Who serves as an image to men of the worst adjustment—
Oxymoron of parasitical glory—
    Cannot even be cursed,
Lacking the only pride of his way of life, not knowing
    That he has chosen the worst.

So even that legion of birds who appear so gladly
Purposeful, with air in their bones, enfranchised
Citizens of the sky and never at odds with
    The season or out of line,
Can be no model to us; their imputed purpose
    Is a foregone design—

And ours is not. For we are unique, a conscious
Hoping and therefore despairing creature, the final
Anomaly of the world, we can learn no method ·
    From whales or birds or worms;
Our end is our own to be won by our own endeavour
    And held on our own terms.

MUTATIONS

If there has been no spiritual change of kind
Within our species since Cro-Magnon Man
And none is looked for now while the millennia cool,
Yet each of us has known mutations in the mind
When the world jumped and what had been a plan
Dissolved and rivers gushed from what had seemed a pool.

For every static world that you or I impose
Upon the real one must crack at times and new
Patterns from new disorders open like a rose
And old assumptions yield to new sensation;
The Stranger in the wings is waiting for his cue,
The fuse is always laid to some annunciation.

Surprises keep us living: as when the first light
Surprised our infant eyes or as when, very small,
Clutching our parents' hands we toddled down a road

Where all was blank and windless both to touch and sight
Had we not suddenly raised our eyes which showed
The long grass blowing wild on top of the high wall.

For it is true, surprises break and make,
As when the baton falls and all together the hands
On the fiddle-bows are pistons, or when crouched above
His books the scholar suddenly understands
What he has thought for years—or when the inveterate rake
Finds for once that his lust is becoming love.

BROTHER FIRE

When our brother Fire was having his dog's day
Jumping the London streets with millions of tin cans
Clanking at his tail, we heard some shadow say
'Give the dog a bone'—and so we gave him ours;
Night after night we watched him slaver and crunch away
The beams of human life, the tops of topless towers.

Which gluttony of his for us was Lenten fare
Who mother-naked, suckled with sparks, were chill
Though cotted in a grill of sizzling air
Striped like a convict—black, yellow and red;
Thus were we weaned to knowledge of the Will
That wills the natural world but wills us dead.

O delicate walker, babbler, dialectician Fire,
O enemy and image of ourselves,
Did we not on those mornings after the All Clear,
When you were looting shops in elemental joy
And singing as you swarmed up city block and spire,
Echo your thought in ours? 'Destroy! Destroy!'

THE TROLLS

(Written after an air-raid, April 1941)

(i)

In the misty night humming to themselves like morons
They ramble and rumble over the roof-tops, stumble and
     shamble from pile to pillar,

[218]

In clodhopping boots that crunch the stars
And a blank smirk on their faces:
   Pretty Polly won't die yet.

Skittle-alley horseplay, congurgitation . . . they don't know
      what they are doing,
All they can do is stutter and lurch, riding their hobby, grinding
Their hobnails into our bodies, into our brains, into the domed
Head where the organ music lingers:
   Pretty Polly won't die yet.

Here they come—I thought we had lost them—
Here they come once more and once too many with their rough
      and
Tumble antics, here they
Are, they are, they ARE:
   Pretty Polly won't die yet,
   Oh, won't she?

(ii)

Than which not any could be found other
And outside which is less than nothing—
This, as they call it, life.
But such as it is, gurgling and tramping, licking their thumbs
      before they
Turn the pages over, tear them out, they
Wish it away, they
Puff with enormous cheeks, put paid to
Hours and minutes—thistledown in the void.

(iii)

Death has a look of finality;
We think we lose something but if it were not for
Death we should have nothing to lose, existence
Because unlimited would merely be existence
Without incarnate value. The trolls can occasion
Our death but they are not able
To use it as we can use it.
Fumbling and mumbling they try to
Spell out Death correctly; they are not able.

[219]

Than which not any. Time
Swings on the poles of death
And the latitude and the longitude of life
Are fixed by death, and the value
Of every organism, act and moment
Is, thanks to death, unique.

(v)

This then is our answer under
The crawl of lava, a last
Shake of the fist at the vanishing sky, at the hulking
Halfwit demons who rape and slobber, who assume
That when we are killed no more will be heard of us—
Silence of men and trolls' triumph.
A wrong—in the end—assumption.
Barging and lunging out of the clouds, a daft
Descent of no-good gods, they think to
Be rid for ever of the voice of men but they happen
To be trying what even trolls
Can never accomplish, they happen
To be—for all their kudos—
Wrong, wrong in the end.

TROLL'S COURTSHIP

I am a lonely Troll after my gala night;
I have knocked down houses and stamped my feet on the people's
        heart,
I have trundled round the sky with the executioner's cart
And dropped my bait for corpses, watched them bite,
But I am a lonely Troll—nothing in the end comes right.

In a smoking and tinkling dawn with fires and broken glass
I am a lonely Troll; my tributes are in vain
To Her to whom if I had even a human brain
I might have reached but, as it is, the epochs pass
And leave me unfulfilled, no further than I was.

Because I cannot accurately conceive
Any ideal, even ideal Death,
My curses and my boasts are merely a waste of breath,
My lusts and lonelinesses grunt and heave
And blunder round among the ruins that I leave.

Yet from the lubber depths of my unbeing I
Aspire to Her who was my Final Cause but who
Is always somewhere else and not to be spoken to,
Is always nowhere: which is in the long run why
I make for nowhere, make a shambles of the sky.

Nostalgia for the breasts that never gave nor could
Give milk or even warmth has desolated me,
Clutching at shadows of my nullity
That slink and mutter through the leafless wood
Which thanks to me is dead, is dead for good.

A cone of ice enclosing liquid fire,
Utter negation in a positive form,
That would be how She is, the nadir and the norm
Of dissolution and the constant pyre
Of all desirable things—that is what I desire

And therefore cry to Her with the voice of broken bells
To come, visibly, palpably, to come,
Gluing my ear to gutted walls but walls are dumb,
All I can catch is a gurgle as of the sea in shells
But not Her voice—for She is always somewhere else.

THE REVENANT

(The last lyric from a Song Cycle: a girl speaks to her dead lover)

The nearness of remoteness like a lion's eye,
    So near in a cage yet so far away,
In this death we are proud to die—
    The yellow eye of a beast of prey.

To die in a moment is a small thing
    Like a sea-shell in a quiet room,
Yet from that shell the sea will fling
    The thunder of uncharted doom.

So large, so small, so near, so far,
    So stark a prison, yet so free—
Nothing now can mend nor mar
    This death you have brought home to me.

The windows of our life were placed
    So that their panes were blurred with breath,
We never saw which way they faced
    But now they open wide on death.

The yellow eye of the beast will close,
    The stolen shell return to the sea;
I thank you, my love, for this repose,
    For the death you have brought home to me.

CONVOY

Together, keeping in line, slow as if hypnotised
Across the blackboard sea in sombre echelon
The food-ships draw their wakes. No Euclid could have devised
Neater means to a more essential end—
Unless the chalk breaks off, the convoy is surprised.

The cranks go up and down, the smoke-trails tendril out,
The precious cargoes creak, the signals clack,
All is under control and nobody need shout,
We are steady as we go, and on our flanks
The little whippet warships romp and scurry about.

This is a bit like us: the individual sets
A course for all his soul's more basic needs
Of love and pride-of-life, but sometimes he forgets
How much their voyage home depends upon pragmatic
And ruthless attitudes—destroyers and corvettes.

WHIT MONDAY

Their feet on London, their heads in the grey clouds,
The Bank (if you call it a holiday) Holiday crowds
Stroll from street to street, cocking an eye
For where the angel used to be in the sky;
But the Happy Future is a thing of the past and the street
Echoes to nothing but their dawdling feet.
The Lord's my shepherd—familiar words of myth
Stand up better to bombs than a granite monolith,
Perhaps there is something in them. *I'll not want*—
Not when I'm dead. *He makes me down to lie*—
Death my christening and fire my font—
The quiet (Thames or Don's or Salween's) *waters by*.

SWING-SONG

I'm only a wartime working girl,
The machine shop makes me deaf,
I have no prospects after the war
And *my* young man is in the R.A.F.
    K for Kitty calling P for Pruc . . .
    Bomb Doors Open . . .
    Over to You.

Night after night as he passes by
I wonder what he's gone to bomb
And I fancy in the jabber of the mad machines
That I hear him talking on the intercomm.
    K for Kitty calling P for Prue . . .
    Bomb Doors Open . . .
    Over to You.

So there's no one in the world, I sometimes think,
Such a wall flower as I
For I must talk to myself on the ground
While he is talking to his friends in the sky:
    K for Kitty calling P for Prue . . .
    Bomb Doors Open . . .
    Over to You.

[223]

BOTTLENECK

Never to fight unless from a pure motive
And for a clear end was his unwritten rule
Who had been in books and visions to a progressive school
And dreamt of barricades, yet being observant
Knew that that was not the way things are:
This man would never make a soldier or a servant.

When I saw him last, carving the longshore mist
With an ascetic profile, he was standing
Watching the troopship leave, he did not speak
But from his eyes there peered a furtive footsore envy
Of these who sailed away to make an opposed landing—
So calm because so young, so lethal because so meek.

Where he is now I could not say; he will,
The odds are, always be non-combatant
Being too violent in soul to kill
Anyone but himself, yet in his mind
A crowd of odd components mutter and press
For compromise with fact, longing to be combined
Into a working whole but cannot jostle through
The permanent bottleneck of his highmindedness.

NEUTRALITY

The neutral island facing the Atlantic,
The neutral island in the heart of man,
Are bitterly soft reminders of the beginnings
That ended before the end began.

Look into your heart, you will find a County Sligo,
A Knocknarea with for navel a cairn of stones,
You will find the shadow and sheen of a moleskin mountain
And a litter of chronicles and bones.

Look into your heart, you will find fermenting rivers,
Intricacies of gloom and glint,
You will find such ducats of dream and great doubloons of
    ceremony
As nobody today would mint.

But then look eastward from your heart, there bulks
A continent, close, dark, as archetypal sin,
While to the west off your own shores the mackerel
Are fat—on the flesh of your kin.

THE CONSCRIPT

Being so young he feels the weight of history
Like clay around his boots; he would, if he could, fly
In search of a future like a sycamore seed
But is prevented by his own Necessity,
His own yet alien, which, whatever he may plead,
To every question gives the same reply.

Choiceless therefore, driven from pillar to post,
Expiating his pedigree, fulfilling
An oracle whose returns grow less and less,
Bandied from camp to camp to practise killing
He fails even so at times to remain engrossed
And is aware, at times, of life's largesse.

From camp to camp, from Eocene to chalk,
He lives a paradox, lives in a groove
That runs dead straight to an ordained disaster
So that in two dimensions he must move
Like an automaton, yet his inward stalk
Vertically aspires and makes him his own master.

Hence, though on the flat his life has no
Promise but of diminishing returns,
By feeling down and upwards he can divine
That dignity which far above him burns
In stars that yet are his and which below
Stands rooted like a dolmen in his spine.

THE NEWS-REEL

Since Munich, what? A tangle of black film
Squirming like bait upon the floor of my mind
And scissors clicking daily. I am inclined

To pick these pictures now but will hold back
Till memory has elicited from this blind
Drama its threads of vision, the intrusions
Of value upon fact, that sudden unconfined
Wind of understanding that blew out
From people's hands and faces, undesigned
Evidence of design, that change of climate
Which did not last but happens often enough
To give us hope that fact is a façade
And that there is an organism behind
Its brittle littleness, a rhythm and a meaning,
Something half-conjectured and half-divined,
Something to give way to and so find.

NUTS IN MAY

May come up with bird-din
And May come up with sun-dint,
May come up with water-wheels
 And May come up with iris.

In the sun-peppered meadow the shepherds are old,
Their flutes are broken and their tales are told,
And their ears are deaf when the guns unfold
The new philosophy over the wold.

May come up with pollen of death,
May come up with cordite,
May come up with a chinagraph
 And May come up with a stopwatch.

In the high court of heaven Their tail-feathers shine
With cowspit and bullspit and spirits of wine,
They know no pity, being divine,
And They give no quarter to thine or mine.

May come up with Very lights,
May come up with duty,
May come up with a bouncing cheque,
 An acid-drop and a bandage.

[226]

Yes, angels are frigid and shepherds are dumb,
There is no holy water when the enemy come,
The trees are askew and the skies are a-hum
And you have to keep mum and go to it and die for your life and
   keep mum.

May come up with fiddle-bows,
May come up with blossom,
May come up the same again,
   The same again but different.

THE MIXER

With a pert moustache and a ready candid smile
He has played his way through twenty years of pubs,
Deckchairs, lounges, touchlines, junctions, homes,
And still as ever popular, he roams
Far and narrow, mimicking the style
Of other people's leisure, scattering stubs.

Colourless, when alone, and self-accused,
He is only happy in reflected light
And only real in the range of laughter;
Behind his eyes are shadows of a night
In Flanders but his mind long since refused
To let that time intrude on what came after.

So in this second war which is fearful too,
He cannot away with silence but has grown
Almost a cypher, like a Latin word
That many languages have made their own
Till it is worn and blunt and easy to construe
And often spoken but no longer heard.

NOSTALGIA

In cock-wattle sunset or grey
Dawn when the dagger
Points again of longing
For what was never home

[227]

We needs must turn away
From the voices that cry 'Come'—
That under-sea ding-donging.

Dingle-dongle, bells and bluebells,
Snapdragon solstice, lunar lull,
The wasp circling the honey
Or the lamp soft on the snow—
These are the times at which
The will is vulnerable,
The trigger-finger slow,
The spirit lonely.

These are the times at which
Aloneness is too ripe
When homesick for the hollow
Heart of the Milky Way
The soundless clapper calls
And we would follow
But earth and will are stronger
And nearer—and we stay.

BABEL

There was a tower that went before a fall.
    Can't we ever, my love, speak in the same language?
Its nerves grew worse and worse as it grew tall.
    Have we no aims in common?

As children we were bickering over beads—
    Can't we ever, my love, speak in the same language?
The more there are together, Togetherness recedes.
    Have we no aims in common?

Exiles all as we are in a foreign city,
    Can't we ever, my love, speak in the same language?
We cut each other's throats out of our great self-pity—
    Have we no aims in common?

Patriots, dreamers, die-hards, theoreticians, all,
    Can't we ever, my love, speak in the same language,
Or shall we go, still quarrelling over words, to the wall?
    Have we no aims in common?

SCHIZOPHRENE

Hearing offstage the taps filling the bath
The set dissolves to childhood—in her cot
Hearing that ominous relentless noise
Which the grown-ups have started, who are not
She knows, aware of what it means; it means
The Dark, the Flood, the Malice. It destroys
All other meanings—dolls or gingerbread;
It means a Will that wills all children dead.

Hearing the gasfire breathe monotonously
She waits for words but no words come, she lifts
A soapstone hand to smooth her hair and feels
The hand is someone else's— the scene shifts
To a cold desert where the wind has dropped
And the earth's movement stopped and something steals
Up from the grit through nerve and bone and vein
To flaunt its iron tendrils in her brain.

Hearing again the telegraph wires again
Humming again and always, she must lean
Against the humming post and search her mind
For what it is they say; in some latrine
She knows she wrote it first upon the wall
In self-incrimination, duly signed;
And, unrevoked since then, that signature
Runs round the world on wires, accusing her.

Hearing the church-bells too, she knows at once
That only she can hear them for it is no
Church or even belfry where they hang,
There are no ropes attached or ringers down below,
These bells are disembodied, they express
The claims of frozen Chaos and will clang
Till this and every other world shall melt
And Chaos be Itself and nothing felt.

Lastly, hearing the cock in the grey dawn
Crow once, crow twice, she shivers and dissolves
To someone else who in the hour of trial
Denied his Master and his guilt devolves

On her head only. If she could speak up,
She might even now atone for that denial
But the grey cock still crows and she knows why;
For she must still deny, deny, deny.

ALCOHOL

On golden seas of drink, so the Greek poet said,
Rich and poor are alike. Looking around in war
We watch the many who have returned to the dead
Ordering time-and-again the same-as-before:

Those Haves who cannot bear making a choice,
Those Have-nots who are bored with having nothing to choose,
Call for their drinks in the same tone of voice,
Find a factitious popular front in booze.

Another drink: Bacchylides was right
And self-deception golden—Serve him quick,
The siphon stutters in the archaic night,
The flesh is willing and the soul is sick.

Another drink: Adam is back in the Garden.
Another drink: the snake is back on the tree.
Let your brain go soft, your arteries will harden;
If God's a peeping tom he'll see what he shall see.

Another drink: Cain has slain his brother.
Another drink: Cain, they say, is cursed.
Another and another and another—
The beautiful ideologies have burst.

A bottle swings on a string. The matt-grey iron ship,
Which ought to have been the Future, sidles by
And with due auspices descends the slip
Into an ocean where no auspices apply.

Take away your slogans; give us something to swallow,
Give us beer or brandy or schnapps or gin;
This is the only road for the self-betrayed to follow—
The last way out that leads not out but in.

THE LIBERTINE

In the old days with married women's stockings
Twisted round his bedpost he felt himself a gay
Dog but now his liver has begun to groan,
Now that pick-ups are the order of the day:
O leave me easy, leave me alone.

Voluptuary in his 'teens and cynic in his twenties,
He ran through women like a child through growing hay
Looking for a lost toy whose capture might atone
For his own guilt and the cosmic disarray:
O leave me easy, leave me alone.

He never found the toy and has forgotten the faces,
Only remembers the props . . . a scent-spray
Beside the bed or a milk-white telephone
Or through the triple ninon the acrid trickle of day:
O leave me easy, leave me alone.

Long fingers over the gunwale, hair in a hair-net,
Furs in January, cartwheel hats in May,
And after the event the wish to be alone—
Angels, goddesses, bitches, all have edged away:
O leave me easy, leave me alone.

So now, in middle age, his erotic programme
Torn in two, if after such a delay
An accident should offer him his own
Fulfilment in a woman, still he would say:
O leave me easy, leave me alone.

EPITAPH FOR LIBERAL POETS

If in the latter
End—which is fairly soon—our way of life goes west
And some shall say So What and some What Matter,
Ready under new names to exploit or be exploited,
What, though better unsaid, would we have history say
Of us who walked in our sleep and died on our Quest?

[231]

We who always had, but never admitted, a master,
Who were expected—and paid—to be ourselves,
Conditioned to think freely, how can we
Patch up our broken hearts and modes of thought in plaster
And glorify in chromium-plated stories
Those who shall supersede us and cannot need us—
The tight-lipped technocratic Conquistadores?

The Individual has died before; Catullus
Went down young, gave place to those who were born old
And more adaptable and were not even jealous
Of his wild life and lyrics. Though our songs
Were not so warm as his, our fate is no less cold.

Such silence then before us, pinned against the wall,
Why need we whine? There is no way out, the birds
Will tell us nothing more; we shall vanish first,
Yet leave behind us certain frozen words
Which some day, though not certainly, may melt
And, for a moment or two, accentuate a thirst.

THE SATIRIST

Who is that man with the handshake? Don't you know;
He is the pinprick master, he can dissect
All your moods and manners, he can discover
A selfish motive for anything—and collect
His royalties as recording angel. No
Reverence here for hero, saint or lover.

Who is that man so deftly filling his pipe
As if creating something? That's the reason:
He is not creative at all, his mind is dry
And bears no blossoms even in the season,
He is an onlooker, a heartless type,
Whose hobby is giving everyone else the lie.

Who is that man with eyes like a lonely dog?
Lonely is right. He knows that he has missed
What others miss unconsciously. Assigned
To a condemned ship he still must keep the log
And so fulfil the premises of his mind
Where large ideals have bred a satirist.

THIS WAY OUT

You're not going yet? I must; I have to work.
Though no one better relished halcyon days
Behind his eyes the winch of will was busy
And dizzy ways led zigzag through the murk.

So deprecatingly he blew a nought
In smoke and threw the stub into the purring grate
And left us, as he always did, to follow
His colonising fate through Africas of thought.

He always broke off so, abrupt but shy
In knowledge of his mission, veered and tacked
To his own breezes—till as a variation
His explanation cracked and threw the words awry:
You're not going yet? I must; I have to die.

THYESTES

When the King sat down to the feast and the golden lid revealed
The human cutlets and the Graces sang
Their lays of love returned and lovers meeting,
Did his blood tell him what his mind concealed?
Didn't he know—or did he—what he was eating?

Thus Here and We, neither of which is what
The mind and map admit, in perfidy are linked;
This green foam frets away our sense of duty
While we, who watch it blossom and bulge, are not
Spectators in our hearts but murderers of beauty.

Cannibalism and incest: such is time,
A trail of shaking candles, such are we
Who garnish to pollute and breed to kill—
Messmates in the eucharist of crime
And heirs to two of those three black crosses on the hill.

[233]

PRAYER IN MID-PASSAGE

O Thou my monster, Thou my guide,
Be with me where the bluffs divide
Nor let me contemplate return
To where my backward chattels burn
In haunts of friendship and untruth—
The Cities of the Plain of Youth.

O pattern of inhuman good,
Hard critic of our thought and blood,
By whose decree there is no zone
Where man can live by men alone,
Unveil Thyself that all may see
Thy fierce impersonality.

We were the past—and doomed because
We were a past that never was;
Yet grant to men that they may climb
This time-bound ladder out of time
And by our human organs we
Shall thus transcend humanity.

Take therefore, though Thou disregard,
This prayer, this hymn, this feckless word,
O Thou my silence, Thou my song,
To whom all focal doubts belong
And but for whom this breath were breath—
Thou my meaning, Thou my death.

PROSPECT

Though loves languish and sour
Fruit puts the teeth on edge,
Though the ragged nests are empty of song
In the barbed and blistered hedge,

Though old men's lives and children's bricks
Spell out a Machiavellian creed,
Though the evil Past is ever present
And the happy Present is past indeed,

Though the stone grows and grows
That we roll up the hill
And the hill grows and grows
And gravity conquers still,

Though Nature's laws exploit
And defeat anarchic men,
Though every sandcastle concept
Being *ad hoc* must crumble again,

And though today is arid,
We know—and knowing bless—
That rooted in futurity
There is a plant of tenderness.

THE SPRINGBOARD

He never made the dive—not while I watched.
High above London, naked in the night
Perched on a board. I peered up through the bars
Made by his fear and mine but it was more than fright
That kept him crucified among the budding stars.

Yes, it was unbelief. He knew only too well
That circumstances called for sacrifice   .
But, shivering there, spreadeagled above the town,
His blood began to haggle over the price
History would pay if he were to throw himself down.

If it would mend the world, that would be worth while
But he, quite rightly, long had ceased to believe
In any Utopia or in Peace-upon-Earth;
His friends would find in his death neither ransom nor reprieve
But only a grain of faith—for what it was worth.

And yet we know he knows what he must do.
There above London where the gargoyles grin
He will dive like a bomber past the broken steeple,
One man wiping out his own original sin
And, like ten million others, dying for the people.

[235]

WHEN WE WERE CHILDREN

When we were children words were coloured
(Harlot and murder were dark purple)
And language was a prism, the light
    A conjured inlay on the grass,
Whose rays today are concentrated
    And language grown a burning-glass.

When we were children Spring was easy,
Dousing our heads in suds of hawthorn
And scrambling the laburnum tree—
    A breakfast for the gluttonous eye;
Whose winds and sweets have now forsaken
    Lungs that are black, tongues that are dry.

Now we are older and our talents
Accredited to time and meaning,
To handsel joy requires a new
    Shuffle of cards behind the brain
Where meaning shall remarry colour
    And flowers be timeless once again.

VIII

1944—1947

What is truth? says Pilate,
Waits for no answer;
Double your stakes, says the clock
To the ageing dancer;
Double the guard, says Authority,
Treble the bars;
Holes in the sky, says the child
Scanning the stars.

THE STREETS OF LAREDO

O early one morning I walked out like Agag,
Early one morning to walk through the fire
Dodging the pythons that leaked on the pavements
With tinkle of glasses and tangle of wire;

When grimed to the eyebrows I met an old fireman
Who looked at me wryly and thus did he say:
'The streets of Laredo are closed to all traffic,
We won't never master this joker to-day.

'O hold the branch tightly and wield the axe brightly,
The bank is in powder, the banker's in hell,
But loot is still free on the streets of Laredo
And when we drive home we drive home on the bell.'

Then out from a doorway there sidled a cockney,
A rocking-chair rocking on top of his head:
'O fifty-five years I been feathering my love-nest
And look at it now—why, you'd sooner be dead.'

At which there arose from a wound in the asphalt,
His big wig a-smoulder, Sir Christopher Wren
Saying: 'Let them make hay of the streets of Laredo;
When your ground-rents expire I will build them again.'

Then twangling their bibles with wrath in their nostrils
From Bunhill Fields came Bunyan and Blake:
'Laredo the golden is fallen, is fallen;
Your flame shall not quench nor your thirst shall not slake.'

'I come to Laredo to find me asylum',
Says Tom Dick and Harry the Wandering Jew;
'They tell me report at the first police station
But the station is pancaked—so what can I do?'

Thus eavesdropping sadly I strolled through Laredo
Perplexed by the dicta misfortunes inspire
Till one low last whisper inveigled my earhole—
The voice of the Angel, the voice of the fire:

O late, very late, have I come to Laredo
A whimsical bride in my new scarlet dress
But at last I took pity on those who were waiting
To see my regalia and feel my caress.

Now ring the bells gaily and play the hose daily,
Put splints on your legs, put a gag on your breath;
O you streets of Laredo, you streets of Laredo,
Lay down the red carpet—My dowry is death.

HIATUS

The years that did not count—Civilians in the towns
Remained at the same age as in Nineteen-Thirty-Nine,
Saying last year, meaning the last of peace;
Yet eyes began to pucker, mouth to crease,
The hiatus was too packed with fears and frowns,
The would-be absent heart came forth a magnetic mine.

As if the weekly food queue were to stretch,
Absorb all future Europe. Or as if
The sleepers in the Tube had come from Goya's Spain
Or Thucydides' Corcyra—a long way to fetch
People to prove that civilization is vain,
Wrapped in old quilts; no wonder they wake stiff.

Yes, we wake stiff and older; especially when
The schoolboys of the Thirties reappear,
Fledged in the void, indubitably men,
Having kept vigil on the Unholy Mount
And found some dark and tentative things made clear,
Some clear made dark, in the years that did not count.

CORNER SEAT

Suspended in a moving night
The face in the reflected train
Looks at first sight as self-assured
As your own face—But look again:

Windows between you and the world
Keep out the cold, keep out the fright;
Then why does your reflection seem
So lonely in the moving night?

AFTERMATH

Shuffle and cut. What was so large and one
Is now a pack of dog's-eared chances—Oh
Where is the Fear that warmed us to the gun,
That moved the cock to tousle the night and crow
In the gaps between the bombs? In this new round
The joker that could have been any moment death
Has been withdrawn, the cards are what they say
And none is wild; the bandaging dark which bound
This town together is loosed and in the array
Of bourgeois lights man's love can save its breath:
Their ransomed future severs once more the child
Of luck from the child of lack—and none is wild.

TWELFTH NIGHT

Snow-happy hicks of a boy's world—
O crunch of bull's-eyes in the mouth,
O crunch of frost beneath the foot—
If time would only remain furled
In white, and thaw were not for certain
And snow would but stay put, stay put!

When the pillar-box wore a white bonnet—
O harmony of roof and hedge,
O parity of sight and thought—
And each flake had your number on it
And lives were round for not a number
But equalled nought, but equalled nought!

But now the sphinx must change her shape —
O track that reappears through slush,
O broken riddle, burst grenade—

Q   [241]   M.C.P.

And lives must be pulled out like tape
To measure something not themselves,
Things not given but made, but made.

For now the time of gifts is gone—
O boys that grow, O snows that melt,
O bathos that the years must fill—
Here is dull earth to build upon
Undecorated; we have reached
Twelfth Night or what you will . . . you will.

BLUEBELLS

She, who last felt young during the war,
This Easter has no peace to be waiting for;
Though coining dandelions from her eyes
Has lost the old enrichment of surprise
And though her man is back, yet feels he has brought
The Desert with him, making her cheeks taut.

So both wake early, listen without words
To the now foreign badinage of birds,
And in the twilight when only the bats fly
They miss those engines overbrimming the sky,
For all green Nature has gone out of gear
Since they were apart and hoping, since last year.

Sun is too bright and brittle, wheat is too quick,
She turns from them to the wood where the slow thick
Shade is becalmed and chill and as a glacial stream
Meeting the sea inlays and weaves a milky gleam
Through the dark waste, so here the bluebells flow
Athwart the undergrowth, a merger of blue snow.

'Oh in this dark beneathness where he and I
Live, let a delta of flowers atone for the sky
Which we cannot face and from my ice-cap, oh,
Let one river at least unfreeze and flow
And through that brine so deep and yet so dim
Let my cold gentleness irradiate him.'

[242]

TAM CARI CAPITIS

That the world will never be quite—what a cliché—the same
    again
Is what we only learn by the event
When a friend dies out on us and is not there
To share the periphery of a remembered scent

Or leave his thumb-print on a shared ideal;
Yet it is not at floodlit moments we miss him most,
Not intervolution of wind-rinsed plumage of oat-field
Nor curragh dancing off a primeval coast

Nor the full strings of passion; it is in killing
Time where he could have livened it, such as the drop-by-drop
Of games like darts or chess, turning the faucet
On full at a threat to the queen or double top.

THE NATIONAL GALLERY

The kings who slept in the caves are awake and out,
The pictures are back in the Gallery; Old Masters twirl their
    cadenzas, whisper and shout,
Hundreds of windows are open again on a vital but changeless
    world—a day-dream free from doubt.

Here are the angels playing their lutes at the Birth—
Clay become porcelain; the pattern, the light, the ecstasy which
    make sense of the earth;
Here is Gethsemane scooped like a glacier, here is Calvary calmly
    assured of its own worth.

Here are the gold haloes, opaque as coins,
The pink temple of icing-sugar, the blandly scalloped rock which
    joins
Primitive heaven and earth; here is our Past wiping the smuts
    from his eyes, girding his loins.

Here saint may be gorgeous, hedonist austere,
The soul's nativity drawn of the earth and earthy, our brother the
   Ass being near,
The petty compartments of life thrown wind-wide open, our lop-
   sided instincts and customs atoned for here.

Here only too have the senses unending joy:
Draperies slip but slip no further and expectation cannot cloy;
The great Venetian buttocks, the great Dutch bosoms, remain in
   their time—their prime—beyond alloy.

And the Painter's little daughter, far-off-eyed,
Still stretches for the cabbage white, her sister dawdling at her
   side;
That she grew up to be mad does not concern us, the idyl and the
   innocent poise abide.

Aye; the kings are back from their caves in the Welsh hills,
Refreshed by darkness, armed with colour, sleight-of-hand and
   imponderables,
Armed with Uccello's lances, with beer-mugs, dragons' tongues,
   peacocks' eyes, bangles and spangles and flounces and
   frills;

Armed with the full mystique of the commonplace,
The lusts of the eye, the gullet, the loins, the memory—grace after
   living and grace
Before some plain-clothes death grabs at the artist's jemmy,
   leaves us yet one more half-solved case.

For the quickness of the heart deceives the eye,
Reshuffling the themes: a Still Life lives while portrayed flesh and
   feature die
Into fugues and subterfuges of being as enveloping and as aloof
   as a frosty midnight sky.

So fling wide the windows, this window and that, let the air
Blowing from times unconfined to Then, from places further and
   fuller than There,
Purge our particular time-bound unliving lives, rekindle a
   pentecost in Trafalgar Square.   .

[244]

LITTORAL

Indigo, mottle of purple and amber, ink,
Damson whipped with cream, improbable colours of sea
And unanalysable rhythms—fingering foam
Tracing, erasing its runes, regardless
Of you and me
And whether we think it escape or the straight way home.

The sand here looks like metal, it feels there like fur,
The wind films the sand with sand;
This hoary beach is burgeoning with minutiae
Like a philosopher
Who, thinking, makes cat's-cradles with string—or a widow
Who knits for her sons but remembers a tomb in another land.

Brain-bound or heart-bound sea—old woman or old man—
To whom we are ciphers, creatures to ignore,
We poach from you what images we can,
Luxuriously afraid
To plump the Unknown in a bucket with a spade—
Each child his own seashore.

THE CROMLECH

From trivia of froth and pollen
White tufts in the rabbit warren
And every minute like a ticket
Nicked and dropped, nicked and dropped,
Extracters and abstracters ask
What emerges, what survives,
And once the stopper is unstopped
What was the essence in the flask
And what is Life apart from lives
And where, apart from fact, the value.

To which we answer, being naïve,
Wearing the world upon our sleeve,
That to dissect a given thing
Unravelling its complexity

Outrages its simplicity
For essence is not merely core
And each event implies the world,
A centre needs periphery.

This being so, at times at least
Granted the sympathetic pulse
And granted the perceiving eye
Each pregnant with a history,
Appearance and appearances—
In spite of the philosophers
With their jejune dichotomies—
Can be at times reality.

So Tom and Tessy holding hands
(Dare an abstraction steal a kiss?)
Cannot be generalized away,
Reduced by bleak analysis
To pointers demonstrating laws
Which drain the colour from the day;
Not mere effects of a crude cause
But of themselves significant,
To rule-of-brain recalcitrant,
This that they are and do is This . . .

Tom is here, Tessy is here
At this point in a given year
With all this hour's accessories,
A given glory—and to look
That gift-horse in the mouth will prove
Or disprove nothing of their love
Which is as sure intact a fact,
Though young and supple, as what stands
Obtuse and old, in time congealed,
Behind them as they mingle hands—
Self-contained, unexplained,
The cromlech in the clover field.

CARRICK REVISITED

Back to Carrick, the castle as plumb assured
As thirty years ago—Which war was which?
Here are new villas, here is a sizzling grid
But the green banks are as rich and the lough as hazily lazy
And the child's astonishment not yet cured.

Who was—and am—dumbfounded to find myself
In a topographical frame—here, not there—
The channels of my dreams determined largely
By random chemistry of soil and air;
Memories I had shelved peer at me from the shelf.

Fog-horn, mill-horn, corncrake and church bell
Half-heard through boarded time as a child in bed
Glimpses a brangle of talk from the floor below
But cannot catch the words. Our past we know
But not its meaning—whether it meant well.

Time and place—our bridgeheads into reality
But also its concealment! Out of the sea
We land on the Particular and lose
All other possible bird's-eye views, the Truth
That is of Itself for Itself—but not for me.

Torn before birth from where my fathers dwelt,
Schooled from the age of ten to a foreign voice,
Yet neither western Ireland nor southern England
Cancels this interlude; what chance misspelt
May never now be righted by my choice.

Whatever then my inherited or acquired
Affinities, such remains my childhood's frame
Like a belated rock in the red Antrim clay
That cannot at this era change its pitch or name—
And the pre-natal mountain is far away.

SLUM SONG

O the slums of Dublin fermenting with children
    Wander far and near
The growing years are a cruel squadron
And poverty is a rusty cauldron
    Wander near and far.

The youths play cards by the broken fanlight
    Wander far and near
The Jack looks greasy in the sunlight
As hands will fumble in the moonlight
    Wander near and far.

And the grown man must play the horses
    Wander far and near
Some do better on different courses
But the blacks will remain to draw the hearses
    Wander near and far.

The bowsey in his second childhood
    Wander far and near
Thumbs his pipe of peace and briarwood
But lacks a light to relight his manhood
    Wander near and far.

Near and far, far and near,
The street-lamp winks, the mutes are here,
Above the steeple hangs a star
So near and far . . . far.

THE STRAND

White Tintoretto clouds beneath my naked feet,
This mirror of wet sand imputes a lasting mood
To island truancies; my steps repeat

Someone's who now has left such strands for good
Carrying his boots and paddling like a child,
A square black figure whom the horizon understood—

My father. Who for all his responsibly compiled
Account books of a devout, precise routine
Kept something in him solitary and wild,

So loved the western sea and no tree's green
Fulfilled him like these contours of Slievemore
Menaun and Croaghaun and the bogs between.

Sixty-odd years behind him and twelve before,
Eyeing the flange of steel in the turning belt of brine
It was sixteen years ago he walked this shore

And the mirror caught his shape which catches mine
But then as now the floor-mop of the foam
Blotted the bright reflections—and no sign

Remains of face or feet when visitors have gone home.

LAST BEFORE AMERICA

A spiral of green hay on the end of a rake:
The moment is sweat and sun-prick—children and old women
Big in a tiny field, midgets against the mountain,
So toy-like yet so purposed you could take
This for the Middle Ages.

At night the accordion melts in the wind from the sea
From the bourne of emigrant uncle and son, a defeated
Music that yearns and abdicates; chimney-smoke and spindrift
Mingle and part as ghosts do. The decree
Of the sea's divorce is final.

Pennsylvania or Boston? It was another name,
A land of a better because an impossible promise
Which split these families; it was to be a journey
Away from death—yet the travellers died the same
As those who stayed in Ireland.

Both myth and seismic history have been long suppressed
Which made and unmade Hy Brasil—now an image
For those who despise charts but find their dream's endorsement
In certain long low islets snouting towards the west
Like cubs that have lost their mother.

[249]

UNDER THE MOUNTAIN

Seen from above
The foam in the curving bay is a goose-quill
That feathers . . . unfeathers . . . itself.

Seen from above
The field is a flap and the haycocks buttons
To keep it flush with the earth.

Seen from above
The house is a silent gadget whose purpose
Was long since obsolete.

But when you get down
The breakers are cold scum and the wrack
Sizzles with stinking life.

When you get down
The field is a failed or a worth-while crop, the source
Of back-ache if not heartache.

And when you get down
The house is a maelstrom of loves and hates where you—
Having got down—belong.

NO MORE SEA

Dove-melting mountains, ridges gashed with water,
Itinerant clouds whose rubrics never alter,
Give, without oath, their testimony of silence
To islanders whose hearts themselves are islands;

For whom, if the ocean bed should silt up later
And living thoughts coagulate in matter,
An age of mainlanders, that dare not fancy
Life out of uniform, will feel no envy—

No envy unless some atavistic scholar
Plodding that dry and tight-packed world discover
Some dusty relic that once could swim, a fossil
Mind in its day both its own king and castle,

And thence conceive a vague inaccurate notion
Of what it meant to live embroiled with ocean
And between moving dunes and beyond reproving
Sentry-boxes to have been self-moving.

GODFATHER

Elusive
This godfather who mostly forgets one's birthday,
Perusing
Old schoolbooks when he should be reading the papers
Or, when he does
Glance at a daily, snooping between the headlines.

Revolving
Doors whisk him away as you enter a café,
Clopping
Hoofs of black horses drown his steps in the High Street;
He signs
Huge cheques without thinking, never is overdrawn.

The air-raids
Found him lying alone on his back and blowing
Carefree
Smoke-rings—a pipe-dream over the burning city;
At the crack
Of dawn he would lounge away, his hands in his pockets.

Adept
At all surprises, disguises, to conjure a Christmas
Packet
Into a stocking unnoticed or make without fussing
His first call ever and leave
Pale stone tablets like visiting cards in the churchyard.

AUBADE FOR INFANTS

Snap the blind; I am not blind,
I must spy what stalks behind
Wall and window—Something large
Is barging up beyond the down,
Chirruping, hooting, hot of foot.

Beyond that wall what things befall?
My eye can fly though I must crawl.
Dance and dazzle—Something bright
Ignites the dumps of sodden cloud,
Loud and laughing, a fiery face . . .

Whose broad grimace (the voice is bass)
Makes nonsense of my time and place—
Maybe you think that I am young?
I who flung before my birth
To mother earth the dawn-song too!

And you—
However old and deaf this year—
Were near me when that song was sung.

THE CYCLIST

Freewheeling down the escarpment past the unpassing horse
Blazoned in chalk the wind he causes in passing
Cools the sweat of his neck, making him one with the sky,
In the heat of the handlebars he grasps the summer
Being a boy and to-day a parenthesis
Between the horizon's brackets; the main sentence
Is to be picked up later but these five minutes
Are all to-day and summer. The dragonfly
Rises without take-off, horizontal,
Underlining itself in a sliver of peacock light.

And glaring, glaring white
The horse on the down moves within his brackets,
The grass boils with grasshoppers, a pebble
Scutters from under the wheel and all this country
Is spattered white with boys riding their heat-wave,
Feet on a narrow plank and hair thrown back

And a surf of dust beneath them. Summer, summer—
They chase it with butterfly nets or strike it into the deep
In a little red ball or gulp it lathered with cream
Or drink it through closed eyelids; until the bell
Left-right-left gives his forgotten sentence

And reaching the valley the boy must pedal again
Left-right-left but meanwhile
For ten seconds more can move as the horse in the chalk
Moves unbeginningly calmly
Calmly regardless of tenses and final clauses
Calmly unendingly moves.

WOODS

My father who found the English landscape tame
Had hardly in his life walked in a wood,
Too old when first he met one; Malory's knights,
Keats's nymphs or the Midsummer Night's Dream
Could never arras the room, where he spelled out True and Good
With their interleaving of half-truths and not-quites.

While for me from the age of ten the socketed wooden gate
Into a Dorset planting, into a dark
But gentle ambush, was an alluring eye;
Within was a kingdom free from time and sky,
Caterpillar webs on the forehead, danger under the feet,
And the mind adrift in a floating and rustling ark

Packed with birds and ghosts, two of every race,
Trills of love from the picture-book—Oh might I never land
But here, grown six foot tall, find me also a love
Also out of the picture-book; whose hand
Would be soft as the webs of the wood and on her face
The wood-pigeon's voice would shaft a chrism from above.

So in a grassy ride a rain-filled hoof-mark coined
By a finger of sun from the mint of Long Ago
Was the last of Lancelot's glitter. Make-believe dies hard;
That the rider passed here lately and is a man we know
Is still untrue, the gate to Legend remains unbarred,
The grown-up hates to divorce what the child joined.

Thus from a city when my father would frame
Escape, he thought, as I do, of bog or rock
But I have also this other, this English, choice

[253]

Into what yet is foreign; whatever its name
Each wood is the mystery and the recurring shock
Of its dark coolness is a foreign voice.

Yet in using the word tame my father was maybe right,
These woods are not the Forest; each is moored
To a village somewhere near. If not of to-day
They are not like the wilds of Mayo, they are assured
Of their place by men; reprieved from the neolithic night
By gamekeepers or by Herrick's girls at play.

And always we walk out again. The patch
Of sky at the end of the path grows and discloses
An ordered open air long ruled by dyke and fence,
With geese whose form and gait proclaim their consequence,
Pargetted outposts, windows browed with thatch,
And cow pats—and inconsequent wild roses.

ELEGY FOR MINOR POETS

Who often found their way to pleasant meadows
Or maybe once to a peak, who saw the Promised Land,
Who took the correct three strides but tripped their hurdles,
Who had some prompter they barely could understand,
Who were too happy or sad, too soon or late,
I would praise these in company with the Great;

For if not in the same way, they fingered the same language
According to their lights. For them as for us
Chance was a coryphaeus who could be either
An angel or an *ignis fatuus*.
Let us keep our mind open, our fingers crossed;
Some who go dancing through dark bogs are lost.

Who were lost in many ways, through comfort, lack of
        knowledge,
Or between women's breasts, who thought too little, too much,
Who were the world's best talkers, in tone and rhythm
Superb, yet as writers lacked a sense of touch,
So either gave up or just went on and on—
Let us salute them now their chance is gone;

And give the benefit of the doubtful summer
To those who worshipped the sky but stayed indoors
Bound to a desk by conscience or by the spirit's
Hayfever. From those office and study floors
Let the sun clamber on to the notebook, shine,
And fill in what they groped for between each line.

Who were too carefree or careful, who were too many
Though always few and alone, who went the pace
But ran in circles, who were lamed by fashion,
Who lived in the wrong time or the wrong place,
Who might have caught fire had only a spark occurred,
Who knew all the words but failed to achieve the Word—

Their ghosts are gagged, their books are library flotsam,
Some of their names—not all—we learnt in school
But, life being short, we rarely read their poems,
Mere source-books now to point or except a rule,
While those opinions which rank them high are based
On a wish to be different or on lack of taste.

In spite of and because of which, we later
Suitors to their mistress (who, unlike them, stays young)
Do right to hang on the grave of each a trophy
Such as, if solvent, he would himself have hung
Above himself; these debtors preclude our scorn—
Did we not underwrite them when we were born?

AUTOLYCUS

In his last phase when hardly bothering
To be a dramatist, the Master turned away
From his taut plots and complex characters
To tapestried romances, conjuring
With rainbow names and handfuls of sea-spray
And from them turned out happy Ever-afters.

Eclectic always, now extravagant,
Sighting his matter through a timeless prism
He ranged his classical bric-à-brac in grottos
Where knights of Ancient Greece had Latin mottoes

And fishermen their flapjacks—none should want
Colour for lack of an anachronism.

A gay world certainly though pocked and scored
With childish horrors and a fresh world though
Its mainsprings were old gags—babies exposed,
Identities confused and queens to be restored;
But when the cracker bursts it proves as you supposed—
Trinket and moral tumble out just so.

Such innocence—In his own words it was
Like an old tale, only that where time leaps
Between acts three and four there was something born
Which made the stock-type virgin dance like corn
In a wind that having known foul marshes, barren steeps,
Felt therefore kindly towards Marinas, Perditas . . .

Thus crystal learned to talk. But Shakespeare balanced it
With what we knew already, gabbing earth
Hot from Eastcheap—Watch your pockets when
That rogue comes round the corner, he can slit
Purse-strings as quickly as his maker's pen
Will try your heartstrings in the name of mirth.

O master pedlar with your confidence tricks,
Brooches, pomanders, broadsheets and what-have-you,
Who hawk such entertainment but rook your client
And leave him brooding, why should we forgive you
Did we not know that, though more self-reliant
Than we, you too were born and grew up in a fix?

STREET SCENE

Between March and April when barrows of daffodils butter the
        pavement,
The colossus of London stretches his gaunt legs, jerking
The smoke of his hair back from his eyes and puffing
Smoke-rings of heavenward pigeons over Saint Paul's,
While in each little city of each individual person
The black tree yearns for green confetti and the black kerb for
        yellow stalls.

Ave Maria! A sluice is suddenly opened
Making Orphan Street a conduit for a fantastic voice;
The Canadian sergeant turns to stone in his swagger,
The painted girls, the lost demobbed, the pinstriped accountant
    listen
As the swan-legged cripple straddled on flightless wings of
    crutches
Hitting her top note holds our own lame hours in equipoise,

Then waddles a yard and switches *Cruising down the river*
Webbed feet hidden, the current smooth *On a Sunday afternoon*
Sunshine fortissimo; some young man from the Desert
Fumbles, new from battle-dress, for his pocket,
Drops a coin in that cap she holds like a handbag,
Then slowly walks out of range of *A sentimental tune*

Which cruising down—repeat—cruises down a river
That has no source nor sea but is each man's private dream
Remote as his listening eyes; repeat for all will listen
Cruising away from thought with *An old accordion playing*
Not that it is, her accompanist plucks a banjo
On a Sunday afternoon. She ends. And the other stream

Of Orphan Street flows back—instead of silence racket,
Brakes gears and sparrows; the passers-by pass by,
The swan goes home on foot, a girl takes out her compact—
Silence instead of song; the Canadian dives for the pub
And a naval officer on the traffic island
Unsees the buses with a mid-ocean eye.

RELICS

Obsolete as books in leather bindings
Buildings in stone like talkative ghosts continue
    Their well-worn anecdotes
As here in Oxford shadow the dark-weathered
Astrakhan rustication of the arches
    Puts a small world in quotes:

While high in Oxford sunlight playfully crocketed
Pinnacles, ripe as corn on the cob, look over
    To downs where once without either wheel or hod

Ant-like, their muscles cracking under the sarsen,
Shins white with chalk and eyes dark with necessity
The Beaker People pulled their weight of God.

THE DRUNKARD

His last train home is Purgatory in reverse,
A spiral back into time and down towards Hell
Clutching a quizzical strap where wraiths of faces
Contract, expand, revolve, impinge; disperse
On a sickly wind which drives all wraiths pell-mell
Through tunnels to their appointed, separate places.

And he is separate too, who had but now ascended
Into the panarchy of created things
Wearing his halo cocked, full of good will
That need not be implemented; time stood still
As the false coin rang and the four walls had wings
And instantly the Natural Man was mended.

Instantly and it would be permanently
God was uttered in words and gulped in gin,
The barmaid was a Madonna, the adoration
Of the coalman's breath was myrrh, the world was We
And pissing under the stars an act of creation
While the low hills lay purring round the inn.

Such was the absolute moment, to be displaced
By moments; the clock takes over—time to descend
Where Time will brief us, briefed himself to oppress
The man who looks and finds Man human and not his friend
And whose tongue feels around and around but cannot taste
That hour-gone sacrament of drunkenness.

HANDS AND EYES

In a high wind
Gnarled hands cup to kindle an old briar,
From a frilled cot
Twin sea anemones grope for a hanging lamp,

In a foul cage
Old coal-gloves dangle from dejected arms.

Of which three pairs of hands the child's are helpless
(Whose wheels barely engage)
And the shepherd's from his age are almost bloodless
While the chimpanzee's are hopeless
Were there not even a cage.

In a dark room
Docile pupils grow to their full for prey,
Down a long bar
Mascara scrawls a gloss on a torn leaf,
On a high col
The climber's blue marries the blue he climbs.

Of which three pairs of eyes the tart's are mindless
(Who pawned her mind elsewhere)
And the black cat's, in gear with black, are heartless
While the alpinist's are timeless
In gear with timeless air.

In a cold church
It flickers in the draught, then burns erect;
In a loud mob
It bulges, merges, feels with a start alone;
In a bright beam
It waltzes dust to dust with its chance loves.

Of which three souls the praying one is selfless
But only for a span
And the gregarious man's is rudderless, powerless,
While the soul in love is luckless,
Betrays what chance it can.

And still the wind
Blows, the ape is marooned, the lamp ungrasped;
Woman and cat
Still wait to pounce and the climber waits to fall;
As each soul burns
The best it may, in foul or blustering air.
Oh would He, were there a God, have mercy on us all?

PLACE OF A SKULL

Earth water stars and flesh—the seamless coat
Which is the world, he left; who from to-day
. Had no more need to wear it. The remote
Metropolis yawned, the parchment flapped away,

Away, and the blood dried in the sand. The bored
Soldiers played for the leavings but even they,
Though trained to carve up continents with the sword,
Approved the weaver who had made night and day

And time and mind a tegument, therefore swore
To hazard it as one lot. The dice were gay
And someone won: *Why the first time I wore*
That dead man's coat it frayed I cannot say.

SLOW MOVEMENT

Waking, he found himself in a train, andante,
With wafers of early sunlight blessing the unknown fields
And yesterday cancelled out, except for yesterday's papers
    Huddling under the seat.

It is still very early, this is a slow movement;
The viola-player's hand like a fish in a glass tank
Rises, remains quivering, darts away
    To nibble invisible weeds.

Great white nebulae lurch against the window
To deploy across the valley, the children are not yet up
To wave us on—we pass without spectators,
    Braiding a voiceless creed.

And the girl opposite, name unknown, is still
Asleep and the colour of her eyes unknown
Which might be wells of sun or moons of wish
    But it is still very early.

The movement ends, the train has come to a stop
In buttercup fields, the fiddles are silent, the whole

Shoal of silver tessellates the aquarium
    Floor, not a bubble rises . . .

And what happens next on the programme we do not know,
If, the red line topped on the gauge, the fish will go mad in the tank
Accelerando con forza, the sleeper open her eyes
    And, so doing, open ours.

CAROL

To end all carols, darling,
    To end all carols now,
Let us walk through the cloister
    With a thoughtful brow,

Pruning what was grafted
    Through ages of blind faith—
The rubrics and the finials
    Drift away like breath.

From Bethlehem the sheep-bells
    Grew to a steepled peal,
The joists of the stable
    Spread an ashlar chill,

The rafters of the stable
    Hooped themselves on high
And coveys of boys' voices
    Burst on a stone sky;

While the wrinkled, whimpering image
    Wrapped in his mother's shawl
Was carried between pillars
    Down endless aisles and all

The doors opened before him
    In every holy place
And the doors came to behind him,
    Left him in cold space.

Beyond our prayers and knowing,
    Many light-years away—
So why sing carols, darling?
    To-day is to-day.

Then answered the angel:
    To-day is to-day
And the Son of God is vanished
    But the sons of men stay

And man is a spirit
    And symbols are his meat,
So pull not down the steeple
    In your monied street.

For money chimes feebly,
    Matter dare not sing—
Man is a spirit,
    Let the bells ring.

Ring all your changes, darling,
    Save us from the slough;
Begin all carols, darling,
    Begin all carols now.

IX

1940—1948

PLURALITY

It is patent to the eye that cannot face the sun
The smug philosophers lie who say the world is one;
World is other and other, world is here and there,
Parmenides would smother life for lack of air
Precluding birth and death; his crystal never breaks—
No movement and no breath, no progress nor mistakes,
Nothing begins or ends, no-one loves or fights,
All your foes are friends and all your days are nights
And all the roads lead round and are not roads at all
And the soul is muscle-bound, the world a wooden ball.
The modern monist too castrates, negates our lives
And nothing that we do, make or become survives,
His terror of confusion freezes the flowing stream
Into mere illusion, his craving for supreme
Completeness means he chokes each orifice with tight
Plaster as he evokes a dead ideal of white
All-white Universal, refusing to allow
Division or dispersal—Eternity is now
And Now is therefore numb, a fact he does not see
Postulating a dumb static identity
Of Essence and Existence which could not fuse without
Banishing to a distance belief along with doubt,
Action along with error, growth along with gaps;
If man is a mere mirror of God, the gods collapse.
No, the formula fails that fails to make it clear
That only change prevails, that the seasons make the year,
That a thing, a beast, a man is what it is because
It is something that began and is not what it was,
Yet is itself throughout, fluttering and unfurled,
Not to be cancelled out, not to be merged in world,
Its entity a denial of all that is not it,
Its every move a trial through chaos and the Pit,
An absolute and so defiant of the One
Absolute, the row of noughts where time is done,
Where nothing goes or comes and Is is one with Ought
And all the possible sums alike resolve to nought.
World is not like that, world is full of blind
Gulfs across the flat, jags against the mind,
Swollen or diminished according to the dice,
Foaming, never finished, never the same twice.

You talk of Ultimate Value, Universal Form—
Visions, let me tell you, that ride upon the storm
And must be made and sought but cannot be maintained,
Lost as soon as caught, always to be regained,
Mainspring of our striving towards perfection, yet
Would not be worth achieving if the world were set
Fair, if error and choice did not exist, if dumb
World should find its voice for good and God become
Incarnate once for all. No, perfection means
Something but must fall unless there intervenes
Between that meaning and the matter it should fill
Time's revolving hand that never can be still.
Which being so and life a ferment, you and I
Can only live by strife in that the living die,
And, if we use the word Eternal, stake a claim
Only to what a bird can find within the frame
Of momentary flight (the value will persist
But as event the night sweeps it away in mist).
Man is man because he might have been a beast
And is not what he was and feels himself increased,
Man is man in as much as he is not god and yet
Hankers to see and touch the pantheon and forget
The means within the end and man is truly man
In that he would transcend and flout the human span:
A species become rich by seeing things as wrong
And patching them, to which I am proud that I belong.
Man is surely mad with discontent, he is hurled
By lovely hopes or bad dreams against the world,
Raising a frail scaffold in never-ending flux,
Stubbornly when baffled fumbling the stubborn crux
And so he must continue, raiding the abyss
With aching bone and sinew, conscious of things amiss,
Conscious of guilt and vast inadequacy and the sick
Ego and the broken past and the clock that goes too quick,
Conscious of waste of labour, conscious of spite and hate,
Of dissension with his neighbour, of beggars at the gate,
But conscious also of love and the joy of things and the power
Of going beyond and above the limits of the lagging hour,
Conscious of sunlight, conscious of death's inveigling touch
Not completely conscious but partly—and that is much.

THE CASUALTY

(in memoriam G.H.S.)

'Damn!' you would say if I were to write the best
Tribute I could to you, 'All clichés', and you would grin
Dwindling to where that faded star allures
Where no time presses and no days begin—
Turning back shrugging to the misty West
Remembered out of Homer but now yours.

Than whom I do not expect ever again
To find a more accordant friend, with whom
I could be silent knowledgeably; you never
Faked or flattered or time-served. If ten
Winds were to shout you down or twenty oceans boom
Above the last of you, they will not sever

That thread of so articulate silence. How
You died remains conjecture; instantaneous
Is the most likely—that the shutter fell
Congealing the kaleidoscope at Now
And making all your past contemporaneous
Under that final chord of the mid-Atlantic swell.

So now the concert is over, the seats vacated,
Eels among the footlights, water up to the roof
And the gilded cherubs crumbling—and you come in
Jaunty as ever but with a half-frustrated
Look on your face, you expect the show to begin
But you are too late and cannot accept the proof

That you are too late because you have died too early
And this is under sea. Puzzled but gay
You still come in, come in, and the waves distort
Your smile and chivvy your limbs through a maze of pearly
Pillars of ocean death—and yet you force your way
In on my dreams as if you had something still to report.

How was it then? How is it? You and I
Have often since we were children discussed death
And sniggered at the preacher and wondered how

[267]

He can talk so big about mortality
And immortality more. But you yourself could now
Talk big as any—if you had the breath.

However since you cannot from this date
Talk big or little, since you cannot answer
Even what alive you could, but I let slip
The chance to ask you, I can correlate
Only of you what memories dart and trip
Through freckling lights and stop like a forgetful dancer.

Archaic gusto sprouted from a vase
Of dancing satyrs, lips of a Gothic imp
Laughing down from a church-top, inky fingers
Jotting notes on notes, and piccolo and tymp
Importunate at the circus—but there lingers
Also a scent of awe, a cosmic pause;

For you were a good mixer and could laugh
With Rowlandson or Goya and you liked
Bijoux and long-eared dogs and silken legs
And titivated rooms but more than half
Your story lay outside beyond the spiked
Railing where in the night the blinded minstrel begs.

He begged and you responded, being yourself,
Like Raftery or Homer, of his kind—
Creative not for the counter or the shelf
But innocently whom the world bewilders
And so they observe and love it till their mind
May turn them from mere students into builders.

Of which high humble company were you,
Outside the cliques, unbothered with the fashion,
And self-apprenticed to the grinding trade
Of thinking things anew, stropping the blade
You never used, your multicoloured passion
Having been merged by death in universal Blue.

So what you gave were inklings: trivial signs
Of some momentous truth, a footprint here and there
In melting snow, a marginal caress

Of someone else's words, a gentleness
In greeting, a panache of heady wines
Or children's rockets vanishing in air.

Look at these snapshots; here you see yourself
Spilling a paint-pot on a virgin wall
Or boisterous in a sailing-boat or bubbling
At a Punch-and-Judy show or a music-hall
Or lugging Clausewitz from a public shelf
To make your private notes, thumbing and doubling

His corseted pages back. Yes, here and here
You see yourself spilling across the border
Of nice convention, here at a students' dance
Pinching a girl's behind—to reappear
A small boy twined in bracken and aprance
Like any goatfoot faun to propagate disorder.

Here you are swapping gags in winking bars
With half an eye on the colour clash of beet
Lobster and radish, here you are talking back
To a caged baboon and here the Wiltshire sleet
Riddles your football jersey—here the sack
Of night pours down on you Provençal stars.

Here you are gabbling Baudelaire or Donne,
Here you are mimicking that cuckoo clock,
Here you are serving a double fault for set,
Here you are diving naked from a Dalmatian rock,
Here you are barracking the sinking sun,
Here you are taking Proust aboard your doomed corvette.

Yes, all you gave were inklings; even so
Invaluable—such as I remember
Out of your mouth or only in your eyes
On walks in blowsy August, Brueghel-like December,
Or when the gas was hissing and a glow
Of copper jugs gave back your lyrical surprise.

For above all that was your gift—to be
Surprised and therefore sympathetic, warm
Towards things as well as people, you could see

[269]

The integrity of differences—O did you
Make one last integration, find a Form
Grow out of formlessness when the Atlantic hid you?

Whether you did or not, the fact remains
(Which I, for all your doubts, could have no doubt of)
That your whole life till then showed an endeavour
Towards a discovery—and if your pains
Were lost the loss is ours as well; for you are out of
This life and cannot start any more hares for ever.

THE KINGDOM

I

Under the surface of flux and of fear there is an underground
    movement,
Under the crust of bureaucracy, quiet behind the posters,
Unconscious but palpably there—the Kingdom of individuals.

And of these is the Kingdom—
Equal in difference, interchangeably sovereign—
The incorruptible souls who work without a commission,
The pairs of hands that are peers of hearts, the eyes that marry
    with eyes,
The candid scholar, the unselfish priest, the uncomplaining
    mothers of many,
The active men who are kind, the contemplative who give,
The happy-go-lucky saint and the peace-loving buccaneer.

These, as being themselves, are apart from not each other
But from such as being false are merely other,
So these are apart as parts within a pattern
Not merged nor yet excluded, members of a Kingdom
Which has no king except each subject, therefore
Apart from slaves and tyrants and from every
Community of mere convenience; these are
Apart from those who drift and those who force,
Apart from partisan order and egotistical anarchy,
Apart from the easy religion of him who would find in God
A boss, a ponce, an alibi, and apart from

[270]

The logic of him who arrogates to himself
The secret of the universe, the whole
Choreography of atoms; these are humble
And proud at once, working within their limits
And yet transcending them. These are the people
Who vindicate the species. And they are many. For go,
Go wherever you choose, among tidy villas or terrible
Docks, dumps and pitheads, or through the spangled moors
Or along the vibrant narrow intestines of great ships
Or into those countries of which we know very little—
Everywhere you will discover the men of the Kingdom
Loyal by intuition, born to attack, and innocent.

II

Take this old man with the soldierly straight back
Dressed in tweeds like a squire but he has not a squire's
        presumption,
His hands are gentle with wild flowers, his memory
Latticed with dialect and anecdotes
And wisps of nature poetry; he is of the Kingdom,
A country-lover and very English, the cadence
Of Christmas bells in his voice, his face like Cotswold stone
Severe but warm, a sureness in his walk
And his blood attuned to the seasons—whether it is the glyptic
Winter turning feathered twigs to stone
And making the Old Bill pollards monuments
Beside the dyke of Lethe—or if it is the frantic
Calf-love and early oratory of spring—
Or peony-time with the midges dancing—or later, sweeter,
That two-in-one of clarity and mist,
Of maidenlight and ripeness which is autumn:
Every case is new and yet he knows the answers
For he is of the Kingdom. Through the serene and chequer
Fields that he knows he walks like a fallen angel
Whose fall has made him a man. Ladders of cirrhus cloud
Lead down as well as up, the ricochet of rain
Makes the clay smell sweet and snow in sunlight
Affirms the tussocks under it. Such changes—
The hedgerow stippled with hips or lathered with elder—
To him are his own rhythm like his breathing
And intimate as dreams. Hirsute or fluted earth,

[271]

Squares of plough and stubble, oatcake and corduroy
Russet and emerald, and the shot-silk evening
And all the folk-song stars—these are his palette
And it is he who blends them with the brush-strokes
Of long experience and sudden insight,
Being mature and yet naïve, a lover
Of what is not himself—but it becomes himself
And he repays it interest, so has had
A happy life and will die happy; more—
Belongs, though he never knew it, to the Kingdom.

III

When she had her stroke the china dogs
Did not even flinch, although they might have guessed
That tomorrow no one would dust them, but the family
Felt that this was an Act of God and did not see
The syllogism slouched across the kitchen table,
The inevitable caller; given poverty,
Given two on the dole and one a cripple,
Given the false peace and the plight of England,
And given her matriarchal pride, her bones
That would not rest, her arrogation of every
Job in the house to herself, given her grim
Good humour—her daily tonic against despair,
Given her wakeful nights trying to balance the budget
And given her ignorance of her own frailty,
What other end was coming? They propped her up
While the canary fidgeted with his seed
And the clock hiccuped, being about to strike,
And someone ran for the doctor: 'Our Mother is taken bad.
Everything in that house was mutually possessive:
She was Our Mother, Dad was called Our Dad,
Connie Our Connie and the cat Our Tiger
But now the most possessing and the most possessed
Was on her way to leave them. They did not see
Even that this was so, they did not see
The tall clock stretch his arms like a rising Cross
Or see the steam of the kettle turn to incense;
Our Mother is taken bad—and that was all.
They did not see that the only cable was broken
That held them together, self-respecting and sane

[272]

And that chaos was now on the move. For they did not know,
Except at times by inklings, that their home
Remained a rebel island in the sea
Of authorised disgust only because their mother
Who thought herself resigned, was a born rebel
Against the times and loyal to a different
Order, being enfranchised of the Kingdom.

IV

'Drunk again! Where do you think you are?'
'I think I am somewhere where I don't belong;
I chanced in here from the Kingdom.' And he crashed
His heavyweight hand among the chipped and dinted
Vessels of false good-fellowship, went out
Into the night with his chin like a bulldozer
Churning a trough of fury; then the Night
Being herself archaic and instinctive
Welcomed his earthy anger, clapped him on the back
And told him stories that were not wit but humour,
Not smut but satyr-talk, not clever but wise,
Not elegant but poetry. And his mouth relaxed,
His head went back and he laughed, hearing the bugle
That blows tomorrow morning, blows for a hard routine,
Blows for the life automatic, for spit and polish and jargon
And deference to fools, but blows also for comrades,
Blows for a gay and a brave unforced solidarity,
Blows for the elemental community, blows for
Knowledge of shared emotion past and future,
(Blows for the static life that suddenly comes to
Life with the smell at dawn of running engines)
And blows as well—to those who have ears to hear
And hands to strike—for the Kingdom.

V

Too large in feature for a world of cuties,
Too sculptured for a cocktail lounge flirtation,
This girl is almost awkward, carrying off
The lintel of convention on her shoulders,
A Doric river-goddess with a pitcher
Of ice-cold wild emotions. Pour them where she will
The pitcher will not empty nor the stream grow warm

But is so cold it burns. Vitality and fear
Are marbled in her eyes, from hour to hour
She changes like the sky—one moment is so gay
That all her words are laughter but the next
Moment she is puzzled, her own Sphinx,
Made granite by her destiny, encumbered
With the dour horoscopes of dying nations
Deduced from dying stars.
So what can you expect? Behind that classic
Forehead, under that smooth Renaissance dome,
The Gothic devils revel around a corpse
Allegedly a saint's and snuff the holy candles
And cackle and deny—and their denial
Torments her with a doubt. She raises once again
Her pitcher, tilts it—Will the water flow?—
And see, it flows, it flows, ice-cold as ever,
Anarchic, pure and healing. For she filled it
One day that is not dead at a lost well
Between two rocks under a sombre ilex
In the grey dawn in a deserted corner
Of the remembered Kingdom.

VI

A little dapper man but with shiny elbows
And short keen sight, he lived by measuring things
And died like a recurring decimal
Run off the page, refusing to be curtailed;
Died as they say in harness, still believing
In science, reason, progress. Left his work
Unfinished *ipso facto* which continued
Will supersede his name in the next text-book
And relegate him to the anonymous crowd
Of small discoverers in lab or cloister
Who link us with the Ice Age. Obstinately
He canalised his fervour, it was slow
The task he set himself but plotting points
On graph paper he felt the emerging curve
Like the first flutterings of an embryo
In somebody's first pregnancy; resembled
A pregnant woman too in that his logic
Yet made that hidden child the centre of the world

And almost a messiah; so that here
Even here over the shining test-tubes
The spirit of the alchemist still hovered
Hungry for magic, for the philosopher's stone.
And Progress—is that magic too? He never
Would have conceded it, not even in these last
Years of endemic doubt; in his perspective
Our present tyrants shrank into parochial
Lords of Misrule, cross eddies in a river
That has to reach the sea. But has it? Who
Told him the sea was there?
Maybe he told himself and the mere name
Of Progress was a shell to hold to the ear
And hear the breakers burgeon. Rules were rules
And all induction checked but in the end
His reasoning hinged on faith and the first axiom
Was oracle or instinct. He was simple
This man who flogged his brain, he was a child;
And so, whatever progress means in general,
He in his work meant progress. Patiently
As Stone Age man he flaked himself away
By blocked-out patterns on a core of flint
So that the core which was himself diminished
Until his friends complained that he had lost
Something in charm or interest. But conversely
His mind developed like an ancient church
By the accretion of side-aisles and the enlarging of lights
Till all the walls are windows and the sky
Comes in, if coloured; such a mind . . . a man . . .
Deserves a consecration; such a church
Bears in its lines the trademark of the Kingdom.

VII

All is well, said the voice from the tiny pulpit,
All is well with the child. And the voice cracked
For the preacher was very old and the coffin down in the aisle
Held the body of one who had been his friend and colleague
For forty years and was dead in daffodil time
Before it had come to Easter. All is well with
One who believed and practised and whose life
Presumed the Resurrection. What that means

He may have felt he knew; this much is certain—
The meaning filled his actions, made him courteous
And lyrical and strong and kind and truthful,
A generous puritan. Above whose dust
About this time each year the spendthrift plants
Will toss their trumpets heralding a life
That shows itself in time but remains timeless
As is the heart of music. So today
These yellow fanfares in the trench re-echo,
Before the spades get busy, the same phrase
The preacher lost his voice on. All is well,
The flowers say, with the child; and so it must be
For, it is said, the children are of the Kingdom.

VIII

Over the roofs and cranes, blistered cupola and hungry smoke-
    stack, over the moored balloons and the feathery tufts of
    searchlights,
Over the cold transmitters jabbering under the moon,
Over the hump of the ocean big with wrecks and over
Our hide-bound fog-bound lives the hosts of the living collect
Like migrant birds, or bees to the sound of a gong:
Subjects all of the Kingdom but each in himself a king.
These are the people who know in their bones the answer
To the statesman's quiz and the false reformer's crude
Alternatives and ultimatums. These have eyes
And can see each other's goodness, do not need salvation
By whip, brochure, sterilisation or drugs,
Being incurably human; these are the catalytics
To break the inhuman into humanity; these are
The voices whose words, whether in code or in clear,
Are to the point and can be received apart from
The buzz of jargon. Apart from the cranks, the timid,
The self-deceiving realist, the self-seeking
Altruist, the self-indulgent penitent,
Apart from all the frauds are these who have the courage
Of their own vision and their friends' good will
And have not lost their cosmic pride, responding
Both to the simple lyrics of blood and the architectonic fugues of
    reason.
These have their faults like all creators, like
The hero who must die or like the artist who

Himself is like a person with one hand
Working it into a glove; yes, they have faults
But are the chosen—because they have chosen, being
Beautiful if grotesque and wise though wilful
And hard as meteorites. Of these, of such is
Your hope, your clue, your cue, your snowball letter
That makes your soft flakes hard, your aspirations active;
Of such is your future if it is to be fruitful,
Of such is your widow's cruse, your Jacob's ladder,
Of such is the garden of souls, the orchestration of instinct,
The fertilisation of mind, of such are your beacons,
Your breaking of bread, your dance of desire, your North-West
    passage,
Of such is the epilogue to your sagas of bronze and steel,
Your amnesty, your advent, your Rebirth,
The archetype and the vindication of history;
The hierarchy of the equal—the Kingdom of Earth.

WESTERN LANDSCAPE

In doggerel and stout let me honour this country
Though the air is so soft that it smudges the words
And herds of great clouds find the gaps in the fences
Of chance preconceptions and foam-quoits on rock-points
At once hit and miss, hit and miss.
So the kiss of the past is narcotic, the ocean
Lollingly lullingly over-insidiously
Over and under crossing the eyes
And docking the queues of the teetotum consciousness
Proves and disproves what it wants.
For the western climate is Lethe,
The smoky taste of cooking on turf is lotus,
There are affirmation and abnegation together
From the broken bog with its veins of amber water,
From the distant headland, a sphinx's fist, that barely grips the
    sea,
From the taut-necked donkey's neurotic-asthmatic-erotic
    lamenting,
From the heron in trance and in half-mourning,
From the mitred mountain weeping shale.
O grail of emerald passing light

And hanging smell of sweetest hay
And grain of sea and loom of wind
Weavingly laughingly leavingly weepingly—
Webs that will last and will not.
But what
Is the hold upon, the affinity with
Ourselves of such a light and line,
How do we find continuance
Of our too human skeins of wish
In this inhuman effluence?
O relevance of cloud and rock—
If such could be our permanence!
The flock of mountain sheep belong
To tumbled screes, to tumbling seas
The ribboned wrack, and moor to mist;
But we who savour longingly
This plenitude of solitude
Have lost the right to residence,
Can only glean ephemeral
Ears of our once beatitude.
Caressingly cajolingly—
Take what you can for soon you go—
Consolingly, coquettishly,
The soft rain kisses and forgets,
Silken mesh on skin and mind;
A deaf-dumb siren that can sing
With fingertips her falsities,
Welcoming, abandoning.

O Brandan, spindrift hermit, who
Hankering roaming un-homing up-anchoring
From this rock wall looked seawards to
Knot the horizon round your waist,
Distil that distance and undo
Time in a quintessential West:
The best negation, round as nought,
Stiller than stolen sleep—though bought
With mortification, voiceless choir
Where all were silent as one man
And all desire fulfilled, unsought.
Thought:
The curragh went over the wave and dipped in the trough

When that horny-handed saint with the abstract eye set off
Which was fourteen hundred years ago—maybe never—
And yet he bobs beyond that next high crest for ever.
Feeling:
Sea met sky, he had neither floor nor ceiling,
The rising blue of turf-smoke and mountain were left behind,
Blue neither upped nor downed, there was blue all round the
      mind.
Emotion:
One thought of God, one feeling of the ocean,
Fused in the moving body, the unmoved soul,
Made him a part of a not to be parted whole.
Whole.
And the West was all the world, the lonely was the only,
The chosen—and there was no choice—the Best,
For the beyond was here . . .

                                        But for us now
The beyond is still out there as on tiptoes here we stand
On promontories that are themselves a-tiptoe
Reluctant to be land. Which is why this land
Is always more than matter—as a ballet
Dancer is more than body. The west of Ireland
Is brute and ghost at once. Therefore in passing
Among these shadows of this permanent show
Flitting evolving dissolving but never quitting—
This arbitrary and necessary Nature
Both bountiful and callous, harsh and wheedling—
Let now the visitor, although disfranchised
In the constituencies of quartz and bog-oak
And ousted from the elemental congress,
Let me at least in token that my mother
Earth was a rocky earth with breasts uncovered
To suckle solitary intellects
And limber instincts, let me, if a bastard
Out of the West by urban civilization
(Which unwished father claims me—so I must take
What I can before I go) let me who am neither Brandan
Free of all roots nor yet a rooted peasant
Here add one stone to the indifferent cairn . . .
With a stone on the cairn, with a word on the wind, with a
      prayer in the flesh let me honour this country.

[279]

THE STYGIAN BANKS

Like a strange soul upon the Stygian banks
Staying for waftage.

TROILUS AND CRESSIDA

I

To keep themselves young—Is that why people have children?
To try and catch up with the ghosts of their own discoveries,
A light that has gone into space? Unscrolling history,
To slip back through the New Learning of adolescence
Into those Middle Ages of nursery masons
Where all the bricks were gay; the rondel of the years
Never changing its burden, only the leader
Changing his lines and time changing the leader.
Now it is Spring, O follow your leader, follow your
Child in his fourteenth-century dance; the wool trade
Is booming still, wool is building churches
And the Black Death has not come. Now it is Spring
And the half-grown wheat in the wind is a ripple of satin,
Let you in your child who is only lately articulate
Throw the lassoo of his sight to the height of some green thing,
    christen it
With a new name which no one has ever used
And call a tree a tree.
                  Oh, we know that the word merry
Is vulgarised and Chaucer's England was not
All cakes and ale nor all our childhood happy;
Still there is something lost. The very limitedness
Of childhood, its ignorance, its impotence,
Made every cockcrow a miracle after the ogre's night
And every sunbeam glad—as the medieval winter
Slow and dense with cold made March a golden avatar,
April Adam's innocence and May maiden's gaiety;
Nor did the burden change though the blossoms fell,
Alison is for ever aged fifteen
Though leasing different bodies. So let your child
Bowl your own life in his hoop; a wandering clerk yourself
Have you not in your time stolen a love-song
And written it down in an abbey? A different body
Yours from your father's and your child's from yours
But now it is Spring and the roll of the drums of the Judgement

[280]

Muffled with foliage, so you can fool yourself justly,
Playing the jongleur; that your songs are an artifice
Is of your nature; that the blossom must fall
Is what keeps it fresh; that lives and pieces of lives
Are cut off is needed to shape them, time is a chisel,
So what was is. If it were not cut off,
Youth would not be youth. This granted, take your stance
Under the high window which will not open—
You have a right to fool yourself; though your children
Cannot keep either you or themselves young
They *are* themselves in passing and the aubade
Though—no, because—the window will not open
Will find itself in the air, cut off as it must be
By the sudden cry of alarm from the turreted watchman
Which also rhymes. Cut off like a piece of sculpture.
This is the dawn. Reality. Fantasy holds.

II

Fantasy holds the child in the man, the lover in the monk, the
        monk in the lover,
The arbour in the abbey, the ages together,
But as notes are together in music—no merging of history;
The aisles of this church have their intervals. Father and son
Do not repeat; this child has different totems
From that one and from his father's. The slab in the floor of the
        nave
Makes one family a sonnet, each name with a line to itself,
But the lines, however the bones may be jumbled beneath,
Merge no more than the lives did. We must avoid
That haunting wish to fuse all persons together;
To *be* my neighbour is banned—and if I could be,
I could neither know him nor love him. Each of us carries
His own ground with him to walk on. Look at your child
Bowling his hoop along that arterial road
Where he cannot read the signpost; as he trundles,
It may, as they say, ring some bell from your past
Or, as Aristotle would put it, by an analogy
Match his private theme with themes of your own
As a waft of roses for one, of beans for another,
Will waft him back not to a general love
But to some girl with a name, herself and no other.

[281]

Analogy, correspondence, metaphor, harmonics—
We have no word for the bridges between our present
Selves and our past selves or between ourselves and others
Or between one part of ourselves and another part,
Yet we must take it as spoken, the bridge is there
Or how could your child's hoop cross it? Strike the right note
And the wine-glasses will ring. I am alone
And you are alone and he and she are alone
But in that we carry our grounds we can superimpose them,
No more fusing them than a pack of cards is fused
Yet the Jack comes next to the Queen. Though when they are
    dealt
You will often fail of the sequence; only you know
That there were such cards in the pack, there *are* other people
And moss-roses and beanfields and in yourself
Monk and lover and a battered hoop
With you for once behind it—and a coffin
With you for once inside it. All these active,
Even that compère of wax who now it is Spring
Jogs your elbow as the blossom falls
Whispering: 'Fulfil yourself. But renounce the temptation
To imbrue the world with self and thus blaspheme
All other selves by merging them. Rather fill,
Fulfil yourself with the Give and Take of the Spring
And honour the green of the grass, the rights of the others,
Taking what they can give, giving what they can take,
Not random pigments muddled and puddled together
But a marriage of light reflected.' Thus from the coffin
The retired life warns us against retiring
Now it is Spring and the roll of the drums of the Judgement
Can still be assumed far off. The hoops are running
A cow-parsley gauntlet, white as though for a wedding,
Alison is fifteen, the labourer's arm
Ripples with muscle, the green corn with wind,
And the glasses chime to a note that we cannot hear
For the frequency is too high. Within us a monk
Copies a love-song but remains a monk
And out there beyond our eyes Tom-Dick-and-Harry
Remain respectively Tom and Dick and Harry
Clapping backs in the sunshine. Granted the word merry
Is out of favour, it is the word's fault;
The thing itself yet sprouts and spouts before you

Calling for a communion. Fill your glasses;
When they are emptied again, the note may be higher yet
And your own glass may break.

III

And what when the glass breaks when the Note sounds?
What when the wind blows and the bough breaks?
Will each life seem a lullaby cut off
And no humanity adult? From the tree-top
Where all our conversation was *Why* and *Mine*
The answer now being *Why Not? Not Yours!*
If so, if we have by a sense no right to be here,
Trespassers, propertyless, never of age,
Branded by thoughts, born with a silver spoon—
With the power of words—in the mouth and smuggling in
To a world of foregone conclusions the heresy of choice,
If, to sum all, to be born man is wrong,
Breaking a closed circle, then let us break it clean
And make two wrongs a right, using the contraband
The genes got past the customs, putting it out at interest
And in the face of Nature's ritual of reflex actions
Riding our heresy high. Look, love! Now it is Spring
And the wind blows, pick what buds you fancy,
Fill your wine-glass, rockabye baby, break the circular world wide
    open;
It is your birthright never to be grown up
But always growing, never yourself completed
As are the brutes and therefore, unlike the brutes,
Able to shape something outside yourself
Finding completion only in othernesses
Whether perceived started without you
Or conceived within you, ending beyond you;
For things that you do or make can win a final pattern
But never yourself—never at least until
The velocity of a wind, the frequency of a note,
End in a topple, a clink, a shutter released
And the dead man gets his exposure. But now it is Spring
And we need not be camera-conscious, we are still doing and
    making
Not to display our muscles but to elicit
A rhythm, a value, implicit in something beyond us.

Rockabye baby! The wind that whitens the cornfield
And lilts in the telephone wires is tilting the tree-top
Further and further—but sing in your cradle,
You can outplay that wind which cutting off your song
Can never cut off itself, merely repeats itself
Where yours will end and find itself in the air
Unlike your body not returning to earth
But There—like a piece of sculpture.
                               Yes, let the teacher of ethics
Reduce all acts to selfishness, let the economist
Confuse conditions and causes and the psychologist
Prove and disprove the rose from manure and the scientist
Explain all value away by material fact—
What do I care? It is Spring and it always will be
However the blossoms fall; and however impure
Our human motives, we can sheer off sometimes
On the purity of a tangent. Let the wind
Lunge like a trombone, draw back his hand to his mouth,
Then lunge again and further; he is welcome
And time and all particulars are welcome
And death which rounds the song. Fill your glasses;
There *is* a distinction between vintages
And heretics must have courage. There *is* a despair
Which the animals do not know, it is chiefly exhaustion
When the bull kneels down in the ring; but our despair
Need not exhaust, it is our privilege—
Our paradox—to recognize the insoluble
And going up with an outstretched hand salute it.
For we, unlike the bull, have a matador within us
More titivated still, more cruel still,
Whom we have known for years and the holiday crowd
Have been waiting there for years and the sand is smooth
And the sun will not go in till the show is over. Yes,
We too are in a ring and gaudy banderillas
May quiver in our flanks; the paradox
Is that we can break out—being about to die
We can salute our death, the consciousness
Of what must be ennobling that arena
Where we have defied what must be.
                               Now it is Spring
And the blossoms fall like sighs but we can hold them
Each as a note in the air, a chain of defiance,

Making the transient last by having Seenit
And so distilled value from mere existence;
Thus when our own existence is cut off
That stroke will put a seal upon our value.
The eye will close but the vision that it borrowed
Has sealed the roses red.

IV

That roses are red is home—and homesickness.
As that men are alive is living—and deathwish;
And that men are dead is a name and a cause.
The hoop takes different turnings, Alison different bodies,
The burden does not change;
Though the spokesman may simulate progress
It must be within that unchanging framework,
Drilling the peas and beans in the garden but not seeing over the
        wall,
The mellow grass-grown wall encircling and forbidding
Too high to climb and no birds fly across it;
Only an incoming wind which unlike the winds of the garden
(The winds which threaten the new-born child in the tree-top
But only can share the name of This by analogy)
Flutters no paper tag on a stick in a plot,
Moves no leaf; the dandelion puffballs
Ignore it and we often. Often—but why are that lover's
Eyes of a sudden distant? He does not raise them—
One cannot see over the wall—Not one hair on his head
Is blown out of place but he ceases to give, give out;
Does not even widen his focus for here is
A movement only inwards, intake of distance.
Until she speaks and the wall is back in its place
Rounding off their vision again with words,
Unchanging burden to which the bees assent
And the thrush with a snail in its beak. A 'real' wind
Yawns—and flicks a tree-top nonchalantly
As if to say 'Look, though half in my sleep,
I can do more than that Other.' So all is well. As it was.
The voices of pigeons are grinding their delicate mills of lust,
Arkwright and Hargreaves are busy changing England,
The hooter sounds at eight, Darwin will sweep away
One code and give us a new one; all is well

As the girl sees in her lover's eyes returning—
'I am so glad you are here. I am so glad you are back.
Now you must stay for ever. Do not be foolish;
Even if a wind from over the wall can reach you,
It is a one-way traffic.' And saying this she smiles
And smiling this she lies and lying knows it,
There is a fleck of distance in her eyes too,
But the mill must grind. Why is it people have children?
So take London to-day: the queues of itching minds
Waiting for news that they do not want, for nostrums
They only pretend to believe in; most of their living
Is grinding mills that are not even their own.
The pigeons are luckier in their significant ritual,
And the dome of Saint Paul's more overt in its significance
But what to these does the word significant signify,
Who are neither autonomous crystals nor willing notes
In any symphonic whole? What they achieve of value
Is mainly in spasms, might be ascribed to chance
Did we not know that all men, even apparent ciphers,
Rough out their own best moments. Moments too rare
For most of these in the queue. Granted the garden,
There are distinctions in soil and in what comes out of it
(To consider means is not mean, so long as a gadget
Is not set up for an end, so long as an end
Can infiltrate into means); but still, above all,
To raise a value gardens must be gardened
Which is where choice comes in. Then will. Then sweat.
And—in the last resort—there is something else comes in
That does not belong and yet—You see that wall?
Many will tell you that is what protects us,
What makes in fact the garden, saves it from not-being
So that, now it is there, we need not think beyond it;
But look at the eyes of that tired man in the queue
In whom fatigue dulling the senses has rendered
Some other part of him sensitive—Intake of distance.
What is it that comes in? Can it be that the wall
Is really a stepping-stone? So that what is beyond it
(That which as well perhaps could be called what is Not)
Is the sanction itself of the wall and so of the garden?
Do we owe these colours and shapes to something which seems
      their death?
It does not bear thinking of; that was not a thought came in

To the tired man's eyes—Look back at him now; he has lost it,
Perhaps we only imagined that *he* imagined—
No matter, the queue is moving. Move along there;
If you want a system the public address is a good one
And you need not ask how came this mechanical voice
Nor by what right it tells you to move along there.
The blue cock pigeon is courting again. The hooter
Will sound at eight. That is the end of the news.

<h2 style="text-align:center">V</h2>

That is the end of the news. The humanist
Thinks he has heard something new and the man in the street
Passing the garish but dowdy hoarding dodges the dripping
    brush
While his brother changes the posters. Now it is Spring
But the know-all blonde on the poster will never know it
For only a few projections of human minds
Are able to give and take. For all that, now it is Spring—
Foaming white edges of roads, white hedges, white
Alison walking the rim of a classical text
Lovingly copied by monks who misunderstood it
But in her arms are flowers, long hours of flowers,
And her smile serene as young and the horned head-dress
Cuts the enamel sky. People have children,
One might say, to be childlike. Munching salad
Your child can taste the colour itself—the green—
And the colour of radish—the red; his jaded parents,
Wise to the fallacy, foster it (for we begin with
A felt unity and, they presume, shall end with
An unfelt ditto but all between is by proxy,
So the more mouthfuls of cress he takes the better,
For *we* can remember . . . can we? . . .) Glory is what?
The remembrance of an effulgence that was illusion?
Or is the illusion now in burnishing the past?
Or building up, in the catch-phrase, for the future
Which, with a capital F, is a catch-phrase too? Nostalgia
Implies having a home. Which heroes die for—
But can they without having seen it? The hackneyed songs
Mislead us—Home Sweet Rose, Last Home of Summer—
The paradox of a sentimentalist
Insisting on clinging to what he insists is gone;

When now is the opposite paradox now it is Spring
And what we insist remains we insist on leaving
After exchange of courtesies. Let the blossom
Fall, that is fact but the fact can be retranslated
To value of blossom and also to value of fall;
While we, who recognize both, must turn our backs on the
    orchard
To follow the road of facts which we make ourselves
Where others, men, will help us to conjure value
In passing and out of passing but always turning
Our backs on the road we have made
Until—which has value too—at a certain point we fall
And the hoop topples into the ditch. The well-worn symbols
Of quests and inns and pilgrims' progresses
Do correspond; the inn-sign clanks in the night
And the windows gild the cobbles—which is merry,
All the more because we meet it in transit
And the next morning Tom and Dick as to-day
May clap each other on the back and Harry may still stare down
Into the tawny well in the pewter mug—
Or so we think having left them but in fact
They too are for the road, they too have heard
The roll of recruiting drums beyond the horizon
However the woods of spring may blur the reverberations
As in the little church the fresco above the rood-loft
Has lost its percussive colours but though faded
The bearded Judge and the horned figures with prongs
Unlike the blonde in the poster still can give. And take.

VI

And take me then! In the dawn under the high window
The burden is the same. And on the black embankment
The lost man watching the lights jig in the water
And choosing the spot to plunge has the same burden
But the lines between are gone; his own invention
They slipped his memory sooner. So the lover,
Once the watchman cries, must kiss his hand
Up to the grille and go. And the lisping child
Envious of a bird stretches his arms to fly
Or to embrace the sea, loving it at first sight:
O air, O water, take me! Thus there are some

Who when the wind which is not like any wind known
Brings to their ears from ahead the drums of the Judgement
Slacken their pace and, not to be taken by That,
Implore all others to take them. As if those others could answer
In the absolute terms required. It is only silence
Could answer them as they want, only the wind
Which they dread, the wind which passes Alison by
Without even ruffling her dress, yet once in a way
Passes not by but into her. Ancient Athens
Was a sparrow-chatter of agora-gibes and eristic
But in the mind of Socrates beneath
His quizzical voice was the daemon, a cone of silence;
And in Imperial Rome in the roaring bloody arena
Linking the man with the net and the man with the sword
Was a circuit of silence, electric. The Middle Ages
Were rowdy with earth and hell, yet in Alison's poise in the
        orchard,
Dripping from the pen of the monk, the lance of the Lanzknecht,
Was a silence, drop by drop. But here to-day in London
Can we—we cannot have—lost it? Talking so much
Our optimism and pessimism are both
Corrupted dialects, divorced from grammar,
Almost indeed from meaning. The hooter sounds,
The busker sings to the queue, grinding of gears,
But if we stopped haggling, stopped as we did in the raids,
The gap in our personal racket, as in the gunfire,
Should become positive, crystal; which is the end of the news
Which is the beginning of wisdom. No captions and no jargon,
No diminution, distortion or sterilisation of entity,
But calling a tree a tree. For this wisdom
Is not an abstraction, a wordiness, but being silence
Is love of the chanting world.

VII

So let the world chant on. There is harsh fruit in the garden
But flowers are flowers and, what is more, can be tended
And here we stay and communicate, joining hands
To share the burden while each in turn can throw
His own lines in between; friar and wandering tumbler
Smuggle a pollen of culture into the villages
And Socrates stands by the sun-dial, talking away

But his soul is calm, moving, not seeming to move,
Like the pointer of shadow and silent. Yes, here we stay—for a
    little—
Strange souls in the daylight. Troilus
Patrols the Stygian banks, eager to cross,
But the value is not on the further side of the river,
The value lies in his eagerness. No communion
In sex or elsewhere can be reached and kept
Perfectly or for ever. The closed window,
The river of Styx, the wall of limitation
Beyond which the word beyond loses its meaning,
Are the fertilizing paradox, the grille
That, severing, joins, the end to make us begin
Again and again, the infinite dark that sanctions
Our growing flowers in the light, our having children;
The silence behind our music. The very silence
Which the true martyr hears on the pyre to darken
The hissing motley flames and the jeers, to make him
In spite of logic a phoenix. From that silence
Are borrowed ear and voice and from that darkness
We borrow vision, seal the roses red.
The hooter will sound at eight till the wall falls
But in the meantime—which is time—it is ours
To practise a faith which is heresy and by defying
Our nature to raise a flag on it. Come, let us laugh
As the animals cannot, laugh in the mind for joy;
Let the west wind lather the tree-top, toss the cradle,
Let the young decant the spring for us, banners of wine
While the Jack sits next to the Queen, let us busily gaily
Build us a paean, mixing for need is the metaphors,
Munching the green and the red, becoming as little children
Whose curls are falling blossom, using the eye
And the ear to fill the orchestra, plant the garden,
Bowling a hoop, braiding a love-song, fighting
A fire that cannot be seen; heretics all
Who unlike anything else that breathes in the world
When feeling pain can be lyrical and despairing
Can choose what we despair of. Glory is what?
We cannot answer in words though every verb is a hint of it
And even Die is a live word. Nor can we answer
In any particular action for each is adulterate coin
However much we may buy with it. No answer

[290]

Is ours—yet we are unique
In putting the question at all and a false coin
Presumes a true mint somewhere. Your child's hoop,
Though far from a perfect circle, holds the road
And the road is far from straight, yet like a bee
Can pollinate the towns for the towns though ugly
Have blossom in them somewhere. Far from perfect
Presumes perfection *where*? A catechism the drums
Asseverate day-long, night-long: Glory is what?
A question! . . . Now it is Spring.

LETTER FROM INDIA

for Hedli

Our letters cross by nosing silver
Place of a skull, skull of a star,
Each answer coming late and little,
The air-mail being no avatar,
And whence I think I know you are
I feel divided as for ever.

For here where men as fungi burgeon
And each crushed puffball dies in dust
This plethoric yet phantom setting
Makes yours remote so that even lust
Can take no tint nor curve on trust
Beyond these plains' beyondless margin.

You are north-west but what is Western
Assurance here where words are snakes
Gulping their tails, flies that endemic
In mosque and temple, morgue and jakes,
Eat their blind fill of man's mistakes
And yet each carcase proves eternal?

Here where the banyan weeps her children,
Where pavements flower with wounds and fins
And kite and vulture hold their vigil
Which never ends, never begins
To end, this world which spins and grins
Seems a mere sabbath of bacilli;

[291]

So that, for all the beauties hoarded
In Buddhist stupa, Mogul tomb,
In flick of hand and fold of sari,
In chant and scripture which illume
The soul's long night, I find no room
For our short night in this miasma

Where smiling, sidling, cuddling hookahs
They breed and broil, breed and brawl,
Their name being legend while their lifewish
Verging on deathwish founders all
This colour in one pool, one pall,
Granting no incense and no lotus.

Whereas though Europe founder likewise
Too close acquaintance leaves us blind
Who by aloofness, by selection,
Have written off what looms behind
The fragile fences of our mind,
Have written off the flood, the jungle.

So cast up here this India jolts us
Awake to what engrossed our sleep;
This was the truth and now we see it,
This was the horror—it is deep;
The lid is off, the things that creep
Down there are we, we were there always.

And always also, doubtless, ruthless
Doubt made us grope for the same clue,
We too sat cross-legged, eyes on navel,
Deaf to the senses and we too
Saw the Beyond—but now the view
Is of the near, the too near only.

I have seen Sheikhupura High School
Fester with glaze-eyed refugees
And the bad coin of fear inverted
Under Purana Kila's trees
And like doomed oxen those and these
Cooped by their past in a blind circle;

And day by day, night upon nightmare,
Have spied old faults and sores laid bare,
Line upon lineless, measureless under
Pretended measure, and no air
To feed such premises as where
A private plot would warrant shelter.

For even should humanism always
Have been half-impotent, debased,
How for all that can her own children
Break from the retina encased
In which our vision here must waste,
Meeting but waste, the chance of Vision?

And a Testator half-forgotten
Still with his will sways you and me
Presuming Jack and Jill so sacred
That though all rivers reach the sea
His course through land's diversity
Is still for us what makes a river.

What wonder then if from this maelstrom
Of persons where no person counts
I should feel frail trusting the ether
With love in weighed and staid amounts
And as the liaising aircraft mounts
Can think its chartered speed illusion?

For though to me an absolute person
Yet even you and even by me
Being clamped by distance in a *burqa*
Cannot be seen, still less can see
How in this earlier century
Dark children daub the skies with arson.

And the small noises that invest me,
The sweepers' early morning slow
Swishing, the electric fans, the crickets,
Plait a dense hedge between us so
That your voice rings of long ago,
Beauty asleep in a Grimm story.

Yet standing here and notwithstanding
Our severance, need I think it loss
If from this past you are my future
As in all spite of gulf and gloss
However much their letters cross
East and West are wed and welcome;

And both of us are both, in either
An India sleeps below our West,
So you for me are proud and finite
As Europe is, yet on your breast
I could find too that undistressed
East which is east and west and neither?

THE NORTH SEA

But not for a king's daughter? Here where Sir Patrick Spens
Went down to survive as a shiver on the scalp, a name,
I forage among the smearbread in the steamer
For the same snacks as a year ago and the same
Gull flies past the porthole while the immense
Eye of this Nordic sea outstares the dreamer,

Until he doubts whether the time between
These trips held any content; until he doubts
Whether the space between is not his all
And Bergen and Tynehead merely ins and outs,
The touch or the dead ball line, since these green
Waves are the only field of play for the ball,

Which makes one think (Sir Patrick went down playing
And a loud laugh laughed he) the laugh is on us
Who assert we are going to or from say Norway,
Who assume (*a quo* or *ad quem*) a terminus,
Who count this course between a mere delaying
And the cold vast between a stooge, a doorway.

Doorway? No more so than your office hours.
Doorway? No more so than your hours in bed
Alone or with a companion. And stooge no more
Than any counted or discounted flowers

[294]

Or stars which you might breed or weed or wed
Or grope for through strange lenses—or ignore.

For this, while we are in it, is an arena,
A perfect blue, green, grey, or pepper-and-salted nought,
In which beneath an indifferent sky the ghosts
Of Vikings board and grapple and the coasts
Which they were briefed to raid shrink to an idle thought
And each long dragon ship like an amphisbaena

Stings with both head and tail—but like a bee
Leaves her sting in time and thereby dies
And thereby lives in legend. The rover drowned
On a Thursday lives on a Thor's Day, the waves agree
To differ in Old Norse, the years rebound
To souse us in a lather of battle cries

And, as these top and vex our engines' pulse,
So hull-down on the horizon we can divine
A chain of round bright shields on a long gunwale
Itching to give the lie to screw and funnel,
To caterpillar up the scarps of brine
Like a tank's bogies, proving progress false.

Thus the Dark Ages like a traversing gun
Cover our own and we are in their sights,
Halvars and Olafs jostle our Esquires
And blood-lust our conventions; what we have done
Elsewhere is nowhere when the North Sea night's
Black single eye turns round on us and fires;

And we the target are the pupil too,
Sighted and sighting, are the central point
Round which the master's hand in strident chalk
Has roughed a circle in the pointless blue
Which timelessly is true like the great auk
But within time the times are out of joint,

And no ideal can be drawn to the life
And no eye gaze on it and never blink;
We saw the new world late yestreen with the old
Troll in her arms and now, shrill as a fife,

The wind is rising, the king's daughter is cold
As well she might be for this ship must sink.

And though Sir Patrick Spens were a man of iron
And master of his craft, he must conform
To the sea's routine; a wife in every port
Is nothing to that unconscionable siren
Whose arms are the lifting skylines and to court
Whom is to court the end, the deadly storm.

A Viking's last battle, their proverb ran,
Is always a defeat (not literally
True but true); just so the skipper's last
Trip is a wreck, settling down equitably
To drown in the arms of his mistress and mother, a fast
Lock of ill luck, an ending where he began.

Thus the wheel of the sea, of life, comes full circle, the gun
Swings in the swinging turret and finds her range
To illuminate, to annihilate, in a flash
Our timebound cargo and in a flash to change
The morse of the mind to changelessness—dot and dash
Be ended and the circle and point be one.

And so between firth and fro Sir Patrick must make his call
To find say a northern queen, say Understanding,
And make her take ship home with him—as must we—
And should our fate preclude both home and landing
Yet to have even embarked her, though not all,
Is all most men can hope for in such a sea.

MAHABALIPURAM

All alone from his dark sanctum the lingam fronts, affronts the
        sea,
The world's dead weight of breakers against sapling, bull and
        candle
                Where worship comes no more,
Yet how should these cowherds and gods continue to dance in
        the rock

[296]

All the long night along ocean in this lost border between
That thronging gonging mirage of paddy and toddy and dung
        And this uninhabited shore?

Silent except for the squadrons of water, the dark grim chargers
        launched from Australia,
Dark except for their manes of phosphorus, silent in spite of the
        rockhewn windmill
        That brandishes axe and knife—
The many-handed virgin facing, abasing the Oaf, the Demon;
Dark in spite of the rockhewn radiance of Vishnu and Shiva and
        silent
In spite of the mooing of Krishna's herds; yet in spite of this
        darkness and silence
        Behold what a joy of life—

Which goes with an awe and a horror; the innocence which
        surmounted the guilt
Thirteen centuries back when an artist eyeing this litter of granite
        Saw it for waste and took
A header below the rockface, found there already like a ballet of
        fishes
Passing, repassing each other, these shapes of gopi and goblin,
Of elephant, serpent and antelope, saw them and grasped his
        mallet
        And cried with a clear stroke: Look!

And now we look, we to whom mantra and mudra mean little,
And who find in this Hindu world a zone that is ultra-violet
        Balanced by an infra-red,
Austerity and orgy alike being phrased, it seems, in a strange
        dead language
But now that we look without trying to learn and only look in the
        act of leaping
After the sculptor into the rockface, now we can see, if not hear,
        those phrases
        To be neither strange nor dead.

Not strange for all their farouche iconography, not so strange as
        our own dreams
Because better ordered, these are the dreams we have needed
        Since we forgot how to dance;

[297]

This god asleep on the snake is the archetype of the sleep that we
lost
When we were born, and these wingless figures that fly
Merely by bending the knee are the earnest of what we aspire to
Apart from science and chance.

And the largest of all these reliefs, forty foot high by a hundred,
Is large in more senses than one, including both heaven and the
animal kingdom
And a grain of salt as well
For the saint stands always above on one leg fasting
Acquiring power while the smug hypocritical cat beneath him
Stands on his hindlegs too admired by the mice
Whom the sculptor did not tell.

Nor did he tell the simple and beautiful rustics
Who saved from their doom by Krishna are once more busy and
happy
Absorbed in themselves and Him,
That trapped in this way in the rock their idyl would live to excite
And at once annul the lust and the envy of tourists
Taking them out of themselves and to find themselves in a world
That has neither rift nor rim:

A monochrome world that has all the indulgence of colour,
A still world whose every harmonic is audible,
Largesse of spirit and stone;
Created things for once and for all featured in full while for once
and never
The creator who is destroyer stands at the last point of land
Featureless; in a dark cell, a phallus of granite, as abstract
As the North Pole; as alone.

But the visitor must move on and the waves assault the temple,
Living granite against dead water, and time with its weathering
action
Make phrase and feature blurred;
Still from today we know what an avatar is, we have seen
God take shape and dwell among shapes, we have felt
Our ageing limbs respond to those ageless limbs in the rock
Reliefs. Relief is the word.

THE WINDOW

I

Neck of an hour-glass on its side—
    Hermitage, equilibrium.
The slightest tilt and a grain would glide
    Away from you or towards you;
So without tremolo hold this moment
    Where in this window two worlds meet
Or family voices from the room behind you
Or canned music from beyond the garden
    Will irrupt, disrupt, delete.

Between this room and the open air
    Flowers in a vase imponderably—
The painter knew who set them there
    The knack of closed and open;
With highlights upon bloom and bulge
    He hung this bridge in timelessness
Preventing traffic hence and hither
And claimed his own authority
    To span, to ban, to bless.

The sands of light within, without,
    Equated and inviolable,
Allow no footprint and no doubt
    Of savagery or trespass
Where art enhancing yet revoking
    The random lives on which it drew
Has centred round a daub of ochre,
Has garnered in a square of canvas
    Something complete and new.

So there it rests the clump of flowers,
    Suspension bridge and talisman,
Not his nor hers nor yours nor ours
    But everyone's and no one's,
Against the light, flanked by the curtains
    No draught nor chatter can discompose
For this is a window we cannot open
A hair's breadth more, this is a window
    Impossible to close.

Thus pictures (windows themselves) preclude
  Both ventilation and burglary—
No entrance to their solitude,
  No egress to adventure,
For life that lives from mind to moment,
  From mouth to mouth, from none to now,
Must never, they say, infringe that circle,
At most may sense it at a tangent
  And without knowing how.

II

How, yes how! To achieve in a world of flux and bonfires
Something of art's coherence, in a world of wind and hinges
An even approximate poise, in a world of beds and hunger
  A fullness more than the feeding a sieve?
For the windows here admit draughts and the bridges may not be
    loitered on
And what was ecstasy there would be quietism here and the
    people
  Here have to live.

Beginning your life with an overdraft, born looking out on a
    surge of eroding
Objects, your cradle a coracle, your eyes when they start to focus
Traitors to the king within you, born in the shadow of an hour-
    glass
  But vertical (this is not art),
We feel like the tides the tug of a moon, never to be reached,
    interfering always,
And always we suffer this two-way traffic, impulses outward and
    images inward
  Distracting the heart.

And the infant's eyes are drawn to the blank of light, the window,
The small boy cranes out to spit on the pavement, the student
    tosses
His midnight thoughts to the wind, the schoolgirl ogles the
    brilliantined
  Head that dazzles the day
While the bedridden general stares and stares, embarking
On a troopship of cloud for his youth or for Landikotal, evading
  The sneer of the medicine tray.

Take-off outwards and over and through the same channel an
     intake—
Thistledown, dust in the sun, fritillaries, homing pigeons,
All to which senses and mind like sea anemones open
     In this never private pool;
The waves of other men's bodies and minds galumphing in,
     voices demanding
To be heard or be silenced, complied with, competed with,
     answered,
     Voices that flummox and fool,

That nonchalantly beguile or bark like a sergeant-major,
Narcotic voices like bees in a buddleia bush or neurotic
Screaming of brakes and headlines, voices that grab through the
     window
     And chivvy us out and on
To make careers, make love, to dunk our limbs in tropical
Seas, or to buy and sell in the temple from which the angry
     Man with the whip has gone.

He has gone and the others go too but still there is often a face at
     your window—
The Welsh corporal who sang in the pub, the girl who was
     always at a cross purpose,
The pilot doodling at his last briefing, the Catalan woman
     clutching the soup bowl,
     The child that has not been born:
All looking in and their eyes meet yours, the hour-glass turns
     over and lies level,
The stopwatch clicks, the sand stops trickling, what was remote
     and raw is blended
     And mended what was torn.

And how between inrush and backwash such a betrothal should
     happen
Of tethered antennae and drifting vanishing filament
We do not know nor who keeps the ring and in passing
     Absolves us from time and tide
And from our passing selves, who salves from the froth of
     otherness

These felt and delectable Others; we do not know for we lose
    ourselves
    In finding a world outside.

Loss and discovery, froth and fulfilment, this is our medium,
A second best, an approximate, frameless, a sortie, a tentative
Counter attack on the void, a launching forth from the window
    Of a raven or maybe a dove
And we do not know what they will find but gambling on their
    fidelity
And on other islanded lives we keep open the window and fallibly
    Await the return of love.

III

How, yes how? In this mirrored maze—
    Paradox and antinomy—
To card the bloom off falling days,
    To reach the core that answers?
And how on the edge of senselessness
    To team and build, to mate and breed,
Forcing the mud to dance a ballet,
Consigning an old and doubtful cargo
    To a new and wayward seed?

But, hows apart, this we affirm
    (Pentecost or sacrament?)
That though no frame will hold, no term
    Describe our Pyrrhic salvoes,
Yet that which art gleaning, congealing,
    Sets in antithesis to life
Is what in living we lay claim to,
Is what gives light and shade to living
    Though not with brush or knife.

The painted curtain never stirs—
    Airlessness and hourlessness—
And a dead painter still demurs
    When we intrude our selfhood;
But even as he can talk by silence
    So, blinkered and acquisitive,
Even at the heart of lust and conflict

[302]

We can find form, our lives transcended
    While and because we live.

But here our jargon fails; no word,
    'Miracle' or 'catalysis',
Will fit what dare not have occurred
    But does occur regardless;
Let then the poet like the parent
    Take it on trust and, looking out
Through his own window to where others
Look out at him, be proudly humbled
    And jettison his doubt.

The air blows in, the pigeons cross—
    Communication! Alchemy!
Here is profit where was loss
    And what were dross are golden,
Those are friends who now were foreign
    And gentler shines the face of doom,
The pot of flowers inspires the window,
The air blows in, the vistas open
    And a sweet scent pervades the room.

INDEX OF FIRST LINES

u   [305]   M.C.P.

Having bitten on life like a sharp apple, 86
Hearing offstage the taps filling the bath, 229
Heart, my heart, what will you do? 202
He carried a ball of darkness with him, unrolled it, 197
He never made the dive—not while I watched, 235
He was not able to read or write, 194
His last train home is Purgatory in reverse, 258

I am a lonely Troll after my gala night, 220
I am not yet born; O hear me, 215
I do not want to be reflective any more, 85
If in the latter, 231
If there has been no spiritual change of kind, 217
If we could get the hang of it entirely, 180
I have no clock, yet I can hear, 62
I meet you in an evil time, 19
I'm only a wartime working girl, 223
In a between world, a world of amber, 68
In a high wind, 258
In cock-wattle sunset or grey, 227
Indigo, mottle of purple and amber, ink, 245
In doggerel and stout let me honour this country, 277
In his last phase when hardly bothering, 255
In my childhood trees were green, 205
In Sligo the country was soft; there were turkeys, 187
In that Poussin the clouds are like golden tea, 60
In the beginning and in the end the only decent, 209
In the misty night humming to themselves like morons, 218
In the old days with married women's stockings, 231
In the Paralelo a one-legged, 208
In this evening room there is no stir, no fuss, 61
Intricacy of engines, 112
I see from the paper that Florrie Forde is dead, 199
It all began so easy, 196
It being in this life forbidden to move, 205
It is a decade now since he and she, 197
It is not enough, 103
It is patent to the eye that cannot face the sun, 265
It's no go the merrygoround, it's no go the rickshaw, 116
It was a big house, bleak, 191
I was born in Belfast between the mountain and the gantries, 89

Just as those who gaze get higher than those who climb, 80

Life in a day: he took his girl to the ballet, 193

Man: a flutter of pages, 181
March gave clear days, 109
May come up with bird-din, 226
Museums offer us, running from among the buses, 77
My father who found the English landscape tame, 253

Neck of an hour-glass on its side, 299
Never to fight unless from a pure motive, 224
No shields now, 90
Now that the shapes of mist like hooded beggar-children, 96
Now the winter nights begin, 93

Obsolete as books in leather bindings, 257
O early one morning I walked out like Agag, 239
On golden seas of drink, so the Greek poet said, 230
Only let it form within his hands once more, 104
On those islands, 52
Ordinary people are peculiar too, 206
O that the rain would come—the rain in big battalions, 216
O the crossbones of Galway, 188
O the slums of Dublin fermenting with children, 248
O Thou my monster, Thou my guide, 234
Our April must replenish the delightful wells, 81
Our half-thought thoughts divide in sifted wisps, 83
Our letters cross by nosing silver, 291

Peace on New England, on the shingled white houses. 204
Popcorn peanuts clams and gum, 200

Refusing to fall in love with God, he gave, 209
Riding in cars, 98

Seen from above, 250
Shall we remember the jingles of the morning, 102
She, who last felt young during the war, 242
Shuffle and cut. What was so large and one, 241
Shuttles of trains going north, going south, drawing threads of
    blue, 82

Why, now it has happened, 189
With all this clamour for progress, 47
With a pert moustache and a ready candid smile, 227
With prune-dark eyes, thick lips, jostling each other, 202

You're not going yet? I must; I have to work, 233
Your thoughts make shape like snow ; in one night only, 78